<u>Thanks</u> for helping to
write the next chapter!

Jim

Eat'n Park Hospitality Group
December 2000

A TOWN WITHOUT STEEL

A TOWN WITHOUT STEEL

ENVISIONING HOMESTEAD

Judith Modell

PHOTOGRAPHS BY
Charlee Brodsky

UNIVERSITY OF PITTSBURGH PRESS

Published by the University of Pittsburgh Press, Pittsburgh, Pa. 15261

Copyright © 1998, University of Pittsburgh Press

Manufactured in the United States of America

Printed on acid-free paper

10 9 8 7 6 5 4 3 2 1

Library of Congress Cataloging-in-Publication data will be found at the end of this book.

A CIP catalog record for this book is available from the British Library.

CONTENTS

PREFACE. Envisioning Homestead: Anthropology and Photography   vii

ACKNOWLEDGMENTS   xxiii

1.   Envisioning Homestead: The Place   1

2.   Setting the Stage: Three Generations in a Mill Town   22

3.   The Curtain Comes Down:
     Living Without a Mill in a Mill Town   57

4.   Women's Activities and Men's Work:
     The Division of Labor in a Steel Town   90

5.   Raising a New Generation in an Ex-Steel Town   132

6.   Harmony and Discord:
     Interpretations of Ethnicity and Religion in a Steel Town   157

7.   Steel and Segregation: Race Relations in Homestead   193

8.   Outside the Mill: Recreation and Residence in Homestead   230

9.   Responses in the Valley: The Aftermath of the Closing   250

10. Beyond the Closing: Changes in Homestead   294

NOTES   325

BIBLIOGRAPHY   333

INDEX   337

PREFACE

Envisioning Homestead:
Anthropology and Photography

The monotony of street after street is broken only by the bits of lawn and flowers in front. Where there are yards in the rear, they serve as play places for the children, and offer rest and refreshment to the grownups. As the men are usually too tired to enjoy working in them, the women often assume the task of keeping the flowers and grass in order and find it a welcome change from the hot kitchen. One garden, hardly 20 feet square, had along one fence a thick row of violets that the daughter had brought from the woods; a pink 'bleeding heart' and several flourishing rose bushes grew beside the house.

—Margaret Byington, *Homestead: The Households of a Mill Town*

Our collaboration

A Town Without Steel consists of complementary representations. These include Charlee Brodsky's visual record, my interpretation of the testimonies I gathered, and, last but not least, the accounts Homestead residents provided as they posed in front of camera and tape recorder. Homestead residents were our collaborators as well, conveying the history of their town in times of prosperity and in times of depression.

Individuals we met in Homestead enjoyed looking at the photographs we brought with us, were comfortable about showing us the snapshot collections they had accumulated over the years, and (by and large) enjoyed having their portraits taken by Brodsky. Looking at pictures prompted individuals to turn to the past with the nostalgic idealization of the "good old days" that provides a major theme in the book. Responses to photographs at once recreated a community of *then* and formed an assessment of the community *now*. Interviews, reactions to visual material presented by them and by us, and modes of posing for Brodsky's camera provide insight into a population's sense of itself as it moves into a future without the mill that guided its past.

The combination of verbal accounts and visual representations in the following pages indicates the complexity of a town's response to crisis. The combination of our methods as anthropologist and photographer, however, did more than elicit diverse responses to the crisis Homestead faces at the end of the twentieth century: the collaboration also altered our own understanding of visual and verbal documentary. This preface discusses the process of working together, its impact on the interpretations each of us made, and the way collaborating influenced the content and form of the book. Discussion of our method suggests the broader significance of combining word and image, which Homestead residents did in our presence. As they became critical social analysts and photo critics, we expanded the terms of our approaches.

The photographs Brodsky took, like the interviews I did, reflect the passing of time and an increasingly visible decline in the town. Over the nearly seven years we spent going back and forth over the High-Level Bridge, Homestead came more and more to resemble other towns along the Monongahela River. Not only did the large mill on our left as we crossed into town first appear empty and then as rubble, but in the town stores closed and house fronts needed more than cosmetic painting. By 1992, no resident or visitor could look toward the Mon River and avoid seeing the meaning of "deindustrialization." Deserted, empty lots met the eye with a painful shock. The landscape of the town had been radically altered since Byington described its "bits of lawn and flowers."

Scholars have begun paying attention to the importance of physical commemorations of complex histories and cultural struggles.[1] These studies tend to focus on the large public monuments and deliberately reconstructed settings that mark a significant event or era. My interviews in Homestead suggest individuals establish a different kind of physical commemoration in pictures, and especially in the pictures they save at home— in albums, shoe boxes, and on living room walls. Like other Americans, residents of Homestead kept archives of visual material; like a public monument, these materials were a way of saving history. But unlike a monument, these materials wove together private and public experiences, and that weaving is a major theme in my text.

Using photography as part of research strategy is particularly vital in rust-belt towns like Homestead. Towns that lose their industries are also losing a big chunk of their landscape; into the place of the old industry will come buildings with different appearances and functions. Photographs are a unique way of getting at the intimate impact of those changes: pictures, I discovered, bring out personal opinions, as even the most open-ended interview does not. Embedded in quick, laughing, and fond reactions to a photo were aesthetic criteria that I treated as a window onto cultural values. In expressing pleasure in one depiction over another, an observer articulated a worldview otherwise too familiar to be spoken.

Charlee's and my collaboration did not have a strict agenda. We conducted the joining of "visual" and "verbal" in different ways—sometimes going to Homestead together, sometimes alone. Sometimes days would go by before we talked about the project, while other times we talked constantly. The loosely constructed nature of the collaboration had advantages, not only giving each of us a chance to formulate our own interpretations but also as a kind of "jog" to our perceptions, as when Brodsky's camera found something I had not seen or when an interview I did revealed a new dimension in the images she had accumulated.

Remembering a town

Behind our documentation of a deindustrializing town lies an earlier documentation of the same town industrializing. The work of Margaret Byington and Lewis Hine in Homestead clearly informs our collaboration. When Byington and Hine did their study of Homestead in 1908 and 1909, Carnegie's Steel Corporation was thriving. The struggles and the stringencies writer and photographer recorded were a consequence of expanding production and of ambitious owners. The conflicts residents experienced then resulted from an influx of immigrants, so that workers competed for jobs and families competed for housing. The town Brodsky and I studied is at the other end of this history, struggling to survive against a different kind of steel crisis.

Byington and Hine started with a vision influenced by the Progressive ideology they shared, by the instructions they received for their "survey" from the Russell Sage Foundation, and by the reputation of America's smoke-filled industrial towns. Byington's prose reveals the strong visual impression Homestead made on her, though the scenes she depicted were not the same as the ones that dominated her collaborator's viewfinder. Margaret Byington saw the domestic aspects of the environment, the alleys as well as the parlors and kitchens where she interviewed women of the steel town. Concentrating on the households, Byington seemed not to see the mill itself or the shops where women and children spent a good part of their time. But she did see, and evoke, the landscape in which the households were situated:

On the slope which rises steeply behind the mill are the Carnegie Library and the "mansion" of the mill superintendent, with the larger and more attractive dwellings of the town grouped about two small parks. Here and there the towers of a church rise in relief. The green of the parks modifies the first impression of dreariness by one of prosperity such as is not infrequent in American industrial towns. Turn up a side street, however, and you pass uniform frame houses, closely built and dulled by the smoke; and below, on the flats behind the mill, are cluttered alleys, unsightly and unsanitary, the dwelling place of the Slavic laborers.[2]

The first Hine photographs in the book show the same cluttered, crowded, smoky landscape, foreground to the "better" houses creeping up the greener hillside. The rest of Hine's photographs push forward the image of the mill, of working conditions, and of men at work. Byington's words, by contrast, bring forward the women of the town—for hers was the story *outside* the mill and Hine's was the story *of the mill*.

Their collaboration was held together by a mutual commitment to the dignity and the vulnerability of America's working people. We have followed their path, respecting the self-presentations of individuals we met. For even when deep in a discussion of budgets and shortages, Byington displays a sensitivity to the emotional energy women expended in running a household in an unreliable economic environment. Hine's photographic inquiries reveal a similar interpretation, emphasizing the courage of the working man who faced his camera. As a documentarian, Lewis Hine interviewed with his camera, the lens pointing at a person as if asking him (or, more rarely, her) a question. And like his partner the social investigator, the photographer commented on the information he elicited. To underline his argument, Hine's photographs always have captions, in his own words and in the words that accompany them in Byington's text. Not tightly intertwined or deliberately juxtaposed, photograph and narrative yet convey an integrated account of a town.

But it is not the whole town. Driven by a Progressive agenda, *Homestead* features one side of a prism, concentrating on one segment of the town's population. Byington did not spend time in the fancy parlors belonging to mill owners' wives or in the garden clubs where ladies of leisure whiled away the hours. Her data come primarily if not exclusively from the crowded alleys of Lower Homestead. Nor did Hine focus on the elegant houses and large backyards near the Carnegie Library of Homestead

HOMESTEAD 1908

KEY

------ Borough Line	● Groceries
⊞ Railroad	✕ Ethnic Hall
® R.R. Station	† Protestant Church
▨ Carnegie Land Co.	✚ Catholic Church
★ Theaters	✡ Synagogue
△ Hotels & Saloons	■ Schools

Homestead, 1908 (Western Pennsylvania Historical Society)

either, except as an occasional contrast to his central subject, the places
and people near the mill. We, too, tended to spend more time with the
working-class population of Homestead, though I did several interviews
with businessmen, merchants, and community leaders.

The combination of interviewing and photographing in *Homestead*
fits a longer tradition of documenting American society by juxtaposing
words and images.[3] The history of America is in part a story of "sights"—of
Western plains and crowded Eastern seaports, of children in schools and of
farmers at the plow. More or less explicitly, such documentation carries a
political agenda, praising the nation or condemning its practices, and sometimes doing both at once. Perhaps the most well-known example of the
union of social analyst and photographer are the projects supervised by
Roy Stryker for the Farm Security Administration (FSA) in the 1930s.
The collaborative work of Walker Evans and James Agee and of Dorothea

Lange and Paul Taylor present insights into the domestic strategies that carry people through the death of what once defined their lives.

The FSA projects demanded a closer collaboration between writer and photographer than the Pittsburgh Survey required. One result of the enforced teamwork was a self-consciousness by participants about the joining of photograph and text. Moreover, working together led to a questioning of the "truth" each form of representation told. If Dorothea Lange's beautiful "Migrant Mother" became emblematic of the Stryker series, the book by James Agee and Walker Evans became its most famous collaborative product. Unequaled in its presentation of verbal and visual insights, *Let Us Now Praise Famous Men* (1941) resulted from critical thinking by both Evans and Agee about what they had accomplished in the Dust Bowl study. Their arguments about ways of seeing were a reference for us as we created a book about a disaster quite different in content but quite similar in proportion to the Great Depression.

Photographs, Evans asserted at one point, give only a "superficial" account of a place or a person. The writer's words complete the story, drawing out the profound inner reality Evans felt it was not possible to capture on film. According to him, a text offers the intimacy a photograph cannot. Fine, precise, and measured, the view through the lens lacks the imaginative penetration provided by a creative narrative.[4] Evans claims he showed what was there and that Agee showed what was "under" the "there," or outside the frame of the photograph. James Agee, also modest, said the photographer finished the narrator's task by showing the "reality" behind a verbal account. In Agee's view, the photographer proved the truth of what the writer expressed, grounding the poetic speculations of the writer in the materiality of a visual representation.

A reader of *Let Us Now Praise Famous Men* finds truth at every level—in visual images that have no correspondence in the text and in detailed descriptions of hard farm labor that have no representation in a photograph. But a profound truth lies in the juxtaposition of image and word, as the reader moves forward from the first striking Evans print in the book. The success of *Let Us Now Praise Famous Men* is perhaps unique, inasmuch as it depended on the powerful geniuses of two artists who were in the same place at the same time.

Since its publication the book has made a dent on almost every American writer and photographer who collaborate, and the high standards set by Evans and Agee are an ideal for those who come after. In subsequent efforts, some collaborators integrate photography into the investigative and interpretive process more closely than Agee and Evans did—or, for that matter, than Byington and Hine did.

Tamara Hareven's and Ronald Langenbach's 1978 *Amoskeag: Life and Work in an American Factory City* inserts photographs into the heart of the research. A historical account of a New England textile town, *Amoskeag* utilizes Langenbach's photographs during interviews, as well as for interpretation and illustration. Describing their method, Hareven makes the point that seeing photographs alters a person's responses to being interviewed. In looking at pictures, she notes, people redefine their roles as social actors and as historians. They see themselves both as important and as experts:

> Interviewing gained new meaning with the opening of Randolph
> Langenbach's exhibit, 'Amoskeag: A Sense of Place, A Way of
> Life. . . .' The exhibit evoked an overwhelming response from former
> Amoskeag and Chicopee workers, some of whom visited the show
> over and over. . . . The former workers of the Chicopee mill whose
> portraits were displayed in the exhibit had become historical symbols.
> As soon as they realized this, it was no longer necessary to explain
> why their lives were important, why we wanted to interview them,
> and why we were writing this book.[5]

Insight into how photographs affect the way an individual presents private and public history distinguishes *Amoskeag* from other studies of industrial America that combine oral history and photography.

Still, the photographs remain at a distance. Like a memento or a diary, the photos serve as a reminder of old days, a jog to the memory and a release of inhibition, not the focus of concentration itself. Looking at Langenbach's photos, the Chicopee workers moved on to tell their own stories. His beautiful evocations were the backdrop for personal, autobiographical details individuals offered the interviewer. Consequently, the photographs appear as stunning illustrations rather than as the material used by townspeople to create history. A book published fifteen years later shows how photographs can be integrated into the very process by which an individual creates an industrial history. In *Portraits in Steel*, oral historian Michael Frisch uses Milton Rogovin's portraits to structure conversations.

Showing the portrait Rogovin had made ten years earlier of the woman or man at work, Frisch elicited detailed and emotional narratives about life in steel. Seeing oneself in helmet and goggles did more than jog memories. A portrait of one's vanished self prompted bitter criticism of the industry and the government that had let steelworkers down. Views of the past inspired pointed commentary on the causes of the national economic disaster and on the possibilities for renewal in rust-belt communities like Buffalo, New York. Rogovin also took pictures after the interview of men and women no longer part of a steel industry and wondering what to make of the future. The book is powerful, much of its truth coming from the contrast between the outpouring of personal testimony and Rogovin's formal, artistically composed portraits.

We expanded these strategies by using people's own snapshots, in albums, boxes, and displayed throughout the house. A 1987 book by Richard Chalfen, *Snapshot Versions of Life*, provided insight into the use of such personal collections. Chalfen explores the significance of family photos and home movies for the people who make them, save them, and upon occasion look at them. In *Turning Leaves: The Photograph Collections of Two Japanese American Families* (1991), Chalfen pushed his insights further by examining the principles by which people select photographs and preserve a "composition" of lives over time in an album or on a mantel-piece. In *Turning Leaves*, he comments:

> But relatively little attention has been given to how these vernacular forms [family albums, for example] present and re-present life in pictorial form—as culturally structured representation. We find a similar neglect of seeing how ordinary people create narratives from sequences of these images found in album form. Few professional observers have attempted a coordinated view of relationships among picture takers, their photograph albums, and the ways family members look at, use, exhibit, and revere their picture collections.[6]

Chalfen argues that snapshots provide data not only through their content but also through the principles of selection that "shooting" and saving reveal. The organization of snapshots in an album, on the wall of a living room, or in plastic envelopes is not random but reflects personal rules about "envisioning." These rules, in turn, open a window onto the cultural ethos and the history of ethnic groups in the United States. Chalfen's regard for snapshot collections adds a significant dimension to the use of photography in research.

He does not, however, consider how principles of selecting and of saving visual material might relate to the way individuals react to crisis and make plans for the future. In the Homestead study, I tried to discover this relationship. This book asks whether, if people have principles for preserving a past in pictures, these can translate into an agenda for change.

Snapshot versions of a steel town

In almost any town in America, one will come across family albums, boxes of old photographs, and framed formal portraits. Such private commemorations offer significant insights into American culture and values, and, I discovered, into definitions of a town's identity. Family photo collections, including the most tattered and puzzling snapshots, often inspired a viewer to analyze social institutions, historical events, and cultural themes with an ease that was not always part of the verbal narrative unaccompanied by pictures. Poring over a pile of photos, in an informal conversation, an individual delineated the terms of life in a twentieth-century American industrial town.

The collections Homestead residents brought out to show me contained little that was surprising. There were pictures of weddings, birthdays, and anniversaries; there were candids of funny moments, remarkably consistent from one generation to the next: in every era, buffoons appear and adorable children make mischief. Occasionally an individual had documented a public moment in Homestead history: the visit of a president, a Fourth of July parade, the snipping of a ribbon at a new building. Rarely did I see pictures of women and men working, engaged in the daily struggles that were so much a part of verbal narratives. In my experience, few people in Homestead had snapshot versions of laboring and learning to labor. Outsiders take pictures of work, but insiders do not.[7]

Mrs. Wozeck described her father, an open hearth worker, in vivid visual detail. She told me of his gnarled, heat-toughened hands, his red face, his bulky arm muscles. She did not expect to find a photograph recording these details and, in fact, was surprised when a picture of him at work surfaced from her collections. Yet this was a man at his retirement ceremony, not covered with dust and reddened with heat. Mrs. Wozeck's reaction to the portrait suggested that this view of her father was unfamiliar. A conventional studio portrait, the man in his vest and tie had nothing to do with the real worker who had done twelve-hour shifts week after week. Mrs. Wozeck was evidently startled by this image of her father, completely unlike the man she had a few minutes earlier described to me. The company photograph turned him into a well-suited citizen, staring uncomfortably into a camera, about as distant from work at the hearth as anyone could be. Revealing how untrue the portrait was to the father she remembered, Mrs. Wozeck put the picture aside with a dismissive, "we must've had it on display."

On the other hand, snapshots of her mother prompted a revision of the story Mrs. Wozeck had told of that parent. Mrs. Wozeck interpreted photos of her mother as pictures of a woman *at work,* adding a dimension to her account of the 1930s steel town in which she had grown up. The content of the photos did not strike me as being about labor, but Mrs. Wozeck saw them that way—partly in order to grant her mother historical importance, I realized. That turned out to be an important moment in my interviewing process, indicating the way "work" classified person and era in Homestead.

One snapshot, for instance, showed a woman in a long skirt standing next to a smaller and younger woman. Mrs. Wozeck pointed to the younger, and explained: "This is one of the girls we took off from Ireland." That started a tale of her mother's enterprise and energy in running a boarding-house. Similarly, a sweet picture of two girls in fancy dresses led to a story of sewing and saving, thrift and calculation. "At the time when we were growing up, OK, dresses, my mother would have—there was a lady and she would have her make our clothes, and this particular dress—" showing me on the snapshot. "I can remember the material my sister had, hers has the whole thing, mine has white on top because they ran out of the blue and white so they just put white on the top. But at the time it was cheaper for her to buy the material and have this lady make them, because she would only charge a dollar a dress."

Interpretations like Mrs. Wozeck's revealed that if work was too ordinary to be photographed, it was not too ordinary to be read out of a photograph. Like Byington and Hine, contemporary residents of Homestead recognized that hard work determined the values and the textures of their lives; in the end, this fed into views of USX's betrayal and of the new people who came to town in the wake of economic collapse. Individuals who while being interviewed shied away from applying the word *work* to domestic activities, saw family members hard at work in the most innocent-looking photos. Like Mrs. Wozeck, other residents took off from snapshots to talk about the labor necessary to keep a household going, especially but not only in the past of their parents and grandparents.

Seeing photographic evidence this way was remarkably consistent across generations, ethnic backgrounds, and gender. No one showed me a snapshot of a father or brother wielding a shovel or a mother hanging laundry in a backyard or a daughter clerking in a bank, but almost everyone was reminded by some image of how hard people in a steel town worked. The pattern was repeated from one interview to the next: a sixty-five-year-old retired steelworker found a working mother in a snapshot of a woman in a schoolyard; a thirty-five-year-old man, glimpsing his brother in a photo, described struggles over who would run the family store. Looking at their own packed family albums, Mrs. Wozeck's children constructed an account of their mother's activities that resembled hers of her mother.

The other aspect of life in a steel town that appeared when individuals looked at photos was Homestead's fame. In talking with me, individuals were not reluctant to mention how famous their town was; photographs proved the truth of what they were saying by placing them in the scene. Pictures conventionally represent the "real," and pictures in family albums testified to public history by linking it with private histories.

Charlee and I spent an afternoon with eighty-year-old Mrs. Tennant and her forty-year-old daughter, Annie. They had spread their family photos over the coffee table in preparation for our arrival, and one by one we went through the large collection. But there was a sticking point, an unidentifiable figure in the midst of a civic parade. Annie and her mother continually stopped at that figure, asking which president it was. Specifically, they argued about whether it was Teddy Roosevelt or FDR. The contest went on, and Charlee and I were both drawn in. "No, that doesn't look like Roosevelt," Annie assured her mother, adding, "This could almost be Wilson." Charlee offered her opinion: "Wilson would be skinnier than that man." Her efforts were to no avail. An hour later, Annie's mother chuckled about her daughter: "She's still tracking down Roosevelt." Charlee finally decided, "No, that's Teddy." "Well, whoever he is." And then the real point was made by Mrs. Tennant: "Oh, we used to have big shots come in to Homestead, once in a while."

By focusing on a presidential visit, Mrs. Tennant and Annie effectively put Homestead back on the map of American history where it had been for decades. They also inserted Homestead's historical role into their own lives, veering from the figure they did not know to all the figures they did know—and gossiped about, as snapshot followed upon snapshot. Whichever Roosevelt it was, the picture was mixed in with their own family photos. The same impulse to historicize the private occurred when Ken, pulling out a formal studio portrait of his son, said, "Here's what I'm proud of. My son was in Truman's—he was in the honor guard. He was in his funeral part. Firing squad."

Using photos as part of my interviewing strategy revealed the different ways individuals "make" history. The snapshot version was not the same as the narrative version of life, and pictures were not simply an illustration of or prompt for memories. Photographs altered an interviewee's interpretations, intertwining the personal and the public so that official steel town history did not dominate the stories I gathered. With snapshots in front of them, Homestead residents forgot the discourse in which steel was the only subject and created their own, full ethnography. The presence of photographs also changed the dynamic of an interview. Interviewees usurped my position as questioner and questioned me; with photos in front of them, they were the experts and I was the pupil to be tested. Beyond taking hold of the album or print, individuals took hold of me, checking my responses to the pages they turned or the portraits they had framed. Ken, an ex-steelworker in his sixties, provided the best example and one that taught me a lesson for other interviews.

The first evidence I had of Ken's control over the exchange of information was when he drove me around town in his comfortable car. He used the occasion to insert particular scenes into my interpretations of the town. "See," he said, "that's where the workers lived." And later, "See, that's Saint Michael's Church."

He had done much the same thing, I realized, when we looked at photographs together. In fact, Ken had instantly changed the terms of that part of the interview by bringing not only snapshots and newspaper photos but also blue ribbons and baptismal certificates—anything that "pictured" his understanding of the town. And then he tested me. Over a lunch table crowded with his mementos, he pushed a small snapshot in my direction: "Here she is," he noted, having just mentioned his mother. "This is the playground over on Second Avenue. She was a teacher over there." Then, making sure I was attentive: "Did you see what I passed to you? 1939." Most often he wanted me to find him in a picture, as if I would not be worth my salt as an anthropologist if I could not distinguish one person from another. More than once I had to locate Ken among a group of schoolchildren looking old fashioned—and alike—in their 1930s clothing. "Here's when I was in sixth grade. See if you can find me. This is down in Lower Homestead." He moved swiftly from one snapshot to another. "We made our First Holy Communion. See if you can find me on there. This is 1935."

Although identifying this or that is a common habit when people look at photographs, in cases like Ken's it also served the purpose of evaluating me as an observer—an especially appropriate thing to do, given how much emphasis I had put on the visual aspect of my study of Homestead. Moreover, his inclination to chortle with pleasure when I failed my test showed the extent to which the exercise raised his confidence as an informant. Not only did Ken discover himself to be important, but he also declared himself to be more visually acute than I was. This was apparent when we looked at historical photos together; these were new to him, but he was able to see details in those photographs that I did not. And like the dates he thrust at me, finding a detail on an archival photograph "proved" the reliability of his memory and consequently the qualifications he had as an historian.

Anthropology and photography

Almost everyone I interviewed enjoyed looking at family albums, at Charlee's elegant portraits, and at the historical photographs we brought. Each of these collections accentuated the inclination to reminisce, to make the past golden, and to bemoan the darkness of the present. "When I was a wee little kid, this was a hotel," one person said nostalgically, looking at an old photo. Another displayed his expertise at identifying buildings here and there: "I'll bet you that's *our* church." And someone else asked: "Where the hell *was* this?" before happily locating a familiar spot in another picture: "Look at this, this is the Avenue!" And the real experts could make out a microscopic title in a movie poster a photographer had included in a shot of Eighth Avenue: "1945, *The Valley of Decision,* with Greer Garson and Gregory Peck."

If a photograph made a viewer sad—and some scenes of course did—this too became a part of the comparison between past and present that is a form of history. In general, photographs disinhibited the individuals I interviewed, so that a range of emotions entered the stories they were telling me about Homestead. Brodsky took photographs of some of the individuals I interviewed, and it was interesting to see how they made themselves the subject of a photo after having discussed existing photographs. Posing is an important theme throughout our book.

Mary Burton was a wonderful person to interview. Full of cheer and seventy years' worth of memory, she was also eager to show Brodsky the photographs she had been saving for nearly that long. We arrived together, one August day in 1989, to find Mary sifting through the photos she had spread out over the dining room table. By the time I turned on the tape recorder, she was already explaining: "And that's my mother-in-law's cousin.

Movie posters, 1935 (Pittsburgh and Lake Erie Railroad)

And that's John's sister. And of course that's my mother-in-law." She took pleasure in using the photos to jog her memories: "This is me when we went to Europe. See, in them days when you were married you had to wear a hankie [on your head]. . . . But that's the girl that you see here [pointing to another snapshot]. See, she was a young lady." Brodsky's comments hardly interrupted the flow. "That's my wedding picture," Mary pointed out. "You don't look that happy in this photograph," Brodsky noted. "Yeah," Mary responded, quickly moving on. "That's my husband. That's John's best friend. And that's the girl—," reminding me of an earlier conversation, "I told you her son was here."

On the other hand, Mary gave her full attention to Brodsky when the camera came out. She was compliant in posing, suddenly listening to Brodsky as she had not when snapshots were the subject. She asked Charlee,

"Do you want to go in the big room or here?" Brodsky responded: "Here is fine." About five minutes later, Mary asked, "Did you take it yet?" Brodsky: "No, not yet. I'm going to ask Judy to move. Can you pull the chair out just a little? Judy, maybe you can help Mary." Mary continued to cooperate, offering to move things and to stop talking. I too had to be posed, directed by Brodsky: "Judy, may I ask you to move? . . . And with the tape recorder. Would you just put it right over there?" We were all posed: me, the tape recorder, Mary Burton, and the pictures on the table.

Watching individuals pose for Charlee's camera, I wondered how they posed for me and what the connections were between posing for a picture and posing for a tape recorder. Everyone did pose in the face of a tape recorder, just as self-consciously as they posed in front of Brodsky's formidable viewfinder camera. They began posing as soon as they knew I wanted to tape, by deciding where we should meet: in their own houses, in a crowded coffee shop or a secluded restaurant, and, occasionally, in a place far away from Homestead. They posed when they decided whether I should ask the first question or when they began without my input. They posed by surrounding themselves with physical objects; above all, they posed by creating a narrative to suit the book I told them I was writing.

"Close study reveals that the subjects have allied with the photographer to help him achieve artistic effect," a commentator writes about Walker Evans. "Although these arrangements allowed Evans to capture a clean, crisp series of images and to bring the entire sidewalk scene into sharp focus, they intrude a question: at what point does fiction begin to masquerade as truth?"[8] Another question, of course, is how easy it is to separate truth from fiction. Posing in front of a tape recorder is not lying; the individual is taking a position as a self-conscious subject and cooperating with the observer in the interests of accuracy. An alliance between subject and ethnographer, like that between Evans and his subjects, leads to the construction of a mutually satisfying representation.

Recording the poses of Homestead residents and composing an interpretation from those unified the work Brodsky and I did in Homestead. Furthermore, in the process of posing, individuals *worked* at interpreting the town for us. Like the shop floor crews I heard so much about, the effort to make this book was cooperative; *A Town Without Steel* is the product of more than one person's labor.

Using photography was sad as well as pleasing and stimulating. People posed, knowing the self they presented *now* was not the one they described in autobiographical reminiscences. Nor was it the self, often, they wanted to be. If photographs and memories revealed patterns in an individual's life, no one could any longer be sure those patterns would carry into the future. All the details of a told story and of commentary on a photo album did not ensure continuity in a setting that had become unfamiliar. Even the passage through time seemed wayward in a town that had lost the reliable bulwarks of community. At the same time, looking back in words and through images offered individuals an anchor for their interpretations. In that regard, nostalgia provides a vital clue to the fate of a rust-belt town.

Dick Wurtz, a man who had drawn the mill, the men in the mill, and "his" town over and over, offered a sharp mirror of our approach to Homestead. He proved the importance of aesthetic commentary and the acuity of social analysis prompted by visual materials. Dick was not alone in this ability, our project shows. Even those less tutored in art and photography than he was saw the town and its history through a set of pictures, remembered scenes, and crucial changes in an envisioned environment. Dick may have been the most startling in his representation of Homestead, but he was not the only one who revealed how complex "envisioning" can be.

Using anthropology and photography, our book documents a community whose passage through the twentieth century is inseparable from the fortunes of a powerful industry. Situated and sighted by its residents, persistent and precarious in its history, this community dominates the text. It is a personal story as well, individual experiences coexisting with—not crushed by—the movement of industry. Comments, reactions, laughter, embarrassment at pictures recalled or seen anew complete the intense verbal narrative residents gave of a radically transformed town. The constellation of viewpoints and of representations evident in the book also suggest the strength of the town—the stamina that carried it from one century to the next, and will again.

ACKNOWLEDGMENTS

We have many people to thank, but most of all we want to thank the residents of Homestead who gave us their time, their stories, and their portraits. We spent nearly a decade in the town and were always welcomed with consideration and attention to our work. We were welcomed into houses and into lives in ways that deserve unbounded thanks and appreciation. The book is theirs as much as it is ours.

We initiated the Homestead project with the closing of the USX Homestead Works in 1986. Modell began interviewing in 1986 and ended in 1992. Brodsky began photographing the town, the mill, and town residents in 1985; her last photographs were done in 1995. The interview material in the book—the reactions of the residents to the mill closing—and Brodsky's photographic documentation of the town cover approximately the same period. Over those years, much changed in the Mon Valley's famous steel town: we have tried to capture the personal as well as the public impact of those changes in our text and in our visual representations.

Some of the individuals who deserve our thanks have asked to be anonymous. Those who can be named include: the Ed Szerbin family, the Michael Szerbin family, Bob Anderson, Richard Wurtz and his wife Velva, the Ferchak family—especially Ryan—and Curt Miner. Kate Bazis spent part of a summer interviewing residents and contributed much to our material.

The project had early encouragement and support from David Demarest, Bennett Harrison, Barbara Lazarus, Gene Levy, and Joel Tarr. Dave Demarest, Bill Donner, Michael Frisch, Albrecht Funk, Doug Harper, Bennett Harrison, John Hinshaw, and Edward Muller read the manuscript at various stages; their comments and criticisms helped enormously. Audiences at the American Anthropological Association meetings, the Social

Science History Association meetings, and the University of Pittsburgh looked at photographs and responded to the collaboration; those events, too, were helpful in the final preparation of the book. For related publications, we appreciate the input of Lori Cole, John Hinshaw, Eva McMahan, John Modell, Kim Rogers, Joe Trotter. Perrin Rowland did preliminary copy-editing. As usual, Scarlett Townsend did a wonderful job preparing the manuscript, checking references, and running small errands. Thanks to Hillman Library, Special Collections, for the Pittsburgh and Lake Erie Railroad photographs. At the University of Pittsburgh Press, Fred Hetzel initially recognized the value of the work, and Cynthia Miller has been an ideal editor, attentive to the project through its several stages. Ann Walston did an excellent job with the design of the book. Kathy Meyer was the kind of copyeditor all authors want, thorough and engaged.

The Dreyfus Foundation provided generous funds for the initial fieldwork. Carnegie Mellon's Faculty Development Fund supported later phases of the project. The Pennsylvania Council on the Arts supported photographic work.

In the end, the book and the photographs belong to the people of Homestead. Without their cooperation, encouragement, and criticisms, the task could never have been accomplished. This book is dedicated to the community of Homestead.

A TOWN WITHOUT STEEL

ENVISIONING
HOMESTEAD

The Place

Even the details of family life depend on whether "the mister" is working day turn or night turn; and the long shifts determine the part the steel worker plays in his household and also in his community. Financially, all time is marked off by the fortnightly "pay Friday." On that night stores are open all the evening. The streets are filled with music.

—Margaret Byington, *Homestead: The Households of a Mill Town*

I drove into Pittsburgh in December 1984, the winter before I was to move there to teach at Carnegie Mellon University. As I entered the city, newscasters on the radio were announcing a startling event: a group of unemployed steelworkers and their families had thrown skunk oil and dye into the Sunday morning services of a prominent Presbyterian church. I listened with fascination, as the stories conveyed what seemed to me a complicated and powerful form of protest—polluting the sacred domain of a church. The event also struck a chord with my anthropological training in the importance of symbolic acts. I knew virtually nothing about the background of this protest and would only later learn its short-term and long-term consequences for people who identified themselves with Pittsburgh's "steel valley."

In the city itself I saw the environment that formed the setting for the events I was hearing about. Emerging from the Fort Pitt Tunnels, I came upon the view that continues to impress visitors to the city: the sudden rise of skyscrapers, including the Pittsburgh Plate Glass cathedral-like structures, the Mellon Bank building, and next to that, the United States Steel tower. A history was written in the tight cluster of buildings, but a history that had its other chapters along the three rivers that met at Pittsburgh's "Point." As I drove to my neighborhood along the Monongahela River, I had a clear view of the steel mills that lined the Parkway as it wound its way east. The mills seemed quiet. It was late afternoon, and the smoke and fire I would later see at night were not visible in the winter sun.

My entry set a foundation for how I subsequently responded to the city. The knot of protesters, disrupting a church service (not their own church, but that of Pittsburgh's "elite" and "first families"), the tall and (now) clean buildings of a commercial downtown, and the mills: mammoth industrial structures that were like nothing I had seen in my suburban New York upbringing. Two years later, I mentioned this powerful visual impression of the city to a colleague, Charlee Brodsky, a photographer. For several years, she had been photographing the industrial landscape of Western Pennsylvania, documenting the steel mills before the devastating closings of the 1980s hit the area. When we had our conversation in 1985, there were already signs of decline in Mon Valley steel towns, where the number of workers being laid off brought dire foreboding to the region.

Slowdowns that led to closings in the American steel industry began in the 1970s, accompanied by ambiguous messages from the steel companies about the meaning of these decisions. By 1985, towns like Monessen, Braddock, and McKeesport had lost the industrial base upon which they had depended for most of the twentieth century. The bombed-out look of boarded-up downtowns and the abandoned houses of residential areas came to represent the death of the Mon Valley for those who documented it in subsequent years. The sight of a stately Carnegie public library building crying out for repainting and repointing of the bricks epitomized the tragedy that hit these communities.

In 1986, under its new USX rather than United States Steel title, the company announced the closing of what was probably the most famous mill along the Monongahela River, the Homestead Works. Site of one of the most renowned strikes in American history, the Homestead Works was as symbolic a structure as any in the region. Occupying a four-and-a-half-mile-long space along the river, the Works inevitably dominated the physical landscape of the town and caught the attention of the most casual passerby. To see it grow empty and silent must have struck residents of the town with a terrible force. That was the assumption with which Brodsky and I began the project, intending to use the visible changes in the landscape to focus people's responses to the cultural and social changes that accompanied the disappearance of steel. We intended to emphasize *perceptions*, theirs and our own, as the route to understanding local interpretations of a major economic disaster. Through concrete references to what looked different, we hoped, residents would analyze a situation whose complexities were not easily put into words—by anyone. This was not mere speculation on our parts. Homestead's physical environment represented the terms of its industrial life: a massive plant along the river, workers' housing in neighborhoods close to the plant, and more elegant residences up the hillsides to the south.

Unlike most studies of deindustrialization, our book focuses on the ways a crisis appears to the people who suffer from it. We show that in instantaneous, sensed, and felt reactions to the changes in a landscape people interpret the crisis caused by a closing. These interpretations, moreover, reveal the lineaments of a town's self-portrait, the core aspects of its identity. Residents liked the photographic dimension of the project inasmuch as pictures constituted a familiar way of constructing history. Through the pictures we showed them, and they showed us, individuals recounted the tangled history of steel, of strikes, and of sociability based on sharp cultural differences between one ethnic group and another.[1] A *Town Without Steel* is part of experiencing Homestead, for those who have lived their lives there and, we discovered, for those who came to the town after USX left.

With Homestead as an example, the story of other rust-belt towns can be traced through individual responses to the transformation in sights, sounds, and smells that accompany the disappearance of an industry.[2]

Public histories—of the Homestead strike, of steel towns along the Mon River, and of the Pittsburgh region—already exist. The background to the closing reflects the personal lessons residents learned as I heard them in the interviews, and there was no mistaking the merging of public and private histories; the threads of the two are so closely intertwined that it would be inaccurate to separate them. Individuals combined the well-known features of Homestead, available in almost any American history textbook, with the knowledge accumulated over generations of the significance of living in a town built around steel. What this kind of history implies for the future evolution of Homestead is a major question throughout this book. *A Town Without Steel* is not the story of *men* of steel or even of steel work, but rather of individuals who see their lives against the backdrop of a mill.

A town of steel

Seven miles east of the city of Pittsburgh, Homestead represents a typical western Pennsylvania industrial town. For most of the twentieth century, its history followed that of a giant corporation. Like automobiles in Detroit or textiles in New England, steel shaped life in Homestead. Homestead proper is actually one of three closely attached boroughs: Homestead, West Homestead, and Munhall. As often as not, the people we met blurred the boundaries among the three, as does much of the literature on steel towns of the Monongahela Valley. There were moments, however, when a speaker would distinguish among the three boroughs, and the sharp division this indicated between an "us" and a "them," as well as the bases for these divisions, became clear. Whether or not Homestead meant all three or just the administrative unit of Homestead depended upon the speaker, the content of his or her narrative, and the point at hand. In fact, the ebb and flow in town boundaries conveys the intricate connection of physical geography, social geography, and cultural mapping for townspeople.

By census, Homestead is the most diverse of the three towns, economically, ethnically, and racially; West Homestead had several integrated neighborhoods, and Munhall was the most consistently middle class and white of the three boroughs. Census reports provide the background for the more subtle and changing identifications of townspeople. Identified with the steel plant, Homestead symbolized all three boroughs in historical writings and in the histories told by residents. Yet each borough separately, like every neighborhood, reflected the presence of the mill.

Company employment practices, restraints on housing, and charitable bequests to citizens formed life for generation after generation in the town. Up the hill in Munhall still stands the elegant public library Andrew Carnegie donated in 1901; closer to the river, a church steeple topped by the statue of a worker commemorates steel in another way. Rows of two-story wood frame houses, their porches running into one another, contrast with the larger houses up the hill which are separated by front lawns and tall hedges. In the 1980s, as in the 1890s, no matter where one walked, shopped, or played, there were reminders of the boss and benefactor under

Population Table: Homestead, Munhall, West Homestead

Year	Homestead		Munhall		W. Homestead	
	whites	blacks	whites	blacks	whites	blacks
1930	20,141	3,606	12,995	83	3,341	211
1940	19,401	3,388	13,900	73	3,418	108
1950	10,046	1,380	16,437	60	3,126	131
1960	7,445	1,359	17,312	39	3,994	161
1970	7,502	1,735	16,674	71	3,674	115
1980	6,309	1,877	14,532	96	3,025	109
1990	2,277	1,828	12,952	154	2,357	111

whose initial vision the town had burst into successful industrial growth. Several streets of Homestead carry the names of Carnegie's kin.

Until Andrew Carnegie appeared on the scene, Homestead was farm-land, but a lucky piece of land near a river and not far from the coalfields of central Pennsylvania. Carnegie, a Scotsman, has become the prototype of the American industrialist, seeing golden opportunities where others had not. He recognized the potential in a flourishing ironworks and in 1883 purchased the Pittsburgh Steel Company in Homestead. As the years went by, through clever conglomerations and partnerships, he turned his Carnegie Steel Company into one of the largest companies in the world. With the help of Henry Clay Frick, Carnegie also built a reputation as a hard boss, one who took no nonsense from employees. When in 1892 the men of the mill walked off the job, Frick took immediate action to protect the fortunes of the flourishing industry. Following a telegram to Carnegie, then in Scotland, Frick called in a force of Pinkerton detectives who drove the men back with random shots and ended a walkout that had had the potential to shut down a plant and strengthen worker solidarity. Instead, the denouement led to the downfall of the Amalgamated Association of Iron and Steel Workers and mill workers were on their own, until the intermittent struggles to organize succeeded nearly half a century later, in the 1930s.

Frick's actions sent the men back to work, the women and children back to their proper places at home, and the mills back to their relentless, twenty-four-hour-a-day production schedule.[3] "Crushing the union helped them [Carnegie and Frick] to establish the powerful, integrated company that, in 1901, became the United States Steel Corporation, the nation's first billion-dollar corporation."[4] Though a failed strike in practical terms, the 1892 struggle was a symbolic victory. For the townspeople, the men of the Homestead mill took on heroic proportions and filled a large piece of the town's self-image. Homesteaders placed the legendary Great Strike at the center of their history and drew upon that confrontation as a way of representing themselves to an outsider even after the mill closing in the 1980s. Then, however, the heroic portraits of strikers became more complex as residents wondered about the role of unions in the turn of U.S. Steel's fortunes.

Growth of the mill, as town residents knew, meant not only increase but also change in the population. That many people I interviewed spoke glowingly of the original immigrants in their families did not alter the impression they also conveyed, that "waves" of immigrants disrupted the town's placid harmony. The story had a reflection in reality. Andrew Carnegie brought in workers without much concern for their social interactions. He placed newcomers in the mill in the strict, and discriminatory, hierarchy he had always enforced, and left townspeople to adjust their relationships as they might. And so individuals I interviewed punctuated the history of steel's expansion with the categorical designations of the shop floor: Anglo, Hunky, Negro, and, finally, Hippie. For townspeople, the history of steel was in part the history of one group climbing on the shoulders of another—though only the Anglos ever achieved success in the management of the corporation.

An especially dramatic change in population, according to those who remembered and reconstructed the town in the old days, was the "importation" of blacks from the South to break the six-month-long 1919 strike. There had been blacks in Homestead before, but these men represented a new type, workers with a "different" relationship to the mill and harbingers—in memory—of the great migration of the 1930s. As residents suffered through the post–World War I strike, management brought fresh workers in to keep the plants running, and those blacks who came ended up settling in Homestead. Eventually, they merged into the heterogeneous population of the town and formed a contrast, in my interviews, to the blacks who arrived after the closing of the Homestead Works in the late 1980s.

Blacks, however, did not always retain their mill jobs or find it easy to buy a house in the steel town.[5] The racial prejudice characteristic of many Mon Valley towns was present in Homestead, though not directly voiced by those who viewed the old days as the "good days." Then, it seemed to whites in town in the 1980s and 1990s, job discrimination and housing segregation did not imply conflict, but rather a solidarity constructed out of acknowledged differences. Older blacks expressed the same perspective on the "good old days," in which compromise with the modus vivendi was tolerable because as long as the mill ran no one starved. Furthermore, from the vantage point of the present, the mill owners of the past emerged as villains, and ordinary citizens—black and white—were seen to be unified against the hands of power. That, too, was nostalgia.

But nostalgia helps to explain the importance of strikes in the colloquial histories of Homestead that I gathered. Strikes were a representation of the working man against the rich, the town against the mill, and offered a chronology that kept other events in order. Even more than the national wars, strikes, for Homesteaders, marked the passing of time and changes in the town. For the story of strikes, it became apparent, was the story of Homesteaders acting on their own initiative—the town backing its men, the townspeople asserting their dignity.

The strike of 1959 stood out in this respect in the accounts I heard. I met men and women who had lived through that strike; their parents compared it with the famous earlier strikes while their children recalled a time of scarcity that was surprising in the otherwise prosperous 1950s. "In the summer of 1959, the union struck the steel industry. The 116-day strike would be the longest one in the industry since the Amalgamated Association of Iron, Steel, and Tin Workers had struck the United States Steel Corporation in 1909–1910."[6] Bitter and long, the strike revealed the stuff Homesteaders were made of and had not lost despite fat paychecks and long vacations. The victory was a mixed one on both sides: an injunction sent the workers back to the mills, but with higher wages and better benefits.

Four years after the strike, union and corporation granted steelworkers a fantastic package. A 1963 contract provided an extended vacation plan in which workers with over five years of service could take a thirteen-week vacation. This extraordinary and rare arrangement imprinted itself on town histories. I was to hear the phrase "thirteen-week vacation" over and over, out of proportion to its actual occurrence, but in proportion to its emblematic quality.

Although residents talked a great deal about strikes, they talked very little about formal unionization or about the role of unions in the strikes. Just as individuals tended to distinguish "household" life from "steel" life, after the closing they distinguished worker stamina, endurance, and opposition to oppressive work conditions from the union that, in fact, supported them in such circumstances. Confusion about the union's role in the postclosing trauma was also evident in the interviews I did in the late 1980s and early 1990s.

There were exceptions to this narrative, and some residents remarked on the importance of the formation of the United Steel Workers of America in 1937. The culmination of long years of struggle, the acceptance of the USW into the CIO marked a substantial improvement in life for workers in steel mills and, by extension, for residents of steel towns. After the closing, for some residents Homestead Local 1397 acquired a distinct character as radical, renegade, and rebellious. In retrospect, that character for some residents represented a highlight of union days and for others a sign of worse things to come. In the face of the 1970s crisis in steel, Local 1397, run by activists and outspoken workers, tried to organize protests against USX policies. Their attempt failed. It was a cry in the wilderness in towns that had traditionally kept their anger at the corporation under control and in a national union that itself had grown conservative and blue-suited.[7]

When USX bought Marathon Oil and began closing steel plants all around the country, residents of Homestead claimed the union could not help. By then, individuals claimed, the national steelworkers union had become the corporation's twin, and Local 1397 was too radical for most tastes. The final blow came in 1986 when the doors of the USX Homestead Works slammed shut and, as some people put it, the town was "X'ed out."

A town of homes and families

Women and children went through strikes with as much endurance and courage as did the men who worked in the mill. Photographs and drawings of the Great Strike of 1892, and the lesser great strikes of the next century, give the impression that the whole town was involved. Yet in historical accounts women and children tend to fade into the background and "men of steel" take over the drama. Residents of Homestead repeated the story of heroic workers and told another story as well. Behind the official tale lay the private stories, told by men about their mothers and wives and by women about their own roles in maintaining household stability through the ups and downs in steel.

Margaret Byington told that story in her 1910 book, *Homestead: The Households of a Mill Town*. After hours in the kitchens and parlors of the households, Byington showed frank admiration for these workers whose shifts seemed never to end. Byington's study was one of six surveys of the

Homestead houses, 1910 (Pittsburgh and Lake Erie Railroad)

Pittsburgh area sponsored by the Russell Sage Foundation of New York from 1908 to 1909.[8] Homestead received not only the attention of Byington but also the respectful eye of the documentary photographer Lewis Hine. Although Hine concentrated on the working men, he took an occasional break to document the alleyways, music halls, and parks that provided a setting for family life in Homestead. Together the two remind readers that life in a steel town was not all steel, not all men, and not all work.

Byington's work captures a perspective I later heard voiced, if hesitantly, that valued domestic life, the celebrations of family events, and the joyousness of a successful Little League game. Interviewees hesitated because they thought I, like most other observers of the town, "really" wanted to hear about steel and because they themselves, regardless of age, race, and gender, had grown up on stories that equated Homestead history with steel.[9] Not only men but also women began their life stories with reference to the mill—the heat they experienced near its walls, the sight of sweaty men rushing to a nearby bar, the standard of hard work set on a shop floor. Whether in their seventies or in their twenties, the women I met spoke of men's work first, and with awe and admiration. The brawny, picturesque hearth worker was a hero to his wife, daughter, and sister, and women were modest about the heroism of their own work.

From these modest accounts grew a picture of women whose coping skills were many, whose adaptations to changing circumstances were creative, and whose lives did not exist in shadow. On the surface, the details of housework seemed to remain the same over generations, and what a woman did in the 1960s differed little from what her great-grandmother had done in the 1900s. The routine of it all, however, masks the impact of two world wars and the chance that was provided to women by war to work outside the home. The sense of routine also masks the impact on women's roles of new ideologies and of federal laws against discrimination. Though women in Homestead did not greet "women's lib" with abundant enthusiasm, the 1960s women's movement offered expanded educational and employment opportunities.

Yet Homestead is a conservative town, and changes in surrounding ideologies mainly gave women (and men) a way to justify a wife's or a daughter's choice to work outside the home. A number of women in Homestead had always worked outside the home, in shops and taverns next to their husbands before World War II, in factories during and after the war, and in teaching and other clerical jobs throughout the twentieth century. After the 1960s, however, with its emphasis on autonomy and individualism, women did not have to excuse their labors as strenuously as before. Nevertheless, when I interviewed women and men after the closing of the Works, a large residue of older attitudes caused even those in their twenties and thirties to claim that a wife ought to work only in dire circumstances. With an American view of upward mobility, some of these same individuals hoped their daughters would work, though in jobs that were "pink collar" and preferably in places where other family members already worked. At the same time, the realization that the mill would never reopen made customary compromises less and less viable.

Threats to existing household arrangements followed fast on the shutdown, driving individuals into a romanticized view of home and hearth and of the semidomestic domains, church and school. Discussion of women's roles, of men's work, and of children's upbringing occurred in the context of a way of life that was summarized in the phrase "below the tracks." This phrase referred to the neighborhoods near the mill and to an existence in which steel remained central even to those who never worked in the mill. "Below the tracks" represented continuities in life, so that a son and a daughter walked comfortably in the footsteps a parent had already trod. Finally, "below" referred to an organization of diversity, a harmony of cultures, that for the Homesteaders I interviewed translated into community.

The importance of the trope—and its nostalgic portrait—deepened precisely because the neighborhood had disappeared physically when the mill expanded in 1941–1942. Now, shocked by the disappearance of the mill itself, residents asked whether they could rebuild a community in Homestead on the model of the one that had vanished fifty years earlier.

Live and let live

"Below the tracks" resonated in interviews with old and young, white and black, female and male. The meaning of the phrase crossed most of the usual divisions in Homestead and was familiar to all except the newest residents, though even they learned the connotation of the phrase as part of Homestead history. Chronologically, "below" referred to the pre–Second World War past and to the settlement of Homestead by men and women with conventional immigrant dreams of "pots of gold."

Geographically, "below the tracks" comprised the neighborhood immediately abutting the Homestead Works, between the Sixth Avenue railroad tracks and the Mon River. Socially, "below the tracks" was home to the working men and women of Homestead, first stop for the immigrants who came to work in the mill or in the businesses that serviced a mill town. Culturally, "below the tracks" meant harmony or, in the phrase I heard often, "live and let live." Not that the individuals I met put it exactly that way; for them, "below" was important as an indication of lost values and of a tolerance for ethnic, religious, and racial differences that seemed to have since disappeared. Also not explicitly stated, "below the tracks" referred to a life that existed vigorously despite the shadow shed by steel and against the domination of economic forces. With the concept of "below," residents of Homestead asserted their independence from "big industry" and "big government."

The growth of the Carnegie empire blurred the boundaries of the three boroughs of Homestead, Munhall, and West Homestead, as all became the sources of labor, objects of patronizing policies, and enclaves of ethnicity, religion, and race that were exploited on the shop floor. At the

Hays Street crossing, 1921 (Pittsburgh and Lake Erie Railroad)

same time, the physical and economic growth of the mill pointed to the differences among the three boroughs: as Munhall prospered and excluded "laborers," West Homestead absorbed a growing middle-class worker, and Homestead remained both the melting pot and the site of the most notable changes in the mill town's history. A majority of newcomers began their lives in the mill neighborhood, in the borough of Homestead and clustered up against the Works.

In the first half of the twentieth century, newcomers came from Eastern Europe and, after World War I, from the American South. These were the Hunky, "Slav," and black workers whose wives Byington interviewed and whose faces Hine photographed, though neither writer nor photographer paid much attention to the small population of blacks. After the mill neighborhood was demolished, its residents spread out over the three boroughs as well as across the river into Hazelton and other Pittsburgh neighborhoods. And for decades after, "below the tracks" symbolized the story of steel, the corporation, and the households of a mill town.

"Below" was a place of distinct subneighborhoods, block by block, where workers separated themselves into the tight clusters historian John Bodnar aptly terms "enclaves," suggesting both the merits and faults of residential separation. Allowing people to celebrate their customs and to display their mannerisms unbothered by others, the enclaves also kept workers from realizing the interests they had in common. "Below" may have been harmonious in the memories of my interviewees, but it was a harmony that often diminished resistance to oppressive working conditions.

On the flats near the river, the area was alternatively called the Lower Ward, in contrast to the more prosperous, greener, and spacious Upper Wards.[10] Although residents of below patronized the developing commercial district on Eighth Avenue, the neighborhood also boasted its own shops, taverns, and places of business—as well as its own churches, schools, and meeting halls. It was the most crowded, lively, and intense part of Homestead, as Byington and Hine noted and as residents assured me nearly a century later.

In my interviews, Homesteaders linked accounts of "below the tracks" to responses to the 1930s Depression. Faced the recent crisis, individuals referred back to the old days when, they said, "people not only lived together but also pulled together." As much a fiction as an accurate portrayal, life below the tracks during the Depression is a story of the present as well as of the past. Descriptions of life in the mill neighborhood immediately before its destruction incorporated town legends of coping, dealing with adversity, and maintaining dignity in the face of fate. Whether remembered, as in the case of the first generation, or repeated, as in the case of the third generation, portraits of the place and time represented by "below the tracks" are a mirror for the contemporary town, again experiencing economic devastation.

But a mirror reverses an image as well, and the details of harmony and of sharing food regardless of racial, religious, and ethnic differences were not imported whole into the present. Memories of a neighborhood destroyed in the interests of national policy are replete with a sense of loyalty and an appreciation of wartime efforts; both elements contrast with the postindustrial mood. Now Homesteaders express a sense of betrayal by a nation and a perception that efforts were made only in the interests of corporate gain. In my interviews with townspeople, "below the tracks" attained more, not less, importance from its unique role in the history of the town.

Only a few physical structures remain to influence the stories an older generation recalled and a younger learned about the Lower Ward. But Brodsky found a cache of old photographs in library archives, and those inspired a greater nostalgia than the verbal narratives alone had conveyed. Looking at photographs of the Lower Ward and recapturing the past, residents emphasized the separation of community life from the broad economic and political forces that shaped that life. When people thought back, they recreated a community that was autonomous—celebrated its own rituals and made its own peace among diverse groups. Underlying this theme was the abandonment of steel towns by the very industry that had compelled people to establish, and nurture, a vigorous nonwork life. Here, too, was the knot in the story: a way of life came about in the face of oppressive work conditions and the townspeople's strength and stamina were severely tested without those conditions when there was no mill against which to form a community of solidarity. The tension between a proud independence and an equally proud expectation of return on labor runs through virtually all my interviews, regardless of the interviewee's age, gender, and years in the town.

The phrase "below the tracks" provided a vivid symbol for communal strategies of survival and for collectively positive self-images and, in the postindustrial era, was the obvious place and time to turn to for residents of Homestead. They skipped over the 1950s, slighting the years of prosperity that expansion of the mill and postwar production schedules brought to town. Or, if they did refer to those years, individuals were likely to paint them in negative colors: the beginnings of restlessness and a breakdown in traditional live-and-let-live practices, a decline that culminated for many residents in the intrusion of civil rights legislation.

Moreover, the years of prosperity might be an embarrassing memory: the times of two cars in every driveway, a boat on the front lawn, and famous (or infamous) long vacations offered an image of the steelworker that was now at best ambiguous. Rather than glorying in the benefits of steel work and the luxuries enjoyed by steelworkers in the 1950s and 1960s, in their personal histories Homesteaders returned to another image: the hardened steelworker who endured long, hot hours and still had time for family and neighbors. Vacations and conspicuous consumption were not part of these histories of a "homey," hardworking town of kin and community.

Nor did I hear much about moving to the suburbs, a phenomenon of the 1950s and 1960s. As the nearby South Hills suburbs grew, Homestead lost population. White families were the ones who primarily moved out, enjoying the salaries that allowed them to buy newly constructed houses and in reaction to federal fair-housing legislation that changed the look of Homestead's residential areas. Blacks did not move so readily; besides being excluded from some suburban developments, blacks often did not have the economic wherewithal to move.[11] Either in low-paid jobs or paid less than their white counterparts, blacks frequently did not have income available for buying houses in the suburbs. Unmentioned in the interviews I gathered was the fact that prosperity did not spread any more evenly than economic depression did.

Yet these changes in Homestead did leave a mark on the landscape. Shoppers on Eighth Avenue were older, as their children left for the suburbs and the growing suburban malls. Age, however, was not the only visible sign of change. One white woman came as close to defining the situation as anyone when she reported, "in the 1960s, Homestead turned dark." Whether her remark referred to race or to a deserted Eighth Avenue, the import was the same. Homestead, she admitted, had lost the look she had known as a child. Her remark also suggests a breakdown in the traditional modes of managing racial and ethnic differences, and her memory placed that breakdown in the 1960s.

Rather than prosperity, what many people I interviewed recalled about the 1960s was a disruptive civil rights movement. Regardless of age, a number of white (and a few black) interviewees complained about the "interference" of outsiders in a racial accommodation that had previously "worked well enough." Federal law about who should work with whom, where people should live and children go to school, entered the memories of Homesteaders as a devastating blow to "custom." Looking back, some residents of Homestead considered this blunt intervention by government the first step toward the chaos and collapse that culminated in USX's decision to "X out the town." A few residents added to the explanation the "trouble" caused by public protests led by nonresidents. Such a narrative took the heat off USX, a force too powerful to blame comfortably.[12]

Homestead: An ex-steel town?

From some vantage points, we could imagine the Homestead that framed memories: a broad, tree-lined main street, wood frame houses clustered just above the business district, and the gleaming spires of church steeples on the hillside. Yet a turn toward the river demonstrated how false this view of continuity was. In 1992, the rubble of torn-down mill buildings lay where the Homestead Works once stood.[13] On Eighth Avenue, displays in shop windows showed the impact of USX's decision: a former shoe store converted into a secondhand store, a clinic whose posters warned against drug use and AIDS, a branch of Goodwill, a junk shop. Pittsburgh buses still used Homestead as a transfer point, but passengers rarely got out to shop—especially if it happened to be after dark. Charlee and I also stopped going to town during the evening hours. For us, as for residents, danger lurked along the side streets, and the greetings of those we encountered no longer seemed as friendly as they once had. Was the famous steel town losing its character as a stable and safe community?

In the early months I spent in Homestead, I often heard the statement, "Homestead is not like Braddock." This contrast with the neighboring steel town gave Homesteaders a sense of hope; their town was not in total ruin, as they perceived Braddock to be. The two towns did look different from one another then, though that had not always been the case. With similar histories, the towns developed similar landscapes: a large mill dominating the river bank, a bustling downtown street, and a hillside covered with houses whose styles reflected the socioeconomic hierarchies of a mill town. But Braddock suffered devastation even without mill closings, when the commercial sector suffered a decline in the 1970s. The business street showed signs of depression as stores closed; housing was neglected and schools boarded up.

The contrast evoked another distinction as well. Homestead's history was different from Braddock's because of the 1892 strike, an event that was celebrated in 1992, in centennial festivities. The great steel corporation, some residents claimed, could not destroy the mill that carried so much history; USX would not abandon Homestead the way steel companies had abandoned one town after another along the Monongahela River. When the mill definitively closed and the structures began to fall under the wrecking crews, these same residents argued that the very "militancy" of Homestead antagonized corporate managers and encouraged the destruction of the famous Works. One way or another, however, the unique importance of Homestead framed assessments of the present crisis.

At the same time, facing the crisis of deindustrialization, Homestead residents expanded the history of their town to include its vigorous nonwork culture. In nostalgic stories, they distanced the town from steel by immers-

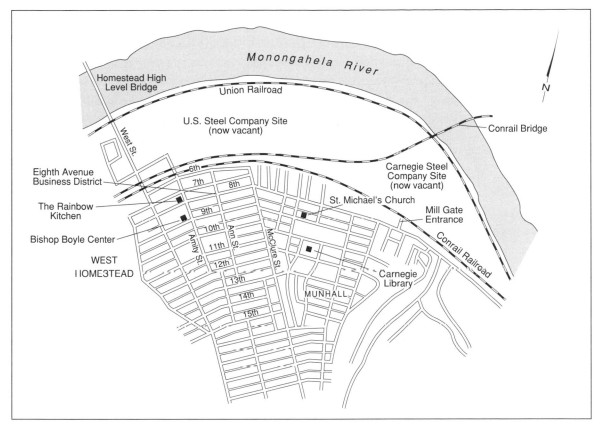

Homestead, 1990 (University of Pittsburgh Press)

ing themselves in memories of a community. Moreover, often a narrator made the community sound rural. Puffs of smoke, an elderly woman said to me, "looked like clouds" in the sky. A young man recalled slag heaps that were like "big mountains" for him and his friends. And one woman told me of deer running through the area called Hunky Hollow. These comments had an ironic echo in the idea proposed by Prince Charles of Britain (in the summer of 1988) that the mill buildings be turned into greenhouses. By 1994, there were no mill buildings in which to test this pleasant notion.

Over three generations: The interviewees

The first person I met in Homestead was a man in his sixties who, it turned out, owned a small business in a residential neighborhood of Homestead. I met him at the Carnegie Library of Homestead on a day early in my exploration of the town. He noticed me reading newspaper articles about Homestead and eagerly began to explain the photographs. That day in 1986 was the start of a long relationship with Sam Wozeck, an amateur historian who relished the chance to inform my interpretations of his town.

I intended to construct the story of the mill closing through the narratives of those who had experienced different phases of the presence of steel in Homestead. From 1986 to 1992, I interviewed members of three different generations in Homestead—the "first generation" being the elders of the community. The second generation was composed of their children, women and men in their forties and fifties for whom reliance on the mill was not always a desirable or a necessary choice. The third generation were young adults, those in their twenties and early thirties who came to maturity with the decline in American steel and who had to make other choices about work.

I started interviewing Sam Wozeck's extended family—both women and men—steelworkers and shopkeepers who had been in Homestead (or the steel valley) since the generation of Sam's own parents. The Wozecks are in many ways the centerpiece of the book, articulating events and perceptions I subsequently found were shared by most long-time residents. Over the years of research, I expanded my contacts with the help of the Wozecks and through other encounters at union meetings, in shops, and as a result of Charlee's contacts with individuals she photographed. The voices in this book follow the pathways of sociability in the town, a method appropriate both to the history of Homestead and to its present fluid social relationships. Depending on informal sociability had two consequences: (1) as members of social networks, the individuals I interviewed were entrenched in the community. They defined themselves as belonging, considered themselves "expert" on the place, and readily took the stage as historians; (2) the significance of networks provided a clear identification of those who were "new" to Homestead, and I included a few such newcomers in my project.

I interviewed forty-five individuals, twenty-one women and twenty-four men. Of these, ten were African American, seven of whom were male. Virtually all interviews were done on tape, and all taped interviews were transcribed; most lasted between an hour and two hours. In the case of seven individuals, I did a second and third interview. In the rare case an individual refused to be taped, or when the tape recorder was not available, I made extensive notes as soon as I could. The array of voices (and opinions) in this book is representative of the age, gender, ethnic, and racial composition of the town at the time of my study.

I have kept the interviewees' names confidential, disguising identifying details throughout. Although the number of people who did not mind being identified slightly exceeded the number who did, it seemed fairest to everyone, and to the town, to respect the privacy of those who spoke to me so readily.

Interviews with members of three generations are complemented by chance conversations with individuals encountered on the streets of Homestead or as they posed for Charlee's camera. Together these sources evoke the sense of a changing town, the perspectives of longtime residents juxtaposed against those of newcomers who often lacked any attachment to steel work. Yet steel was rarely missing from anyone's story as it is the image of and symbol for life in this Mon Valley town—even for those who came when the mill had turned into an empty lot. As a shopkeeper said to me, "everything derives from the steel."

The story I tell is not simply about steel and steel families. It is, however, about how steel framed the experiences of anyone who grew up in Homestead or came to live there after rents fell and the town offered inexpensive housing. The Homestead Works forms the background in historical and cultural as well as economic terms to everything residents claimed about the community.

One ex-steelworker instantly recognized the thrust of our project. Dick Wurtz had an astonishing visual record of the Homestead Works in its decades of prosperity—his own drawings, paintings, and cartoons, as well as notes of his comings and goings as clerk on the shop floor—and he was quite aware of their historical and cultural significance. As clerk in the Homestead Works, Dick had documented in precise and humorous detail the activities of men (and by the 1970s, women) on the shop floor. In a gesture of generosity, he gave me copies of his cartoons for our book. Dick knew his stuff was good, as art and as document, and he was pleased to have the material reach a wider public. He had always treated his cartoons and sketches as precious. He showed his cartoons around the mill, pinned them to his walls, and gave them as gifts to their subjects. "Nobody threw them away. They all kept them. . . . [One man] took the original and his wife took it down there to Pittsburgh and had the guy blow it up big, about two to three feet and had it framed and everything else. And it's hanging in their game room, she liked it so good."

Both the pictures and Dick's explanation of each one told a story of life in the mill. Moreover, his exegesis of the collection confirmed the importance of imagery to the way people understood the events and changes. Dick was aware of how closely he replicated the project Brodsky and I were doing: "I used to have my own darkroom and everything," he said. "I used to develop my own pictures and so on and so forth. I haven't fooled with photography for years. . . . So that's the way that goes. So, but as far as an anthropologist is concerned, I study the human race around me." His drawings manifest an anthropological as well as a photographic view of the cast of characters and their social interactions in a steel mill.

Dick drew everyone he met, and most of the drawings are individual portraits. "This guy, Natali," he said, pulling a cartoon out, "I used to tease about dandelion wine and the taste of it. I used to draw Natali—he was a little short guy—standing on an orange crate talking to the bigger fellas. Someone used to tell me, 'he's not that short, why don't you draw him standing on the ground?' So I drew him standing on the ground because the box caved in and he fell down inside the box." Natali had something to say about the image: "I don't look like that." Dick's response revealed his affiliation with the anthropologist and with the photographer: "I said, 'what the artist sees, the artist draws.'"

His portraits do not simply depict individuals; they also suggest the complicated ethnic and racial relationships in a milltown: "A janitor came up to me and, 'Dick,' he says, 'you got all those pictures out there and you only got one black man.' And he says, 'you got to do one for me so that people know it's me.' He says, 'I'm part of this group.'" Dick told the anecdote on purpose, to remind me of his tolerance—and, more subtly, of the potential for racial conflict in the mill. Usually, however, on the matter of race and ethnicity, the artist let the drawings speak for themselves, adding only an identification: "This is Natali," he would say, "this is Dubaczek, this is Weisman." Sometimes, as in the janitor story, Dick "captioned" his cartoons with commentary for the anthropologist, posing as a social scientist himself.

In our conversations Dick proved the importance of visual materials for analyzing a place and a time. My interviews with him indicated how effectively "seeing" turned a person into an expert on industrial policy, town history, and community relationships. His talk around his collection conveyed a culture beyond that of the shop floor: "They're good solid people. I tell you what, there's a whole cross-section, the Pittsburgh melting pot that they speak of. When you tease an Italian guy about dandelion wine, he knows that you're teasing, just like that Greek fellow teasing me about my gimpy leg."

Dick was not alone in telling the history of a town through the faces and interactions of workers, residents, and families. Even those less tutored in art and photography saw Homestead through pictures, remembered scenes, and perceived alterations in a physical environment. Dick may have been the most self-conscious in his visual representation of Homestead, but he was not the only person who revealed how complex "envisioning" can be.

The following chapters reflect the visual dimension in the way residents have responded to changes in their lives from the early years of the century until its (near) end. Throughout the book, the voices informing my argument are those of individuals whose lives depended on steel, regardless of whether they had ever stepped into a mill. Their voices constitute an ethnography of disastrous change that shows the necessity of fitting change into familiar patterns and expected turns of fate. How people see their surroundings is a cogent interpretation of circumstances. Describing the look of a neighborhood, an individual delineates taken-for-granted discriminatory practices. Evoking the sad scene of a weed-filled mill site, another reveals the depth of her condemnation of a corporation that seemed too big to fight against. Remembering himself as the small boy pictured in a family snapshot led another to recreate the components of a vigorous and diverse community.

Most importantly, from the many memories and retellings of "below the tracks" came the picture of life apart from the mill and its cycles of production. With or without photos to remind them of the "good old days," residents remembered those days as if they were deindustrialized—in a positive way. The image of Homestead that emerges from the intertwining of public and private histories is one of community, of a town that had the stamina and the strategies to survive regardless of steel. At the same time, as responses to Brodsky's photographs and the residents' collections of family snapshots reveal, the existence and expansion of the Homestead Works and its downfall and destruction unmistakably determine every resident's vision of Homestead.

SETTING THE STAGE

Three Generations in a Mill Town

The sons may work a little further up than their fathers; a man told me with pride that his son, who was a foreman, had secured for him a job in the mill, and a mother was eager to relate how her boy had taught the new assistant superintendent the way to do his work. Only rarely, however, do they secure an education that fits them for an entirely different kind of labor. The mothers, too, expect that their daughters will eventually marry mill workers.

—Margaret Byington, *Homestead: The Households of a Mill Town*

"I have over two hundred years in the mill." I did not understand this statement when I first heard it from an ex-steelworker, a man in his late thirties. His meaning emerged during the interview. He was the child in a family whose men had, among them, accumulated two hundred years in the mill. I was to hear a similar calculation from others, who totted up their lives in Homestead in terms of the members of all generations who had lived there. "And I'm the son of a steelworker who was the son of a steelworker," another man said to me, giving an almost biblical rhythm to the notion of generations stretching back in time. But it did not require work in the mill to utilize this mechanism; the vocabulary was available to any Homestead resident who claimed a long ancestry in the town. The wife of a shopkeeper began her life story with the phrase: "I have over a hundred years here." Individuals whose families have been in Homestead for at least three generations take a primary role in the following pages.

These are the individuals, too, who insist they will never leave Homestead. They plan to stay where their parents and grandparents put down roots: "Nobody wants to leave, let's put it that way," said a man in his thirties. "Once you get your roots—I've noticed that about a lot of people." Once you get roots, he meant, you stay through the bad times as well as the good. The concept of roots and the related idea of tradition link personal stories and public history; recalling one's own life is a way of presenting Homestead's fame and glory. Memories, autobiographical fragments, and anecdotes constitute a history of the steel town, and "roots" indicates the loyalty that is part of this history.

Accounts of births and deaths, christenings and weddings blur the lines between private and public and merge the experiences of one generation with another. An image of Homestead threads through the narratives, as distinctly evident in words as it is in the landscape of the town. For residents, the image conveys a sense of permanence and the conviction that they will stay in town no matter what. The image of Homestead also brings forward values and customs that individuals attribute explicitly to the past and implicitly to the possibilities for the future. The phrase "below the tracks" conjures up a perfect town and a place of genuine harmony. Expressed memories of the good old days testify to the conviction that the town will be able to survive an industrial crisis—that lessons learned *then* can help in circumstances confronted *now*.

A vision of the good old days ran through the interviews with individuals who knew "over a hundred years" in town. Most residents pictured an idyllic past based on the terrible years of the Great Depression, which were recalled as a time of courage, coping, sharing, and solidarity even by those who had not lived through the period. Composed for the tape recorder, the "good old days," according to interviewees, illustrated the best of life in Homestead and highlighted elements of life that were independent of industry in one of the most famous industrial towns in America. The good old days represented a reason for staying, and anecdotes of the past proved steel was not the only source of survival in a steel town.

Inhabitants of the deindustrializing town of the 1980s and 1990s described earlier decades of community and of bold response to crisis.[1] For them, views of what Homestead had been formed a legacy, the reward that came with being in a place forever. From this perspective, loyalty to the town ought to carry residents through the recent collapse into a future whose only certainty was the disappearance of a mill. Having that certainty, individuals filled their memories with references to scenes and settings that rendered "steel" either invisible or a harmless, cloudy background to real life. Rather than commemorating history by emphasizing the town's most notable structure, individuals referred instead to the shops on Eighth Avenue, the bleachers at a Little League game, or front porches crowded with "friendly" neighbors. In one way, they neglected official public history; in another, individuals appropriated the public text of "steel" into private testimonies to households and family. Nevertheless, when the Park Corporation began demolishing the Homestead Works in 1989, residents realized the loss of a huge physical inspiration for what they remembered—and how.

With or without the sight of the mill, those who remained in Homestead portrayed a town whose livelihood did not only depend on steel. This image was a source of hope for the interviewee and an insistence that Homestead differed from other towns dying along the Monongahela River. Beyond that, the image captures a version of history and conveys a quality of chauvinism essential to any complete account of deindustrialization. For it makes clear that people who live in a town do not necessarily perceive the demolition of a plant as the death knell for a community. If a house were repossessed by the bank, the owners would find another location and plant the flowers and arrange the religious statuary that sustained a way of life. A mill lot covered with weeds did not signal the end of a town for those whose parents and grandparents had spent their lives there. This pose of optimism, however, required increasing effort in the decade after 1986.

The collapse in the present threw people back to the past—sometimes a past as recent as ten years earlier. Regardless of when the past was, the details of life then—from sweeping front porches to enduring one hundred degrees of heat at the open hearth—represented popular history, a warp in the woof of official histories of the steel town. Details of daily life brought the fate of a giant industry to human proportions.

In residents' narratives, the past represents harmony and diversity, patterns transmitted from parent to child, and agreement about the town's best interests. Above all, the good old days stood for the sentiment that kept residents where they were despite the lack of opportunity and possibilities. *Then,* people shopped where they lived, supporting Eighth Avenue and not deserting it for outlying malls or downtown Pittsburgh department stores. Another rationale for staying became apparent: To save a town, it must be peopled by homeowners, families, consumers, and churchgoers.[2]

Homesteaders envisioned community in various guises. The crowds on Eighth Avenue, for instance, represented not only prosperity but the unity of spirit that followed a hard day's work. According to the people I interviewed, the whistle blew and men, women, and children crowded the sidewalks. No one *then* complained or feared for their pockets. Moreover, such accounts created a picture of Homestead as a town of shops, restaurants, ice cream parlors, and bars. Making a living did not entirely take place in a mill, and did not have to. In emphasizing this to me, residents were looking forward as well as back.

Family albums and responses to archival photographs revealed the recreational side of life. The railroad crossing photos taken by an insurance company elicited stories about "below the tracks," and about the tracks themselves: young boys, I was told, climbed freight trains to steal coal or other "stuff." Older boys walked near the tracks, hoping to catch a glimpse of a prostitute sauntering toward Sixth Avenue and her customers. On Sundays, some residents crossed the tracks to attend church in the "Upper Wards" of Homestead. Family albums documented customs closer to home—weddings, birthday parties, and christenings that comprised the domestic history of Homestead. Not recorded in snapshots and only reluctantly reported in life stories were the ethnic, religious, and racial conflicts that constituted steel town history in the twentieth century.

Romanticization of the old can serve a purpose. When the mill neighborhood was razed during World War II, Mark took the bricks from his original tavern and rebuilt the place, piece by piece, in a new location. In doing so, he claimed the power of an individual to buck the tide of change by reconstructing the central elements of an institution. The Homestead Works cannot be similarly rebuilt, but other pieces of town history might acquire a more appropriate preservation than the building of a water park called Sandcastle on the site of a mammoth machine shop. In West Homestead, Sandcastle symbolized change for residents of all three boroughs, and painful perceptions erased the boundaries between municipal units. "You know, but they say that they're going to be rebuilding and make new high-rise apartments, and the Sandcastle that they made down there, that

Below the tracks, 1941 (Pittsburgh and Lake Erie Railroad)

brings in a lot of people from out of town." No Homestead resident, this woman implied, would pay to slide into the water all afternoon; no Homestead resident, others told me, could afford the entry fee.

Nor did the management of Sandcastle offer real job opportunities to the younger Homestead generation. These children of steel families could not support themselves on the summer salaries paid by an amusement park. Would they leave the town their families had lived in for decades? Or, having heard the tales of solidarity, companionship, and kinship, would they stay?

"So we had a very good thing going"

"Thus a whole world ends when its metaphors die."[3] Was steel a metaphor in the sense this author suggests—the embodiment and representation of a complex worldview? In many ways, yes; both the corporation and the product can be construed that way: "The essence of metaphor is understanding and experiencing one kind of thing in terms of another."[4]

Like a metaphor, *steel* represents a complex history and culture. The word evokes the nineteenth-century transformation from farmland to industrial area, the twentieth-century experience of newcomers, and the perpetual accommodation individuals make to diversity and discrimination. *Steel* also explains the looks of the town, for urban planners as well as for residents. In the 1960s, at the height of Pittsburgh's "renaissance," a brochure presenting plans for renewal in Allegheny County described Homestead: "Clusters of homes on hills and slopes are criss-crossed by laces of grayish streets, with tufts of trees here and there, as though the natural green carpet were neatly rolled up to make way for man's structures."[5]

Homestead was experienced in terms of steel for those who did not work in the mill as thoroughly as for those who did. The spillover from industry to town was palpable in the heat and noise that came from the mill, in the pulsating rhythm of "turns" and the sudden sharp whistle of disaster, in the crowds on Eighth Avenue, and in the crowded houses in every neighborhood. Steel meant prosperity or, as residents put it, a *flow* of money—maybe a trickle in periods of downturn but then a flood in times of war and national expansion. In retrospect, the connotations of the metaphor were good, obscuring the oppressiveness of conditions in and around the mill. Steel provided the foundation for a life that was reliable, bearable, and uplifted by moments of joy. Looking back, the fear of accidents, the endless hours that kept a man from his family, and the arbitrary decisions of a profit-making corporation did not seem so bad.

"When, you know, you have people walking all over you, like shopping center atmosphere, they do business in spite of themselves," said the owner of an appliance store, remembering back to when he began work in the 1950s. "People just buy impulse buying. Well, we had that for many years." He continued in this vein: "On a shift change you couldn't walk down the sidewalk hardly. Both before the shift going in and after the shift coming out. And that happened in the morning, in the afternoon, and in the evening." John did not need to mention steel in order to emphasize the importance of the mill; steel sent people out with money in their pockets, and that benefited every shopkeeper in town. Implicit in this man's remarks, too, is a notion of safety and trust. Steel created a community so that "people walking all over you" was posed as a delight, not a threat.

John glanced out his window. Eighth Avenue did not look like the scene he had created in the interview. A scatter of people wandered by, few interested in the large purchase of a television or refrigerator—though in hot weather, a number would come in for the fans and air conditioners

John also sold. His "crowds" were gone, or different. Impulse buying had disappeared as noticeably as the mill itself, and his patrons were often, he told me, strangers from outside Homestead. Money from steel was not even a trickle by the time I met John, and his customers were no longer his neighbors.

The 1986 closing of the Homestead Works signaled a downturn, the proportions of which were incredible: thousands of men and women lost their jobs.[6] If John missed the pedestrians with money in their pockets, others missed the "dark clouds" of a mill smokestack or the noise of a steel plate running its track. When I interviewed John in 1988, the mill buildings were standing and his memories had visual cues. Moreover, as long as the physical plant remained, the world had not yet died.

"They're opening a machine shop down there," Peter, a young, laid-off steelworker told me in the spring of 1987. "It's supposed to have been, when it was completed in the late seventies, which wasn't that long ago for a machine shop, the newest in the nation. . . . Now they're trying—the mayor of Homestead, and they have a private company, are trying to get the—in fact, the mayor of Homestead was the foreman at the Big Shop [machine shop], so he's gonna help them set the machinery back up." Better than nothing, a machine shop evoked the glories of steel production and preserved the town's image of hard work and regular shifts. But the employed work force was small and, a skilled carpenter, Peter was not among those hired.

Peter had grown up on steel and defined himself by mill work. He had grown up in a steel town and he experienced the pulsating rhythms of production as background for his movement into adulthood. Peter's good old days were recent—less than ten years before I met him—and he expressed his sense of sudden emptiness and monotony throughout several interviews in the late 1980s. Laid off and despairing about finding new work, the fact that he had time to be interviewed at length had a bitter quality. He had too much leisure, too many opportunities for recreation, he said; the theater upon which his life took place had lost its usual parameters.

"Life space is at once the theater of life, understood as a convivial life, and an expression of it," writes a scholar of urbanism. Life space exists as a distinct domain, separated from the activities of making a living and, Peter might have noted, sustained by the fact of making a living. The scholar adds another point relevant to residents' understandings of Homestead: "Life spaces . . . are typically bounded, territorial spaces"—neighborhoods, in other words, places of freedom from the travails of the job.[7] In Homestead, "below the tracks" evoked the conviviality of life space, a loss that Peter mourned.

"'Cause mostly down below the tracks where we lived, it was mostly all either Slovak, Russian, Hungarian, but they mostly all spoke Slovak," remembered a woman old enough to be Peter's mother. "And we were like one big, happy family, we sort of knew each other, and what we did, they did. They had the same culture, they celebrated their Christmas and their Easter and the holidays same way like we did." Her account was repeated not only by women and men of an older generation; their children and grandchildren provided similar accounts of "below the tracks." They had learned to identify "below" with the genuine culture of Homestead, independent of the pressures imposed by corporate production schedules. "Below" was shorthand (or metaphor) for the values, beliefs, and social interactions that represented the heart of Mon Valley steel town life.

Tavern owner Mark told me that when he grew up "below the tracks" fifty years ago, "We all got along, life was a pleasure." He painted a picture of harmony and of mutual tolerance for different customs—or intolerance, where the misbehavior of children was involved. Everyone brought up the kids, he recalled. "If I stepped out of line and old man Flannagan saw me do something wrong, he smacked me in the fanny. And likewise if my father saw one of them do something wrong, he reprimanded them. Everybody got along nice." Not mentioned were the strict neighborhood boundaries, so that Mark's "everybody" probably referred to whites and not to the blacks and Mexicans who also lived "below the tracks." In the good old days, it seemed, residential segregation came naturally.

Often when someone wanted to convey how "convivial" life was, he or she described a wedding. On those occasions, according to an interviewee, people celebrated who they were, free of economic exigencies: "Weddings, kids got married. They would start maybe on a Tuesday. Saturday was the big day. But on Tuesday they got started. The gypsies came and they played all day and all night. The old man would pass booze around to guests coming from out of town. And ladies were down in the cellar sweating, working, cooking." Thus Mark underlined his story of fellowship and joy in 1930s Homestead, despite the Great Depression. Others had similar memories. Celebrations and ceremonies stood for community for most people, including those whose past was less than a decade earlier.

"Every time there was a church dance or weddings, even if we weren't invited, as little children we'd hear that music and we'd go to the hall and we'd go in, which nobody objected—the children'd come in and dance," a Slovak woman in her sixties told me. "Everybody was welcome. Long as everybody was having a good time. That was the main important thing. Everybody just enjoy themselves and be happy with everybody, cause the bride's there and, you know, a special day for her. So that was a big thing with us." And, of course, there were always photographs of weddings for those who forgot the joy of life in a steel town or needed a reminder of days gone by.

There were fewer photos of other life space activities, of events that symbolized the harmony and solidarity of a community, but there were some. A snapshot of a small boy holding a baseball bat, for instance, reminded an elderly man of the "goodness" of sports: "There were many more sports activities amongst different groups within the area," he told me. "You had baseball leagues within these three, four, five areas. You don't have that any more. You had softball and all that stuff. Competitive stuff between groups. Police departments, fire departments, and everything. You don't see too much of that any more." Like weddings, sports events drew the three boroughs together and separated town from mill.

"And we'd be rooting—everybody, oh, was so nice about it," a grandmother told me. "A lot of parents put a lot of time in, even the mothers," said a younger woman, whose experiences on the playing field had occurred in the late 1950s. This woman continued, presenting the good life of three decades earlier: "We had the ladies' auxiliary and sold candy down the baseball field there, and we had—at the end of the season—we had banquets for the young boys and gave trophies out. So we had a very good thing going there at that time." She concluded, "But now, nothing!"

Yet the shadow of the mill had historically hovered over these activities. The U.S. Steel Corporation supported town leagues, and its departure left teams without resources and, as poverty spread, without spirit. Life spaces were distinct from work spaces, but the corporation had provided the wherewithal for the rituals and recreation Homestead residents remembered.[8] When USX left, sustenance drained out of nonwork domains; a town without jobs had a hard time playing, whatever the locus of play.

"The red lights were lit"

"Below the tracks" had its own cultural as well as economic institutions. Residents of the mill neighborhood could earn a living in numerous ways besides entering the gates of the mill or pursuing new white-collar jobs. The Lower Ward offered numerous sources of income—casual, illegal, semi-legal, and haphazard. These attracted individuals deprived of access to conventional means of survival or, perhaps, bored by such conventions.

"They were flourishing businesses," a man began a pointed anecdote, "every one of them. And even with red lights on the front of them. They had them, too." His point was not to criticize houses of prostitution or those who patronized them, but to convey the economic diversity of a once prosperous steel town. From his perspective, all economic activity was beneficial and the wealth spread around: "And when the dirt was on the sidewalks and the red lights were lit, we were making money up here too. . . . I mean, it was a lot of bars and that down in there, that they never even had licenses. That's how they operated. But nobody seemed to ever bother them. They didn't bother anybody else, so no harm, no foul—, I guess."

For him, even "dirt" meant something good in the old days, in the same way that residents fondly recalled the heavy, dark smoke hanging in the skies. Such "filth" evoked prosperity and not pollution: "It would have been comfortable when it was dirty, financially-wise, for all the people around here." He also may have meant, as others did, that that kind of dirt was the town's own, not the mill's, the government's, or the politicians' to supervise and, ultimately, condemn. Dirty activities included gambling, prostitution, and the stealing and pilfering that was part of an underground economy in good times and bad.

According to older Homestead residents, a bakery truck did not make its deliveries unscathed: "Bull's Baking Company would pull up with their truck in front of the bakery to deliver nickel pies and cakes and so forth," a steelworker in his late fifties remembered for me. "And these guys would case them, you know. They'd watch. And they'd go in the bakery and tell the boss, 'you know I got this delivery for you.' But by the time he came out, that truck was cleaned out." Thinking back, such illegal activities seemed entertaining, not harmful or dangerous. Moreover, these anecdotes were a reminder that workers differed from bosses and bankers, who could buy all the cake they wanted. Taking credit for being a pilferer, this man concluded: "And we went down and everybody got a nickel cake."

Versions of these stories run through published accounts of Mon Valley towns. In Thomas Bell's *Out of This Furnace,* Johnnie does his stealing at the river: "The procedure was to get aboard a barge and throw the biggest lumps he could manage ashore. He risked falling into the river and being chased by a watchman, and occasionally the coal hoist operator would scoop up a bucketful of river water instead of coal and shower him with it, but that hardly detracted from the sport."[9] Work in the mills was bitter and brutal, but these stories argue that there were ways of circumventing troubles. The humming of the Works gave alternative economic strategies a vital background noise.

The same stories transformed the meaning of being poor; those interviewed said a person did not have to be rich to survive in Homestead or to enjoy its pleasures: "The Avenue was the heart-throb of the community." In the old days, the narratives went, Eighth Avenue presented a panorama of desired and desirable goods. Shop windows were crowded with dresses, shoes, and hats, lunch counters jammed with patrons, and shops with large household items not lacking customers—a picture of Homestead as urban, a parallel to the stories of "homey" neighborhoods. It did not matter, in memories, that some residents could buy whatever they wanted and others only yearned. As people thought back, Eighth Avenue took on the air of a marketplace in which contacts and conviviality were as important as actual purchases.

In an effort to persuade me of the commercial success of Homestead, individuals I interviewed recited the names of stores that existed when they were children. These recitations occurred regardless of age and whether or not photos were present to jog a memory. "Bakery, five-and-tens—oh, they're like five five-and-tens—two Isaly's [ice cream parlor], three shows—three theaters." Going up and down Eighth Avenue in memory, however, was also sad since so much had changed and so many of the remembered storefronts had vanished: "At one time there were seven appliance stores on Eighth Avenue out here," a man in his forties assured me. "Seven of them. And probably five furniture stores. Maybe even more if I think a little bit. It's, well there was Ruben's, Half's, and then some other ones up on the hill." Later, this same man said, "There used to be, I got to say, five movies on this avenue within a three-block area. I can't think of the names—yeah, there was a good five of them over the years at one time. A couple of Isaly's. . . . I mean, banks, my gosh, one, two, three, four, I guess it was five banks here at one time."

Over and over, residents named the same stores, suggesting that some institutions "down street" were more important than others. The five movie theaters, all the five-and-tens, the ice cream parlors—I heard the list from generation to generation. "There was Ruben's," a woman in her late twenties told me, "and there was Half Brothers [furniture store]. We had five five-and-tens. Five. Woolworth's first, Newberry's, Grant's, McCrory's, and Wheelwright's." Few people named the bars and taverns, though in other parts of an interview it became clear that these institutions thrived through the worst economic downturns of the century.

When things were going well, Eighth Avenue was "jammed" with people so "thick you couldn't see the sidewalks." "Oh, at that time [pre-World War II], they had wall-to-wall people," said a woman, remembering how she had ventured up to Eighth Avenue when she was a girl in the 1930s. Crowds represented the past for younger women and men—an indication of how much Homestead had changed. A woman in her twenties used almost the same words: "It was so crowded there Saturdays, oh, it's a big day. Even if you weren't buying anything, we would just go down the avenue, just look at the windows. We'd go from one store to the other, look at the clothes that are out on display in the windows." A businessman said nostalgically, "On a shift change you couldn't walk down the sidewalk hardly."

Set against a depressed present, it did not matter to the speaker that income was not equally distributed and that not all residents could buy what they wanted. Thomas Bell's account of a steelworker family's need to balance necessities with pleasures did not play a role in the reminiscences of Eighth Avenue I gathered; compared with now, everyone was better off then. Bell's descriptions bring up the other side of the story, the one that was obscured in my interviews. He talks of husbands and wives yearning for new silverware, regretting not being able to buy the children clothes, foregoing the winter coat. "Leisurely, carefully, they shopped for the needed underwear and dress goods and what not, remembered to stop in the five-and-ten for a bag of candy for the children," but did not buy the work shirts a steelworker needed.[10]

Like my interviewees, Bell points out that at least there were crowds and excitement, even if a person could not buy everything she or he needed. "We didn't like it then, but now we miss it," someone said about the noise, racket, and dirt that were a by-product of "wall-to-wall" people. To the third generation I interviewed, the changes on Eighth Avenue seemed dramatic and abrupt. From their perspective, shops and movie theaters had vanished into thin air when the mill closed. Capturing this sense, a young woman told me "everything" had burned up: "There were fires all over!"

"They're still opening things up down there"

For several years, Homestead residents expressed hope that the town would not go the way of its Mon Valley neighbors. Looking across the river, they observed Braddock, a town that appeared totally devastated. "We are not like Braddock," residents said to me in the first interviews I did in Homestead. In those early months, references to Braddock maintained the distinctiveness of Homestead; America's famous steel town, people implied, could not die like an "ordinary" industrial town.

In the late 1980s, the contrast was visible. Abandoned businesses and For Sale signs dotted Braddock, while Levine's Hardware and Caspar's Appliances still attracted customers to Eighth Avenue. "We have a nice hardware store, I think," a young man told me. "And we have a restaurant. You take Braddock, now they didn't fare as well. I don't think they have anything. They have a bank, still." Then, with a note of fondness for his hometown, he added, "We have a bakery. I can [smell it]; in fact, when they bake bread on Sunday night and that, it wakes me up."

Right after the mill closed, Homestead did not seem to be sliding into the depression experienced by towns like Braddock or, further away from Pittsburgh, isolated mill towns like Aliquippa. Homestead was close to Pittsburgh and to alternative jobs; it was the site of several bus routes, and passengers transferring from one bus to another had time to stop and shop. Homestead was the famous American steel town: would politicians and planners just let it go? More to the point, would residents simply abandon Eighth Avenue for the malls in the expanding South Hills suburbs? During the years of optimism, individuals not only mentioned the Eighth Avenue shops but also, as if to persuade me of their loyalty, suggested we meet for interviews in Isaly's ice cream parlor or at the local branch of the Eat'n Park coffee shop. Other customers drifted in, looking curiously at the stranger with her tape recorder and asking why I was there. In the late 1980s, there was still a perceptible feeling of community in the town.

People I talked with in those first summers of research referred to the good old days to indicate Homestead's ability to survive into the future. A town that maintained over forty church congregations could count on the energy of residents to help each other through hard times. "I think the potential to build this place up is still there because there's enough people around here that are willing to stick with it," a woman in her late twenties explained to me. "A lot of people did bail out, but there's enough people around here like me, coming from a family, generations that—I think something's going to work out, I really do." Her view was that individuals with over a hundred years in town would "stick to it." She finished with the final proof, a comparison to the neighboring steel town: "I think Braddock's a lost cause. But I think Homestead can still, I mean they're still opening things up down there [on Eighth Avenue]. Ten years ago, all we probably had was Winkies. Now there's Long John Silver's and Kentucky Fried Chicken, so somebody else must think that there's something worthwhile."

"Sticking to it" and enduring were part of Homestead's background, interpreted positively by residents who wanted to see the town move into a future without steel. From this vantage point, the qualities that had carried workers and their families through the oppressive conditions imposed by a greedy corporation would carry their children and grandchildren through the consequences of a shutdown. I met a woman in her forties who was insisting her daughter go to college in order to make a living in a new way in the former steel town. She only needed to wait a while, this mother said to me, with a thin strand of hope in her voice, "I think maybe in about five years or so things will be picked up. You know, and I think people that left are going to regret leaving. Everything takes time."

That interview was done in 1991 when, in fact, the appearance of Homestead had worsened, planners had not yet recognized the full brunt of the disaster, and residents needed radically to alter their understandings of the town. After 1991, I heard negative and occasional despairing remarks from an increasing number of residents. Even Mark, generally upbeat, criticized his neighbors for "living in the past." He said, "Many a times you hear all these people who lived there [the Lower Ward] say, 'Boy, what I wouldn't give to go back there again. I'd just love to be in that situation again.' Even though we've improved our lot, I think they still would have preferred being there, because it was a big family, a fellowship affair, you know." In fact, Mark closely resembled his nostalgic neighbors; he himself relished the memories of "fellowship" when he was growing up "below the tracks." It was Mark who rebuilt a tavern brick by brick in order to maintain the old feeling in a new location.

Others were sarcastic and frankly impatient with the notion of looking back in order to move forward. They were the few who looked at the archival photos we brought and considered those days "gone by." They tended to be college-educated and middle-class women and men who hoped to rebuild a town they had always seen in a different light from their working-class neighbors. Ideas for beautification and renewal that came from this segment of the population distressed residents who considered such plans the first wedge in a total transformation of the once-familiar town. The problem, I was told by these critics, was joblessness, not an ugly town. A carpenter felt that renewal in Homestead would take more than nails, painting, and new storefronts: "I'm a carpenter," he announced early in his interview, "I don't have to look very farther than the front of my nose to see that this whole town needs a massive amount of work." One can read his last phrase as having multiple meanings: a "massive amount of work" was what Homestead needed—and the influx of money that would shore up a failing economic system.

By the early 1990s, residents had an increasingly difficult time distinguishing their town from Braddock. The windfall of short-order restaurants had ended. A new bridal shop on Eighth Avenue stood lonely, its splendid white gowns a sad touch of life next to Goodwill and secondhand stores whose windows were a chaos of household items. "That's the difference," a woman began explaining in midstream of her thought: "When they knocked a building down, say, ten years ago, somebody put another one back up. Now when they knock a building down, it stays—there's a hole there. Nobody has the money."

Members of the older generation saw the decline of Homestead as particularly significant for their children and grandchildren. What would bring any "young person" to Eighth Avenue when the malls were livelier, more exciting, and safer? "So because the mall has such a bigger variety, naturally you just run out to the mall," a mother said, her *you* referring to her three daughters. "But for the younger people, or even the middle-aged people," explained a somewhat older woman, "there's really nothing down there on Eighth Avenue for them to do. I mean, they would have to get more stores, you know." Without a new generation shopping down street, these comments implied, there was not much hope for the town.

And even for an older generation, used to running down to one of the five five-and-tens or into Moxley's for a quick soda, the decline and the unfamiliar look of Eighth Avenue were depressing. Like their children and grandchildren, these old-time Homestead residents drove to the malls. "But it's just so sad when you go down into Homestead now," the wife of a retired steelworker remarked. "It's just as though, you know, you see the town as a whole, but the body, it's empty. There's something so sad, so depressing about it. And it's hard, you know, it's hard to believe . . . it's just incredible to believe that there would never be any more steel produced." When her husband wandered into the room, she underlined the powerful image she had already used with me: "I was telling her how when you go down into Homestead now, it just seems like a town with an empty shell inside."

The empty shell of Eighth Avenue had an echoing resonance in the empty lot near the river. By 1992, the familiar man-made structures of a steel mill were wiped away. Maintaining the eloquence with which she had described Eighth Avenue, Joanna repeated to me a conversation she had had with her husband: "While we were sitting there I said, 'You know, look at it down there,' I said. 'I can remember not too long ago when I was picking you up and men were coming out.' And it, even though they were tired, I mean they were tired, there was still like a spirit that was buzzing all around, just people from everywhere. And they had a little restaurant there. . . . It was like a railroad station-type thing, and the men used to go in there. They'd stop in and get a drink, get a beer or something like that after work." But now, she concluded, "It's just so eerie. There was such an eerie feeling down there."

"Oh, I was proud of my job"

The men coming out, with a spirit "buzzing all around," was a loss not easily remedied. And as Joanna implied, it was not only the work but a "spirit" that disappeared when the mill closed in 1986, including the identification with steel that gave the town its character. This spirit was carried by the men who spent hours in the mill, and it pervaded the rest of the town through the stories uncles told nephews and fathers told sons and daughters. The way to work was defined by work in the mill, regardless of whether one had actually gone onto the shop floor, or wanted to, or wanted a child to. And though no one I met called the vast Homestead Works a family, as the workers in the small Sieberling Tire Plant did, a number of men and women I met talked of having "grown up in steel."[11]

In retrospect, too, individuals who worked in the mill minimized the dangers of long hours and stressed the fellowship found on a shop floor. An ex-steelworker in his mid-sixties put it this way: "But overall I think the people help, help make it. Because you work with the same guys, I worked with the same people like for—" he said, forgetting to finish his sentence. He went on to what was his important point: "The camaraderie—would that be the right word?—was great. Like you knew them. You knew their kids, you went to their daughters' weddings, you know, and I think a lot of that helped out, you know."

But mill work represented far more than "fellowship" in a town like Homestead. Reminiscing out loud, men and women expressed the pride that carried a town through the worst—disasters, deaths, and depressions—which a great profit-making corporation introduced into their lives. "Oh, I was proud of my job," another ex-steelworker bragged. "Yeah, we had a good feeling. Not every day, you know. I didn't like going out there when it was fifteen below zero, because I worked outside. All year round. And I didn't like going out when it was ninety-three in flame resistant clothing, hard hat and metal-tie shoes, nails around your waist, and goggles on. I mean, that wasn't a very pleasant feeling." Ken's statement was less a com-

"After the Midnight Shift"
(R. Wurtz collection)

plaint than an announcement of his stamina. In his generation's memories, work existed apart from the policies of the corporation.

Individuals remembered labor in the old days as if their tasks were voluntary, not ordered by a boss. The details became familiar to me, and I could recite them myself: the overwhelming heat, the steady noise that only a real worker could tolerate, the relief of an after-hours shot-and-beer. The stories portrayed manliness, but in the democratization of memory, women could be as tough as men in the mill: "Then again they had some riggers, they had some boilermakers," an older man chuckled, and, "some of these women I wouldn't want to meet 'em in a bar drunk, because they might just smack you and knock you down!"

Like Paul Bunyan tales, these were tales of extremes: the heat, the size of machinery, the endless hours, the flaring tempers. And the tales were crucial to one autobiography after another. I was not startled when an otherwise mild man in his late sixties said to me: "What made it, you were on three turns, what made it hotter yet, you come in at four o'clock and the other fellas kept rolling for eight hours. They didn't have no break down there. That place was just like a regular furnace. We had guys come and check. It was 130, 135 degrees all day long working there." A former supervisor drove me around the mill one afternoon and filled his tour with remarks on the "enormous" height and weight of machinery. "And we made it the greatest maintenance machine shop in the country. In the world." Little was left of the mammoth tools and cranes, though photographs scattered throughout the town showed the dwarfing of men posed next to heavy equipment.[12]

Work in steel formed the legends a whole town knew and recited with new significance after USX pulled out. Told in times of disaster, such tales knitted together the generations who were left to survive without the "one horse" a community had depended upon for decades. Individuals whose positions as shopkeepers, bank clerks, or teachers had once separated them from the mill worker, and men and women who never could "take the heat," united under the mystique of a labor no longer available. Under these circumstances, wives and daughters talked of steel with the same relish and regret at its passing as their husbands and fathers did. Like the men, the women of Homestead forgot their struggles against the corporation when there was no corporation to battle.

Mrs. Wozeck began her own life story with a portrait of her father, an open hearth worker. For him, doing a twelve-hour turn was "nothing": "There were a lot of men that couldn't work there because they just couldn't take it. So, yes, he felt very, very proud of that part, too. Also his hands were very, his skin was tough on his hands. And he could touch hot things that you or I would get burnt right away if we touched them. It just wouldn't penetrate his hand."

Another woman, wife of a man who had been in the mill for over forty years, marveled, "It's a miracle that on the whole that their bodies withstood the heat as well as it did. I mean, you know it's a wonder you didn't hear, come to think of it, you didn't hear more about people dropping from exhaustion or their bodies—you know." She, too, mentioned the challenge, the rite of passage that entering the mill represented to those who knew steel when it rolled continuously. "It was the kind of a thing if a young person went in there, they knew immediately if they were going to be able to hack it, because that's it. The ones that couldn't—." Her husband chimed in, "Those guys didn't even, didn't stay there long enough to pay for their metal-tie shoes."

Despite the mention of women workers, mill work was a test of manhood, with implications for the division of labor and for the definition of masculinity and femininity in a mill town. One wife of a steelworker penetrated the complicated connection between mill work and male work and added another dimension to the stories about steel: "This is my opinion, now, okay, strictly my opinion. The different men that I have encountered in this period that, especially like in my husband's age bracket [mid-sixties], I mean, they got into the mill, they made a good living, and they were proud that they worked hard. But, like, to ask them to explain their feelings or even now, they just won't do it. I don't know. It's not that they really don't have feelings, but that's it: 'We were at the mill, we made a good living, and nothing's like it was before.'"

She was hinting at something that would become more prominent when individuals talked of how likely Homestead was to move into a non-industrial economy. Steel work, according to her, bred a hardness that was temperamental as well as physical—perhaps not the best preparation for service or high-tech jobs. "There's sort of like a brawny, a brashiness about them being in there, and they feel that that's like, I don't know, sissified. Do you know what I'm trying to get at?"

Anything other than mill work came to be regarded as "sissy" work by residents and, to an extent, by outsiders who looked at lives in steel towns. As Byington and Hine demonstrated in prose and in photographs, resistance to "sissyhood" has long been a part of Homestead history, sweeping women and children along in its wake. To be frail, unable to stick to it,

"The Tool Room" (R. Wurtz collection)

and timid was anathema in a steel town, for any one, of any age, race, class, or gender. The women I interviewed, when they finished talking about the men, described their lives in terms of hard work and trials, borrowing the language of the mill to describe their own household chores.

As a counterpart to the one-hundred-degree heat stories, women told of trips to the "hole in the wall." The phrase referred to the arch in a stone wall where the pay desk stood. Townspeople called it "the hole," and from some vantage points the space did evoke a gaping black hole.

"They used to pay by cash," I learned from one steelworker, "and the hole-in-the-wall was the payments, because that's all you'd see was armed guards, security, shotguns, rifles. Because they had all that money, you know. And you'd see the wives down there with the kids." The women I interviewed who went to collect wages remembered other dangers: catcalls, stares, burglary, and an occasional rape.

But the women did it anyway, just as the men walked into the mill gates even after reports of the most horrendous accidents. Some women tried to protect themselves: "But we had a dog and he was a big German Shepherd dog," a wife who made regular trips "down there" told me. "I used to take him a lot in the car with me because even if I'd go up to pick him [husband] up like at midnight or something like that. Because, see, he said they used to wait around and people used to try to jump someone and take their pay and things like that." A younger woman did not specify the dangers but, like generations before hers, remembered her discomfort at having to wait at the gates. "You just didn't go in there at the end of a turn because you just never knew what you were going to encounter." She went, having been assigned the task of collecting her father's pay envelope. The women went so (it was said) the men wouldn't drink away their pay.

Beyond the real and the exaggerated dangers, the mill exerted an incredible pull on the children of the town. For the boys who went down to find jobs and the girls who picked up their father's and then their husband's paychecks, the Works had a magnetic force. An older woman remembered hanging around, looking for chalk with which to play hopscotch. "I don't know whether you've ever seen it, it was flat-like" she said to me, forgetting for a moment what a stranger to steel I was. They, she explained, "used [it] at their work, to mark this hot steel, they used that hard chalk for that." Drawn to the heat and flames, she recalled swiping hunks of chalk and running off, ignoring the frowns of the men who kept an eye on passers-by.

An emphasis on hardness, heat, and an ability to "take it" served the town well for nearly a century, and served the townspeople well as they remembered their histories for me. They had developed expectations, a culture, and a vocabulary of their own by the time the mills shut down. And outsiders did not always understand. "And when they used to say that, my dad used to, like, before he became a craneman, that he used to be like a laborer and he used to be a hooker. Now if you would say 'hooker' to somebody, you know, out of the Mon Valley community, they wouldn't—they'd think you were talking about a lady of the night," said a young woman, chuckling. "'My dad's a hooker down the mills'—they knew what you were talking about."

What truly distinguished the mill towns before the closings was a sense that the mills would never close. The source of identity and of livelihood, steel seemed to be a permanent fixture in every resident's life, from a hopscotching six year old to an adolescent girl impatient with the chore of picking up her father's wages. And wages there were, the most pervasive extension of the mill into town life and imagery. A shop owner who voiced his appreciation of the prosperous times under U.S. Steel provided a wonderful image: "The sidewalk used to be like snow in the morning with graphite," he said. "I mean, you'd sweep the sidewalk, it would be all glittery silver, like diamonds."

It *was* like diamonds in Homestead for some years, with a glitter that cheered even those excluded from mill work or unable to take the heat.

"My dad's business was more prosperous, you know, peoples' fathers were getting thirteen weeks vacation, they were making exorbitant amounts of money, I mean relative to what other people were doing," a young woman said about the old days which, for her, were only ten years earlier. "So even though everybody says you came from a steel town, you never really wanted for anything. I never wanted for anything. It was always there for me, not to the point of being spoiled or anything like that, but I think we all realize that now. We had it pretty good because of the, you know, our parents working in the mill or being affiliated with the mill."

"Our business," a young ex-steelworker said succinctly in 1987, "is steel." By then, this was a wish as much as a reflection on history. The men and women of Homestead who had grown up in steel, who had learned who they were in the shadow of mill work, had to face the disaster they did not believe would happen. The gates of the famous Homestead Works slammed shut in 1986. The few years of hope that USX might change its mind and renovate the plant died by 1992.

TOWN

THE CURTAIN COMES DOWN

Living Without a Mill in a Mill Town

The stories of these months of idleness and privation were pathetic. Remittances to wives and old people in Europe dropped off, bank deposits lessened, and goods were purchased on credit till future wages were heavily mortgaged. As Americans were sometimes given laboring work formerly done by Slavs, the latter bore more than their share of a burden that seriously affected the whole community.

—Margaret Byington, *Homestead: The Households of a Mill Town*

teelworkers in the United States had won a great deal in the post–Second World War decades: good benefits, high wages, and long vacations. It was not surprising that, in thinking back, a Homestead resident might downplay the oppressive work conditions or translate them into the stuff of heroism. Accidents and danger were mentioned, but not so often as anecdotes of a foreman's anger or a fellow worker's insults. In memories the mill certainly had an aura, and it was evoked to convey the character of the town and the townspeople. Women and men in Homestead shared an image of steel and reconstructed the image to fit the crisis they now faced. Thus, strikes were remembered as signs of solidarity, extra turns a proof of stamina, and black smoke an indication of prosperity.

In narratives, townspeople also dealt directly with the most recent event in their experiences of the mill: its final closing in the late 1980s.

The corporation was portrayed as playing fast and loose with employees and with the towns it dominated. More than once a resident used the interview to get a handle on what "really" had happened, trying out explanations for an event that at some level could not be fully comprehended— at least not immediately.

Family albums did not document the downfall, and Brodsky's photographs only fixed in place the scenery of a way of life USX had taken away. Visual images did little more to explain the crisis than did official company reports. Photographs do not detail an industrial policy or an international trade agreement, nor do they present a plan for dealing with those responsible for implementing decisions—corporate personnel. Often, in fact, when townspeople explained the closing to me, they spoke of rifts in the community—divisions that did not appear when "below the tracks" controlled the narrative. At the same time, "below" did not vanish, and the chauvinism of a steel valley town introduced a note of optimism into an otherwise tragic tale.

In the early 1970s the giant steel corporation began to lay off workers, change its investment policies, and neglect equipment in major plants like the Homestead Works. A decade later, the signs were clearer: rusted machinery, empty machine shops, a sky without smoke. By 1990, the condition of Eighth Avenue added further signs of distress: window shoppers who never went beyond looking, gangly adolescents on street corners, and the open door of a soup kitchen. In residential neighborhoods, For Rent and For Sale signs competed with rhododendrons and religious statuary. When Brodsky and I started our project, Homestead did look different from Braddock. By 1992, when I stopped doing interviews, neither we nor town residents could claim a distinction between Homestead and every other rust-belt community in the nation.

"U.S. Steel wants to forget Homestead altogether"

Residents tried to explain the final closing. A merchant, who in the 1940s chose to work in his father's store rather than the mill, compared his work to that of steelworkers: "True, we were always, you know, I was always envious of them [steelworkers]. The things that were in—when my cousins and uncles, they would have three-, four-, five-, six-week vacations. And all their Blue Cross–Blue Shield was paid, their eyeglasses, they got glasses, they got—they had, all their pension money was in there. And they were looking forward to the day when they had enough time and where they could retire. Well, you didn't have that in business." His expression of envy was not innocent, it turned out. Excessive privileges and benefits, according to this man, led the company to decide to put its resources elsewhere. Steelworkers, he said, had demanded too much from the corporation. Steelworkers, in his opinion, expected the world to be handed to them on a silver platter.

In general, however, Homestead residents avoided blaming steelworkers for the decisions made by a steel corporation. Those who did were often individuals who had chosen work other than at the mill, and though they benefited from its presence, they did not identify with the Works. Occasionally, an older steelworker would voice disgust at the benefits a strong union won, but this became a comment on the "younger generation" and not on "men of steel." The young crop of steelworkers asked for more than they gave. These "kids," older steelworkers said, "caused the trouble."

Individuals forgot the stories of struggle from one generation to the next when they complained about lazy kids in the mill. "That was the biggest thing, I think that lured most people in the mill, was the pay, the pay especially for an unskilled person," the wife of a steelworker told me. "Those were good wages for not having any college." The mill was a temptation, and a boy did not have to think twice about his future or his skills. "Lured" in by money, the new workers thought only about wages and not (as in the old days) about the rewards of being a hard worker. Bad work attitudes, she implied, had done in the steel industry. Attributing the view to her husband, she went on with this analysis. Young workers did double and triple shifts, he told her, just to get money and not because they cared about the product or had any loyalty to the job. "He said it was just incredible the way they went after a dollar, you know, like they did." Others searched for a reason for the closing and ended up blaming "others": men in the mill if you were a shopkeeper, younger men if you belonged to the older generation of mill workers, outsiders if you were a longtime town resident.

"I think that when my father's generation, that they took pride in their work and they did work hard and they put in their time and they really deserved their pay and everything," Mrs. Wozeck began her story of the closing. "I think the next generation, they would just put in what they had to. They would just do what they had to. If the boss wasn't looking, they didn't work. Which, in my father's generation, it wasn't like that. I mean, you didn't need to have anybody around. You knew what you had to do, and you did it. I think it was a difference in people." She too suggested that this kind of loyal good work went by the wayside when steelworkers got more benefits. She did not go so far as to blame the union; as a child of a steelworking family, she knew the advantages the union had brought to mill workers. Yet she was critical of what union protections had done: "I know someone personally who worked on a crane, and he would say, 'Ha, I sit there and I read books and I take a nap for a couple of hours, and you know, when they need me, they wake me up,' and things like that." Her son was an exception to the rule of a lazy younger generation, she said, repeating his criticism of his co-workers in a steel plant: "The waste, he said there was an awful amount of waste. And when he'd be working, the other workers would say, 'Slow down, slow down, you're making it bad for the rest of us,' and I don't think they had that years ago."

Most residents avoided blaming either the corporation or the union.[1] They blamed bad workers, individuals who had no sense of the value of hard work and who turned USX against the town. These explanations preserved the spirit of Homestead as a community while making the closing comprehensible, and they had the virtue of shifting attention to town life and away from work life.

Those who expressed a negative view of the union did so cautiously. One young ex-steelworker, for instance, came close to blaming the union, but his phrases were vague—nothing he could be caught out on if by any chance steel came back to the valley. "You get the job and you stay in there, after thirty years you get a little pension. And there's nothing wrong with that thought. But then you get to the point where some people think they don't have to give 'em a day's work." Like others, he attributed the end result to individuals who exploited union gains: "The only way to stop all that is—shut it down." Warming to the theme, he remembered other ways men avoided work and got away with it: "Another fella working down there, he would order a pizza and go across the tracks, pick up the pizza, take it in the mill with a six-pack of beer. He would tell the boss, 'I'm done after 2:00. I'm not doing another tap.' And you got to pay this man for eight hours. And it got so bad, that they just—well, they figured, well, there's only one way to stop it."

An older steelworker was cautious about expressing the idea that unions and strikes might have been at the root of the problem, but he wondered out loud whether the Homestead Strike of 1892 had cursed the town forever. "I think that they're trying to forget the Strike of 1892," he said. "That comes up all the time, and I think they were trying to get

Homestead out of the way." Then, backing down a little, he added: "That's *my* theory. I think U.S. Steel wants to forget Homestead altogether because of that 1892 strike and these other strikes." His explanation, of course, ignored the fact that steel plants were being shut down all over the country, regardless of the history of strikes.

Residents who pointed to corporate policies as the villain were usually not members of steelworking families. "That mill right there you're looking at is 1942—, '52, '62, '72, '82—that's about what? Forty-some years old," began the owner of an Eighth Avenue store. He went on: "And you know how quick technology changes. My gosh, I hate to buy electronics in today, it changes so quick. And the same way in the steel industry. We may have made steel for forty years or fifty years one way. Then all of a sudden our technology starts to take off in this country, and changes came yearly. So, it's just something that they [U.S. Steel] didn't change. They [other companies] found furnaces that could make steel three times as fast as those."

This was an accurate reading of the circumstances of the past two decades. USX had failed to improve its steel-producing equipment, letting cheaply made Japanese steel flood the American market and turning its attention elsewhere.[2] As profits from steel diminished, maintaining a plant like the one in Homestead was inefficient. But in the eyes of workers in Homestead, a neglect of tools was unforgivable on more than an economic level; the importance of well-kept machinery stood out in every context, from the household to the mill—and occasionally expressed itself in admiration for Charlee's fine cameras. By neglecting the machinery in the Works, USX scorned the values workers held dear.

"Never in a million years"

All explanations paled in the face of the shock of recognition that the closing was final. The pink slips did not mean lay-offs, but firings. The weeks without turns were life, not a vacation. The individuals I interviewed claimed it happened without warning. "Who in the hell would have thought this would shut down?" an ex-steelworker asked me rhetorically. "Who would have thought it would end up like this? I never did. Never in a million years. See, when you have a one-horse town with one industry and it falls, you're done." A member of a steel family, this man had experienced lay-offs and slowdowns before—as had his father and uncles. Each time the mill had started up again, and life returned to normal.

A cyclical pattern of good years and bad, high employment and low had been part of Homestead history. The look of a mill running at less than full power was familiar and blinded people to what really was happening. Not naive, women and men in Homestead drew on past experiences to hope 1986 was just another down time. "By the end of World War II, steelworkers in the Mon Valley assumed that their industry always would provide a source of more or less steady work at good wages," wrote one commentator. "There were ups and downs, layoffs and recalls, but these cycles occurred in a lifelike rhythm that embedded itself in the valley psyche. So strong and deep was this feeling of security that many unemployed steelworkers in the 1980s would not accept the idea that their jobs were gone for good."[3]

Hope for a reopening persisted in Homestead for two or three years after the Works emptied out. Residents of the town would give a litany of the closings in the Mon Valley and then express hope that the Homestead Works would roll steel again.[4] "Now Homestead's . . . completely shut down. Duquesne's completely shut down. McKeesport's completely shut down. J & L Southside is completely shut down. Mesta Machine Company was completely shut down. Carrie Furnace was completely shut down." Interviewed in 1987, this steelworker concluded, "maybe Homestead might roll again, but they'd have to put a lot of money in there."

The mill was so enormous and so famous that residents found it hard to take in its demise. Some expressed ideas they once would have been ashamed to voice: "I'd like to see the Japanese come in and take it over." According to this ex-steelworker, the Japanese knew what they were doing, and USX did not. "Somebody. It's there, the property's there, the buildings are still there. The only thing you'd have to do is the Japanese would have to bring their machines in, their technology."

Not until actual demolition of the plant did such dreams die. "For a long time, people—a lot of men would believe, still believe, well, they'll be called back, they'll be called back." The wife of a steelworker took a more measured view than the steelworker himself could: "Hoping, I guess they had that hope. Hoping. Where a lot of people says, no, they're not gonna be called back, but they're still pushing, still hoping something'll turn up. Maybe there'll be orders, they'll get orders from somewhere and they'll be called back, but it didn't happen that way." Unlike the men whose lives and identities were enmeshed in steel, wives and mothers saw the handwriting on the wall and the desperate self-deception in their husbands and sons: "They were all hoping and praying that everything could be resolved and they would go back. And little by little, you know, you could just see the way things were shifting that it was just getting more and more, well, you know, not a fact that things were going to work out and the mill would work out." A few minutes later, this middle-aged woman concluded with gentle wisdom, "It was the kind of a thing that I think just gradually had to sink in."

And sink in it did, for virtually everyone in the three boroughs. The spread of disaster became palpable as steelworkers and their families realized the corporation had washed its hands of the community. Finding ways to circumvent pension plans and deny health benefits, USX ran away from a place whose health and livelihood had long been bound up in its policies. A woman told me about her struggle to get the benefits her husband deserved after giving virtually his whole life to the mill. Like others, he had been let go just before his pension plan would have kicked in: "And he needed, oh, I mean, we had so many medical bills. And even now we carry Major Medical, which we pay for, and you have no idea what they went through under U.S. Steel, because when I called not too long ago, she said, 'Say no more, it's U.S. Steel.' That's exactly the words she gave me at the credit office at the hospital."

Typical of American corporate industries, USX left without leaving anything in its place—not a reliable form of insurance or programs for retraining or any acknowledgment of responsibility.[5] By the end of the 1980s, the town was on its own, lacking jobs, a substantial tax base, and any prospect of new industry in the near future. Looking out from a house in Homestead or a shop on Eighth Avenue, a longtime resident could be forgiven for expressing confusion about the causes and the consequences of an unmistakably radical change in the economic and social landscape.

"A bagger down at Shop 'N Save"

Some people coped while others fell into depression. Younger steelworkers entered job training programs, believing the promises that positions would be available once they learned new skills. Women of all generations reconsidered their own skills and capabilities and the possibility of working outside the home. Earning money was not the only problem; filling up long and empty hours was another. Hobbies might distract an older, relatively optimistic man, but they did not satisfy the needs of an individual in her or his mid-thirties with children to support and a mortgage to pay.

The wife of a steelworker who had retired early, while pleased with her husband's energetic devotion to his hobbies, worried about his weak heart: "He does a lot of things that he's not even supposed to do. But he said, 'What am I supposed to do, lay down and die? I'm used to working all my life and it's real, really hard.'" These comments came out of a despair this man was fortunate enough to be able to keep at bay. In my observations, he did keep up, mending fences and planting flowers, interfering in his daughters' households—but anything was better than boredom. Moreover, he had worked in the mill long enough to have some retirement benefits.

For men who had not given a full complement of years to the mill, the closing was much harder. They did not receive even minimal retirement and health benefits, and they were not ready to take advantage of "leisure."[6] They had not passed the stage of proving their manliness in the mill town way, as sole support of a family, and they could not (as some older ex-steelworkers did) turn easily to domestic activities. "But it's like I says, that's our business here, to be making steel," the man with "two hundred years" in the mill asserted. "And your life revolves around that mill. No mill and no life." That was the point: for younger men, everything had vanished, not just their job. An older woman, perhaps thinking of her own children, talked about the "young adults" in the community whose worlds had toppled to the ground: "So many of the young fellas that went in, oh, I would say like in their twenties, and then they had like that, say, that thriving period for, say, a period of eight to ten years, and then they had little ones." After 1986, men with families were left high and dry and turned to the most reliable resource they had—their own parents. As in every other rust-belt town in America, in Homestead "young fellas" moved back home with the children they had had and hoped to raise in a house of their own.[7] Ken's wife told me, "When we meet, like, their parents, that is, that's all we heard was, 'Well, they're not making the money anymore, and they purchased the house, and the children are involved,' and it was really the grandparents that were trying to help them over the hump."

Grandparents might help children and grandchildren over a "hump," but what was happening in Homestead was more like a mountain. The resources of the older generation were strained, and it was not easy to incorporate into the old household a young family that had their own TV, stereo, and car. "I had a girlfriend who had it all," a woman in her early thirties told me. "Her husband worked down the mill, and they just had it all when they were first married. They had, you know, the TV in every room and gorgeous cars. They could buy anything they wanted, and they bought a house, and they had two children. And now, they had to sell the house and, you know, it's just kind of—it comes full circle backwards because I guess everyone thought it was always going to be there."

When speaking about the actual closing of the mill, residents portrayed the disaster as one without respect for rank or status, ethnic or religious background, even race: "I don't understand it, though, a lot of guys like that—and they still zapped 'em anyway, after they became like company men," was one ex-steelworker's comment on the disregard for job status. "They were the first ones that got fired. All the ones that became foreman, fought tooth and nail, and turned people in and were snitches and everything—and they were the first people they let go. After they cut their pay 15 percent, they let 'em go." Rather than making him more tolerant of the corporation, the fact that they had fired "even" their snitches only increased the evil in his eyes: "I even saw this one kid, I couldn't believe when he got laid off. His father was in charge of accounting in the U.S. Steel Building. Now you talk about clout, that's clout!" From his point of view, USX betrayed all its workers, even those with clout.

USX had "X'ed" out everything, it seemed, starting with the work force. Moreover, the finality came suddenly and left no time for preparation. Longtime residents and workers wondered whether they had ever understood anything about the inner workings of the corporation. Ex-steel-

"You Think You're
Quite a Foreman"
(R. Wurtz collection)

workers told me repeatedly they saw no warning signs of the tragedy that was to come: "And then [I] worked another year, and the day she [his daughter] was born, I called 'em up to tell 'em I had a little girl, and that's the day I got laid off. August the fourteenth. That was the end of me."

Yet these comments *were* explanations—not of management decisions, but of the spread of despair in the town. If there had been no warning from USX, then it was no wonder individuals could not cope: no one had called in the lifeboats. And even afterward, in the ensuing calm, weaning away from steel seemed impossible to many men and women: "I'm the son of a steelworker who was a son of a steelworker," thirty-eight-year-old Peter began his interview. "My cousin was a tinner. My other cousin was a machinist. My other cousin was a pipe fitter, and I was a carpenter. All in the same plant. Most of us going in and out of the same gate. Was, practically the sun never set or rose that there wasn't somebody with my last name in that plant. And now there's none of us. There's not a one."

Peter had never doubted, nor had his parents, nor, apparently, had his teachers, that he would go into the mill: "After taking four years of Latin, chemistry, Spanish, Latin, and I thought—then all of a sudden at eighteen years old, you put down the books and picked up a shovel. 'Cause two weeks after I graduated from high school, I started." Later in the interview, he told me he had never learned to write a resume. Self-reflective in the aftermath of the closing, Peter noted how ill-served the young people of a mill town were, having never learned how to get a job except through personal contacts—following a parent or assuming the route to adulthood followed by generations before. "See, that's the thing, when you go to school your parents worked in the mill. It's a job sitting there. Hey, what do you do? Your daddy brings you an application home, you fill it out and take it in and work in the mill."

If you were like Peter, the boy in a family of successful steelworkers, that was what you did. Moreover, he belonged to a family of skilled laborers, not sharing the experience of generations of Hunkies whose efforts were more strenuous or of blacks whose struggles did not open the same doors. Still, most men and women in the steel valley had learned that getting a job involved asking a friend, a neighbor, or a relative, "'Cause word of mouth, or whatever they call it, is the best way to find a job," said an ex-steelworker of Peter's age, who by 1990 discovered that it wasn't.

Peter knew that being used to the mill affected everything about a job search. Not only had he not been taught how to write a resume, he had also learned to expect on-the-job training and a high wage. Peter's discussion of mill work versus other work also revealed how closely being in the mill was attached to his definition of being a man. Talking of ex-steel-workers he knew who had taken newspaper delivery routes, his tone was both critical and condescending. At the same time, he was acutely aware of the limitations in the Mon Valley job market and of the limitations in the preparation a Homestead person received for a wider world. "Today I love to read. But at that time [high school]—it just didn't hit me like that until I got older."

Peter's struggles to find a job were not unique. He entered a job training program only to discover there was "nothing" at the end of it. He went faithfully to the local employment office, to be told he was overqualified or that a job was too far away or simply that there were no jobs that day. "You go to the job services, hand in three one time, five—." Peter paused as he thought about the humiliation of this experience. "I go up and fill out these papers, go over to the lady, and she looks at it, and she says, 'That's too far for you to travel.' So she threw them in the trash can. 'Why the hell do you think I come down here for? Do you think I love coming down here? You treat us like assholes.' So I burned her ears a little," gaining some of his own dignity, perhaps, but losing the chance to have her help him.

He tried to start his own repair and construction business, but that meant competing with men in Homestead and the steel valley who were in the same position he was; it also meant laying out capital for a truck, tools, and an answering machine, capital he did not have. "Like, how do you go about paying the taxes on this? Or finding the right insurance company to insure you? Or how do you even write out a simple legal contract if you don't know how? Now some of these skills I do have. I mean, I *could* write out a simple legal contract." As he went on, Peter summarized the whole bad situation he, and others, faced. "But you need advertising, you need an answering machine on your phone so while you're down at Shop 'N Save you don't miss a three-hundred-dollar job. You need an ad in the Yellow Pages—when you're going through the ad in the Yellow Pages and you call John Doe here and his line's busy, you just drop right down to the next one."

Peter was angry, about the closing, about the failure of USX to warn its workers, and, profoundly, about the town's reluctance to bring its children up so they could do (and find) other jobs. In this opinion, in the early 1990s, Peter was by no means alone. One young man explained his move into steel in a lethargic manner that was undoubtedly not there when he actually entered the gates of a running mill. Looking back from the crisis he now faced, he conveyed to me the sense that he had slid into steel work: "So I figured, well, what do you do? You don't want to pump—I had a job in a gas station the whole time I was in high school," though he admitted there was another reason as well: "So I liked having money."

The looming mill may have cast a dark shadow over the town when its smokestacks were operating, but it also offered the lure of good money, especially for the generation coming to adulthood in the 1950s and 1960s. "They just went there, and there were many of them in this area, and I think maybe it's just because, like I said, because we were in a steel town." This was the opinion of a woman who herself never "just went there," though she remembered her friends finding the money irresistible: "Even the girls are the secretaries there. They made good money. At that time, when a girl come out of school, that was good wages compared to what other girls were getting, like, in downtown Pittsburgh. They were making triple, just to start out at."

Peter too mentioned the rewards of a job in steel: "Because we kept getting benefits, more vacation, more—we got United Nation's Day off as a holiday. Nobody in the whole country gets United Nations Day off!" Benefits of being a steelworker, he went on, "spoiled" a person for other work. The divorced wife of an ex-steelworker offered her interpretation: "Like, what would they have to do, be a bagger down at Shop 'N Save? From working in the mill, getting like twenty bucks an hour? That's not going to cut it."[8] Then she added, with somewhat more sympathy for men like the husband she had recently left, "You know, that's where everybody shops, and you don't want everybody to know that's where you have a job."

Of course, it was not simply the $4.50 an hour or shame in front of their neighbors that kept men back; it was the fact that bagging groceries did not offer the risk, danger, and challenge those tales of ninety-three-degree heat had conveyed: "I worked in a bigger shop than most of these people ever saw. And they were gonna pay me $4.50 an hour. No benefits, no vacations. With fifteen years experience, I don't think—. So I just told them I didn't want the job." As a Barberton resident put it to Gregory Pappas: "I used to get kind of psyched to go to work at the plant, but how psyched can you get about emptying a bedpan?"[9]

Just as Braddock stood for the decline Homestead residents feared, so did a friend who delivered newspapers or bagged groceries represent the route an ex-steelworker dreaded. References to "my friend who . . ." served as a reminder of the sad options available in Homestead: "My other friend, he was a—I know he made more money than I did, he made about thirty-

The
Curtain
Comes
Down

five thousand dollars a year" in the mill. "Now," this steelworker told me, "He drives a cab. Another friend of mine drives a cab. A lot of security jobs, you know. Seems like steelworkers make good security guards for $3.35 an hour."

I met some ex-steelworkers who drove cabs, repaired roofs, or delivered newspapers. They did not tell me of these jobs with pride, but not with shame either, since the situation was not theirs to control. They were resigned. "I guess I'll go back to delivering papers at night, the *Wall Street Journal*," an ex-steelworker in his thirties told me. "They're looking for people like that. I guess I'll go back to that. It'll be the third time that I'll have gone back to that." I detected no pattern in the choices different men made. A man with three children to support might refuse a job as "beneath my dignity," while one living with his parents might take a job bagging groceries.

If men did not explain their choices, they did describe the best way of finding a job in a steel valley town: try everywhere and everyone. "I have an application in just about everywhere—Port Authority, Pitt [University of Pittsburgh], Carnegie Mellon." Peter paused. "Let me think. I went down when they opened up the Vista Hotel, I was one of the thousand people that stood in line for three openings for a carpenter position." Though such a job was better than nothing, such a search often resulted in nothing. Peter had participated in job training programs, but ultimately found them useless: "But *that* came through the JP—Federal Job Program—which I think is a big, big farce," he recalled about a job he had quit right away. Given the hardships, he told me he was proud he had not succumbed to depression, drink, and drugs, as he saw happen to some of his friends and neighbors.

Job training programs have not been a success for ex-steelworkers in the Mon Valley partly because such men and women were used to manual labor and partly because employers feared a steelworker would ask for too much, do too little, be unhappy with a "less brawny" job. Not surprisingly, many Homesteaders I met concluded that being a good steelworker marked you as a risky employee anywhere else. "Before I was forced to go on welfare, I put an application in at Kennywood [an amusement park], and they told me I was overqualified for that job," said a man in his mid-thirties. "Now it doesn't take—. You're overqualified or you're underqualified," he had been told repeatedly. He offered me a final explanation for the bad luck he had in finding jobs: "the fact that I was a—that I worked for U.S. Steel."

"The roots are here"

"I put applications in everywhere. I put applications in the Port Authority Transit, to wash buses. Two years I've re-upped [resubmitted] it. They sent me a nice letter. They say they thought they would have hired me, but they have more people that are more qualified. Now what kind of qualifications does it take to clean stains off of bus windows, you know?" Whatever the hardships steelworkers and their families faced in the Mon Valley, moving away was not an appealing option. "Nobody wants to leave, let's put it that way. Once you get roots . . . ," I heard from a man in his thirties. He continued, "I've noticed that about a lot of people—because it doesn't always work. And there you are picking everything up, going, and 80 percent of the time it does work, and 80 percent of the time it doesn't. You go get started and you get laid off there. Then you don't have any friends where you're at." Generalizations about roots, jobs, and friendship framed his own strong desire to stay put, and he was not wrong: a person who moved could not be certain of a job or that a job would last. Lacking family, a man would be lonely as well as impoverished.

Residents of rust-belt communities puzzle analysts who see moving away as an optimal solution. It makes economic sense to leave a depressed region and resettle in an expanding one. The very dependence upon family and friends a resident of Homestead considers pragmatic, an outsider calls conservative or cautious. Over and over again, I heard Homestead residents describe leaving as the irrational, impractical choice; it was rational to stay home. Behind the view that a move was risky was a strong attachment to Homestead and an emphasis on the importance of belonging. "I went down there to try to work, and I got the mental impression down there that there's work but there's work only for people who live in Tennessee. They didn't seem like they like Yankees as much as it's supposed to be put up to be."

In Peter's words, "Yeah, they wanted me to go to Connecticut, work in a steel mill. I don't want to go to Connecticut and work in a steel mill, you know. They wanted craftsmen, they were searching everywhere. Texas, anywhere they could get, 'cause they're having an unemployment problem in Texas, you know, in the oil industry." But, he concluded, "I like it around here. The roots are here."[10]

"What deindustrialization ignores is that 'people want to improve their community not abdicate from it.'"[11] This was true in Homestead, though many of the people I interviewed were baffled about how to make improvements when there was no money and no government financing. Yet they stayed, and they condemned those who "jumped ship" in whatever form, from using drugs to escaping to a presumably prosperous sunbelt area. If the people I met were uncertain about what they wanted for Homestead, they knew what they did *not* want: cosmetic tinkering. Individuals chose to stay, but they did not always choose to participate in the political processes that led to urban renewal.

Individuals turned inward, worrying about improving their own situation, about bringing up children in a time of scarcity and danger, and about adjusting a household to its dearth of supplies. Men who had worked long hours in the mill also worried about boredom, restlessness, and a loss of self-esteem. They stayed home and inevitably reconsidered gender roles: "I've been here [at home] since—I've been laid off since '84, off and on, off and on. So they [his children] pretty much think of me as part of the household. I'm here when they get up, I'm here when they eat their breakfast, I'm here to put 'em in bed. And I don't know what they'd—how they would react if I had to start, if I started swinging shifts. That would probably give 'em some kind of mental breakdown, because that's how much they love me. And they all the time, 'Daddy, Daddy, Daddy.' So that's one of the good points about being laid off, anyway, is you get to spend time with your family."

"Then your wife divorces you"

Being a father did not fill Peter's time or make up for the job he had lost. Unlike the men who in the mid-1980s had to retire early but who had had a full working life, he felt cheated. Much as he claimed to enjoy fatherhood, he wanted to be the breadwinner in the family. "I'm sitting here today and I don't have any work, you know. Can't make, I tried making it on my own as a private businessman, you know, but I don't have the—I really don't have the background, I don't think, to handle it. 'Cause I'm not too successful. Lots of times I bid jobs and I end up, not losing money, but just breaking even, and that's not too successful, you know."

There was the alternative of dependence on family, on welfare, and, for those who would go, on the soup kitchen at Eighth and Amity. The Rainbow Kitchen had come to Homestead in 1982, before the Works actually closed. Food banks already existed in the area, serving individuals whose incomes did not provide what they needed or whose families could not offer the more familiar help from kin traditional in a steel town. Parents picked up canned goods, milk, and diapers for children; individuals without families found meals, company, and perhaps some comfort in the place. But the Kitchen was public, located on a busy street corner, and most Homesteaders preferred private help when it was available.

Adult children moved back with their parents or did odd jobs for relatives for small amounts of money. The system of sharing did not work perfectly anymore, as references to the better days of the 1930s revealed: again, "below the tracks" brought up an image of what communal solidarity could "really" be. Now, it seemed, tensions tore at even the closest relationships. One woman complained about her adult son: "I have, like, a boy. He worked there [the mill] for twelve years. And to this day he doesn't have a steady job. Here and there, nothing to make a living out of." She told him to turn to the government: "I mentioned to him, 'why don't you go on welfare? You probably get more on welfare.' He—they have too much pride. They wouldn't—like they give free food, he won't go over there and get any food." Accepting free food from a parent preserved a man's dignity; going to a soup kitchen did not. On the other hand, over the years residents more boldly claimed they "deserved" welfare; support was their due for years of hard labor. "That was one thing, though, the whole time I worked in the mill, it was always a fair share with the United Fund. So now, I figure, they're helping me. Which is great."

Of course, it was not "great." The bravado in such statements was belied not only by the rationalizations I heard for going to a soup kitchen at all, but also by the careful rationing of trips "down there." "And Rainbow Kitchen—not so much. They [wife and children] go down there for lunch, and they go down there like we do, every two months they give us food. And like tonight, today's the end of the month, we get our welfare check tomorrow. So we do have a few things. But we're running real low." Regardless of justifications and of the genuine need for a place of charity, going to the Rainbow Kitchen was not a *good* choice, only a necessary substitute for a job and for an adequate welfare check. "I'm visiting the Rainbow Kitchen now, for free food. I got my food, get my free food from the borough, I don't even get it from my mother. It's bad."

There was a difference between those who ate lunch at the Rainbow Kitchen and those who stopped in for food and clothing. The lunchtime crowd was largely male, and silence and downturned faces pervaded the atmosphere. Women and men who came for food and clothing came in pairs or with children; they chatted with the volunteers, who were neighbors and fellow townspeople. Possibly, as I was to hear, those who came for canned food and clothing came mainly at the end of the month, when the welfare check simply did not stretch far enough. I also heard expressed, in increasingly ominous tones, the view that those who ate at the Kitchen were "strangers."

For Homesteaders, evidently, regulars at the Rainbow Kitchen exemplified the worst of what mill closings did to individuals. From the perspective of a number of residents, the Kitchen was a gathering place for those who could not make it in any way. These comments exposed rifts in the community and new divisions between groups; the harmonious diversity of "below" had given way to the harsh differences among people now around Eighth Avenue. By the early 1990s, joblessness and drug use were wreaking a toll in Homestead, as in every other Mon River town, and it was convenient to have a population upon which to pin the problems. But what was attributed to outsiders was happening to insiders as well, and householders experienced chaos in a variety of forms.

"You lose your job first, then you lose your house, then your wife divorces you, and then where're you at?" a man commented, excepting himself with pride: "I'm one of the lucky guys—my wife sticks with me. Money didn't make a big difference in our relationship. Whether we have it or not, we love each other. But a lot of my friends, they—whoosh—broke up, it broke up, they broke up." Divorce, suicide, and mental collapse ran through Homestead along with other towns in the Mon Valley. Love could carry a person through only so much, not making up for a total loss of income and the toppling of customary patterns. For men in these steel towns, staying home and taking care of the children might be a pleasure at first, but eventually such behavior too severely transgressed the norms for marriage and a family. Then such men faced boredom, dependency, and a lack of self-esteem.

The closing of the mill was equally threatening for women. Not every wife appreciated having a man around the house, interfering in her domain or demanding the attention he may once have gotten on a job. One woman in her mid-thirties who had left her husband after the shutdown told me why. "Yeah, because even when your mate, who's working in the mill and they tore the mill down, then you had to put up with him. You know, and it wasn't always pleasant. Because then they get discouraged and they feel bad because they don't have a job. And now they look at their family and they can't provide like they used to provide, 'cause you made good money when you worked in the mill. So now here they are, either on drugs or drinking. You know? Where do you go?" She left her husband to live on her own. Her husband, she said, became an alcoholic, sitting at the bar with his buddies hour after hour. After the shutdown, a change occurred in how people regarded drinking; what once had been treated as a harmless activity, a well-needed relaxation after work, came to seem—as well as to *be*—dangerous and destructive. By the early 1990s, alcohol seemed just another hard drug and equally a sign of vulnerability, despair, and escapism. A woman told me her sister had run away, "'Cause my sister was into drugs. . . . She has a low self-esteem. And, um, it's due to a—not belonging, not having nothing to do. . . . You can't even find a job here." Drugs were not something to do, they were a response to having nothing to do. For adolescents and young adults, the future in Homestead looked bleak. One afternoon I talked with a volunteer at the Rainbow Kitchen. Glancing out the window, she explained what happened to the kids in Homestead. The boys, she said, go there, and pointed to the Army Recruiting Office across the street. "The girls," she said, "have babies."

Families were different in a deindustrialized Homestead. The foundation of enduring extended families shook with the closing of the mill. Husbands left wives, and wives walked away from husbands; adult children occupied spaces parents thought would be empty nests. Households were headed by single women and sometimes by single men. There was little a parent could tell a child of any age to go out and *do*. But people stayed, in and around the area. Loyalty to one's hometown was a hard habit to break. A man told me, "I'm divorced and she's living with—. The last time I saw her was about a year and a half ago. I stopped to see how she was doing. One of my weaker moments, I guess. But other than that," this man continued, "I don't really want to move. If I were to move from here, I'd move up to where my uncle has his cottage. It's way back in the woods, where nobody would bother me."

"It made me look toward other things"

In fact, the shutdown was not bad across the board. For some individuals in Homestead, having no mill meant exploring other opportunities, trying out things one might otherwise not have done. From the vantage point of early retirement, a steelworker talked about the positive side of a shutdown. "My neighbor was a craneman. That was a good job. He was making good money working six days a week, double and a half, working sixteen hours—[they would] call him out early. And now he's driving a truck across the road. And he likes it, his wife and his two daughters live at home. His niece is living there with her two kids. And he's happy. He's home two days a week, and he loves it."

For women and men who hated manual labor, a plant closing could be a blessing. Gregory Pappas writes about Alex, an ex–tire worker: "Alex Davison had found his seven years at Sieberling intolerable and was more relieved by the closing than threatened. He had hated the boring work, the harsh foremen, and the demands of shop-floor politics, but the steady income had kept him from trying anything different. The shutdown was a chance for Alex to open a home remodeling business."[12] I did not meet anyone in Homestead with quite this happy a story; nor did I meet anyone who admitted hating mill work so much. But some people were definitely relieved: a father who did not want his children to go into the mill and threatened to break their legs if they did; a boy who did not have the stamina to take the heat; a girl who hoped she would be sent to college, since marrying a rich steelworker was out of the question.

The advantages of a closing were experienced mainly by the third generation in relatively prosperous white families. A number of these children would have simply gone into the mill had the mill been standing—picking up a shovel regardless of the Latin and Greek they had learned in high school. Now they were forced to do something else. "Well, now since there aren't the mills, you know, it made me look towards other things," said a young man whose family had been mill workers. "And, you know, just automatically, well, if you aren't that good in academic [subjects]—and you would automatically go into the mills. And now it's—you have to really start thinking about, well, there's not the mills anymore, what are you going to do? You can't, you have to look elsewhere, you've got to get other skills or find a job and work up your skills within the job." His sister, present at the interview with us, finished the story: "We all [three siblings] ended up in banks."

The children in the Wozeck family were successful. They had been prepared for a future that did not necessarily include a mill by a mother who told each one of them to move ahead, consider the world an open arena, and work for a college degree. How effectively her plans would have worked out had USX not made its fateful decision is a mystery. Then, even her children might have been lured in; now, they took other jobs, but they stayed in Homestead. Each of the three siblings told me, "I would never move away." They were at once lucky and resilient. Some members of the older generation also found the closing an opportunity. After Ken was forced into retirement, Louise took the job she had always wanted but Ken forbad as long as he was hard at work in the mill. These instances, however, are small glitters in a bleak landscape.

They are individual instances. Few residents I met tried actively to influence political decisions. Most people simply endured. Aware of this, an ex-steelworker in his late thirties said, "I should be doing something here but I'm not." He described himself as "sitting around," and wondered out loud whether he should try to "organize" fellow unemployed workers. By 1992, when he mentioned the idea, political activism had faded from the Mon River region; the vast, unemployed work force had other things to do. Instead, residents thought back to the old days, an image of community that served as a beacon of hope if not a concrete agenda for change.

Mark relished the episode in his story in which he rebuilt his tavern "brick by brick." Torn down when the mill expanded, the tavern provides a lesson for the reverse situation, the damage caused by the tearing down of the mill. Like Mark, Ken talked about rebuilding the community after the World War II mill expansion with a view to what might be done *now*. He took me to his church, Saint Anne's, located in the "good" section of West Homestead; it had been rebuilt there after the original structure in the Lower Ward had been demolished. In Ken's account, the move up and out of the ward represented solidarity and an erosion of the geographical and the class boundaries separating below and above the tracks. Like Mark's tavern, Saint Anne's preserved precious elements from the original structure: a glorious rose window, old and mellow wooden pews, a stately altar.

There is nothing trivial about commemorating the culture and history of a place through the preservation of physical structures.[13] Utilizing the landscape to incorporate values made sense in a town that had always looked upon a mill and the stretch of neighborhoods from "flats" to hilltop to remind itself of the core of life. Keeping something visible of that past offered a road into the future. By contrast, building a water park where a machine shop had stood or garden apartments where mill houses formerly occupied the ground was a travesty on the steel town's identity. Putting an amusement park where men and women had endured long hours of work produced an incongruity not missed by the townspeople I interviewed.

Against the backdrop of improvement projects, institutions like Goodwill and a soup kitchen dramatized the tragedy that had struck Homestead. "It doesn't make you too proud to know that you have a soup kitchen," a man said to me. "'Cause usually whenever I thought of a soup kitchen, it reminds me of reading in one of my history books about the 1930s. Poverty, people sleeping in doorways, which there is. People actually sleep in the doorway."

The soup kitchen struck an odd note opposite a classic marble-fronted drugstore and across from a Greek-style Mellon Bank building. A reminder of the devastation in the valley, for some residents the Kitchen represented the failure of a city council to "do anything." Dan was the most bitter about the lapse in political responsibility on the part of citizens and council members. In his view, politicians were pompous, self-important little men. "You just say that and pound your gavel and go home and that's it. Nothing's ever done." He was also angry at the federal government and Ronald Reagan, who was then president: "I don't like his policies. He surrounds himself with millionaires. He's a millionaire. He wrote us off. Us steelworkers and farmers, we're all wrote off."

Reagan was an easy man for the townspeople to hate, with his inclination to preach persistence and to cut the programs that allowed the unemployed to sustain a semblance of normal life. "I'd like to see Ronnie Reagan out of there because he's cutting programs," Peter began his critique. "One thing you should never mess with is education, for one thing. We're so behind the rest of the world and we—you can't even buy a VCR that's made in this country. I think we better get on the ball and get some engineers and get people with this ability." As he talked, his fury mounted: "And then when the steel mills—you know, he's [Reagan] only been to Pittsburgh one time in this whole thing, and he came in the back door of the Hilton Hotel. I mean, he don't even know this part of the country exists. So where they throw government contracts makes a big difference, you know. Because they've got—when they order something, they don't order like a hundred, they order big time. And I know we're still making ships and tanks, and somebody's making that steel. Or we're still buying jeeps, and somebody's making that steel. It's not Homestead." Nor did Homestead rise up armed to fight this most recent injustice: "I wonder if that was, if that [violence] *is* maybe what it'd take. 'Cause most of us steelworkers all have deer rifles. And if there's enough of us, it could make a difference. 'Cause most of us, well, not myself, but a lot of my buddies, they all belong to the national guard and the marine reserves. They're all soldiers or ex-soldiers." But there wasn't going to be violence, and Peter knew that. At the end of his interview, he asked, "So you know somebody in administration that could help me get a job over at CMU?"

Sources of work and rhythms of life were changing profoundly. Ask-

ing an interviewer for a job was as unfamiliar to a man of "three generations in steel" as being put out of a mother's kitchen: "I get my food from
the borough, not from my mother." Faces on the streets of Homestead
particularly, but also West Homestead and (least of all) Munhall, looked
different too. The disappearance of the mill weakened boundaries, dimin-
ishing the solidarity of kin, of neighborhoods, and of the town itself. Moreover, men's work was no longer distinct from women's activities. Men stayed
home and women waited on the corners for buses to take them to Squirrel
Hill or downtown Pittsburgh. Women organized the distribution of food
and clothing in the Rainbow Kitchen and church basements. Women argued at PTA meetings that their children should be trained for high-tech
jobs, not manual labor—women who themselves had "over two hundred"
years, in their cases doing the budgets, coping with downturns, and tiding
the family over during crises.

EIGHTH AVENUE

WOMEN'S ACTIVITIES AND MEN'S WORK

The Division of Labor in a Steel Town

It is through the households themselves that the industrial situation impresses itself indelibly upon the life of the people. The environment of the home afforded by this checkerboard town tilted on the slope back of the mill site, the smoke which pours its depressing fumes to add their extra burden to the housewife's task, the constant interference with orderly routine due to the irregular succession of long hours—these are outward and visible signs of the subordination of household life to industrial life.

—Margaret Byington, *Homestead: The Households of a Mill Town*

T he bulk of Byington's book shows how little household life was "subordinated" to industrial life. Spending her time inside the households of a mill town, and with the women who managed those households, Margaret Byington created a portrait of a vibrant and vigorous institution: the kitchen hearth was as significant a part of town life as the mill's furnaces. Her text shows the women at home engaged in demanding tasks as time-consuming and strenuous as the men's.

Byington does not deny the intricate connection between mill and household; she insists upon the strength of the household and the part it played in counteracting the depressing, deadening, and often deadly labor of the mills. Good household management was crucial to shoring up the unsteady incomes of families dependent on a national and, eventually, an international industry. That women stood behind the men with no less power in their stance is evident in a famous drawing of the women of the town rushing to the riverbank when the Pinkerton men arrived in 1892 to suppress the steelworker protest.

Nearly one hundred years after that strike, the importance of households and the stamina of the women of a steel town emerged from our interviews and our observations. Though the mill dominated the riverbank, the houses running up the hillside constituted an equally strong visual image. Block after block, dotted with church steeples, the residential neighborhoods of Homestead, West Homestead, and Munhall rose above the mill. By the end of the 1980s, the well-kept gardens of a number of these houses contrasted with the weed-filled lots fast filling the land a mill once occupied. Though households in the past were the domain of women and children, unemployment is now challenging a division of labor that had for generations been written into Homestead life. In the 1990s, men stay home and women enter the public domains of work.

When I interviewed old-time families, those who had been in Homestead for over three generations, women as often as men began by talking about work in steel. They assumed I was mainly interested in the mill—investigators before me were mainly interested in the mill and its impact on the town—but it was also comfortable for most residents of a steel town to begin their personal accounts with the (sometimes impersonal) story of steel. Photographs changed that thrust; so did the age, ethnicity, and race of the interviewee—characteristics which provided viewpoints on the continuity of work patterns and perceptions of labor from one generation to the next. African-American residents, for example, offered a variant interpretation on life in Homestead without straying too far from the dominant white view of the world of work in a mill town.

Over the course of an interview, the role of women—the mothers at home and the women who went out to work—filled more episodes in the narrative. The order reflected the town's history. Steel had long been Homestead's claim to fame, and it was not surprising that people chose to tell that story first. Men were considered the heroic workers, and work in steel framed discussions of any other work a man or a woman did. Town legends highlighted male work, and so did events. Only during the crisis of

World War II did women enter the steel-making world in any numbers, and again after the Consent Decree of 1974 compelled the corporation to change its hiring policies. By then, the image of hard, tough, stressful, and ceaseless turns dominated the language of labor in Homestead. Women's work gained importance by being described in imagery drawn from mill work, a description often prompted by a snapshot of a domestic event. Home was not only a haven from the rough world of work but also the training ground for it, for girls as well as boys watched their mothers do chores and listened to tales of their father's long hours.

Snapshots threw individuals more deeply into family life than my open-ended queries had. This was not surprising: most albums were full of family pictures, domestic scenes of one sort or another, and few individuals had photographs of men (or women) at work outside the home. In addition, looking at pictures freed a person from self-consciousness about history and opened the way to spontaneous autobiographical anecdotes. I think, too, that while we looked at photographs an individual considered that his or her opportunity to lead the interview in a particular direction.

Most of the people I interviewed, however, tended to interpret personal events in the light of the mill's ups and downs, a reminder that steel was the background for virtually every family story in Homestead, white or black, well off or working class. Domestic life flowed on, parallel to the production of steel, and scholars have too frequently slighted this side of Homestead life.

Histories of the town tend to start with the mill and move to the household; they start with men's work and add on women's work.[1] Residents knew the public history, in which steel dominated. Brodsky's photographs offered individuals a wider and a more intimate view of the place colloquially called Homestead, while including West Homestead, Munhall, Whitaker, and Homestead Park. Pictures of a man in his garden, a woman overlooking her front yard, a child in a wading pool all evoked accounts of domesticity, expanded by the incidents recorded in family albums. In this "inside" view of Homestead, women were heroes and hard workers.

Byington had informed her readers of this fact decades earlier, though in the book Hine's stark portraits of working men easily distract from the details of budgeting, planning meals, and caring for children, which constitute Byington's argument. The photographs we looked at during my interviews brought out the importance of family and supported an individual's attribution of significance to what mothers and daughters did. Yet a dichotomy remained beyond the customary division of labor and revealed the persistent habit of according male work more honor. The distinction in Homestead was that men *worked* while women did *activities*. The closing of the mill threatened this distinction, along with everything else.

"You and I would get burnt right away"

Mrs. Wozeck—I never heard her referred to by her first name—and I sat in her living room as she prepared for an interview she was clearly nervous about. Unlike her shopkeeper husband, the self-appointed amateur historian for our project, Mrs. Wozeck was not used to discussing the town or, even, herself. Like her husband, she had spent all her life in the Mon Valley, though she grew up not in Homestead but in the neighboring town of Braddock. Her father, a big, husky Irishman, had worked in the Homestead mill from the time he came to America until he retired. She began her story with his story.

Her childhood in the 1920s, she remembered, was dominated by the rhythms of the turns, or shifts, her father had at the mill. His comings and goings, and his work, framed the memories she chose to tell. As she portrayed him, Michael Flannagan fit the stereotype of a steelworker: red-faced and toughened by the fires of the open hearth where he worked. Large in her memory and undoubtedly large to a child, Flannagan could have been an industrial Paul Bunyan or a model for the mythic Mark Michalak in the steel valley—except he was not a Hunky.[2]

Half a century later, Mrs. Wozeck recaptured the feeling of his arrival home. He would stride in the door, undaunted and untired at the end of a hot, twelve-hour shift.[3] "My father was very proud that the heat never bothered him, you know; well, it got to him in that he felt hot and everything, but he never passed out." At various moments in the interview she came back to this: the unflagging energy her father displayed, the "toughness" of his hands, his ability to do what others could not do.

As he loomed large in Mrs. Wozeck's narrative, he must have loomed over the household. Mike dominated the interview, and there might not have been a Mrs. Flannagan for all that her daughter reported. It was as if the house existed to rescue the man from his toils and turmoil. The character Mrs. Wozeck painted was as one-sided as Hines's portraits of men in a mill town, without the tenderness of a father and husband. Affection was not part of the story of mill families that Mrs. Wozeck had inherited.

Family members
(family collection)

Self-consciously telling history and even more self-consciously trying to make her autobiography interesting, Mrs. Wozeck turned to the figure of the steelworker.

Her words echoed the anecdotes that circulated around Homestead: the drama of the man returning home, calling for food, hot water, or quiet. Women rushed to the door, their own activities put aside. In his novel, *Out of This Furnace*, Thomas Bell similarly describes the return home of the steelworker, his needs overshadowing those of women and children. There, perhaps more realistically, the man often simply fell into bed, not a word said to the others who occupied his home. "I work, eat, sleep, work, eat, sleep, until there are times when I couldn't tell you my own name. . . . Dorta has only half a husband."[4]

Like Mrs. Wozeck, Louise was in her mid-sixties and the daughter of a steelworker. Her life story, too, accorded primary importance to male work and to her father's hard labor in the Homestead Works. Like other women of her generation, she eliminated the story of oppressive work conditions and brutal, backbreaking hours from her narrative. Louise's father had been a mill worker all his life. He was a Hunky, the name given to any Eastern European who settled in the Mon Valley. As a Hunky, he stood low on the steel company ladder; nevertheless, he faithfully reported to work day after day, week after week, year after year. And, his daughter remembered half a century later, fatigue dropped off his shoulders when he returned to his family and neighborhood. Once home, this heroic figure celebrated community with no thought for the aches and pains of his long day. He threw himself as energetically into amusements as he had into labor. "He would always sing—their Slovak songs that they had brought from the old country. They had a little button accordion—he used to play that and little kids used to come over and watch him and listen to him play." In anecdotes like this, Louise placed her father in a larger context; his world opened beyond the mill gates, her father was more than a laborer, and Louise transformed being a Hunky into something positive: a celebration of ethnic identity.

Louise did not talk about her mother. Nor did she portray the discrimination and hardships her father must have suffered, incidents that would have affected the household as well. A generation of women in their sixties recalled a generation of fathers, tireless workers who did not complain about the discrimination they suffered. Thomas Bell's novel, with its tale of anti-Hunky remarks, accidents, and deaths represents the negative aspect of life in a steel town; with the mill gone, residents tended to emphasize the glories of work now vanished.

The nostalgia of these accounts became evident when older women talked about their husbands. Louise, for instance, did not memorialize her husband as she had her father, though her husband had put a hard forty years into the Homestead Works. Forced into early retirement, he currently had little to do, and perhaps his aimlessness dented his image as a steelworker in her eyes. Still, obeying the gender stereotypes in a steel town, Louise gave his role in the mill more attention than she gave her role at home. At moments, her account of his work echoed stories of her father; like her father, she said, Ken kept going hour after hour after hour. Not only did he work hard, but he played hard, supervising Little League games in the evenings. This part of her narrative suggests that mill families were not demoralized by mill work, but able to revive community spirit in song, celebration, and sports. That part of Homestead was the workers' own.

Women talked about their fathers, husbands, and sons because they thought that was what I wanted to hear and because in a steel town men were viewed as the primary actors. Moreover, women talked about men at work, whether in steel or elsewhere, not about men as fathers and husbands; emotional life was left out. Joanna was an exception. Young enough to sympathize with feminism, she also embraced the image of the brawny steelworker. She said men of steel did not "admit to their emotions. . . . Like that macho image—that's the way men looked upon that, you know," she said. "That was it. If you could stand that rigorous schedule and put up with that, you were a man. You were a man."

Joanna, like others, was ambivalent. If the man of steel did not reveal his feelings, he was still the type of man a town had grown up valuing. "I mean, they got into the mill, they made a good living, and they were proud that they worked hard. But, like, to ask them to explain their feelings, even now, they just won't do it. It's not that they really don't have feelings, but that's it." This was the type of man that the whole town recognized, old and young, black and white. Joanna's assessment also hints at the transformation in "maleness" that may be necessary in a nonindustrial economy.[5]

Her personal history of Homestead fell between generations, just as her life did. Born in the early 1950s, she married a man older than she was and partly adopted the attitudes of his generation. A child of the 1950s and a young woman in the 1960s, she also voiced "modern" ideologies as present in a steel town as in any American city. Once, she said, Luther had been offered a promotion. Knowing the position would keep him out of the house even more, she discouraged his acceptance: "I mean, you know he had the chance to be a foreman, but they could all see that it was such a demanding life." Luther refused the promotion, "And I don't know if it's [refusal to be promoted] because most of the men felt like the mill had such a hold on you as it was. I mean, you were at their mercy with these shifts and they [supervisors] were already doing, playing so much havoc with your body that they [workers] just felt like they just couldn't take that final step to be a foreman and then be actually possessed by them. That's exactly what it was: you were totally under their control."

This was the true picture of work in steel, a view that could only be temporarily covered over by fond memories of stamina and autonomy on the shop floor. Admire her husband as she might, Joanna recognized the toll steel work took on his life and on hers and the children's. The continuity between her statements and those Byington heard is striking. Like her predecessors, Joanna managed the household for the sake of her husband. According to her daughters, she was "there" when Luther came home, meals prepared, house clean, children quiet. "It was the wife waited on the husband," the daughters told me. "And the wife—and the husband provided for the wife, and the wife wasn't supposed to go out and work." By contrast, these third-generation women had full-time jobs and expected (they said) their husbands to help around the house.

Yet when they and their peers thought back to childhood, memories highlighted the work in steel. It was hard to grow up in Homestead and not be captivated by the mill. Physical commemorations reminded every child of men's bravery and of the role steel played in world events. Street names kept Andrew Carnegie and his accomplishments in the mind of any pedestrian. An old billboard that once recorded mill accidents completed the drama. The Wozeck children recalled their fascination with the sign:

Jim: "I remember one of my favorite things, as we were driving along Eighth Avenue when you see the sign—how many days without an injury."

Rosie: "Oh, yeah."

Jane: "Yeah."

Rosie: "How many days—like, 'thirteen days now.'"

Jim: "You see, like, 'one day without an injury,' and you're like, 'Oops, somebody got hurt.'"

Rosie: "Every Sunday we'd drive home from my grandmother's house in Swissvale, and we'd drive past that sign, and that was the big thing. I don't know why but we all, all little five heads would pop up out of the station wagon and see how many numbers, what the number was on that sign."[6]

"Wives and children in their homes came to dread the sound of whistles, the screaming sirens that meant that an accident had occurred," writes labor journalist William Serrin, making male labor the central event in town.[7] There were no signs announcing the perils and the relentlessness of women's labors. Nor did laundry, cooking, and taking in boarders prompt the media attention that a walkout or a union speech did. But that women in all three generations valued their labors and knew the importance of women's work to the survival of the town became evident as I looked over family photos in Homestead households.

"She only had herself to depend on"

Mrs. Wozeck plunged into a vivid description of her father with relish and with ease. She was initially silent about her mother, having long ago learned that a woman's life was "routine," her activities conventional. "Almost everybody did the same thing, you know. Most of the women didn't work in those days and just stayed home and took care of the family." When a picture of her mother popped up out of the shoe box collection, this version of history vanished.

Snapshots told the true story of women in Homestead. They recorded women at birthday parties, weddings, backyard picnics, and, occasionally, standing alone in front of a house. Formal portraits put women forward, too, in elegant dresses and dignified poses, a husband's hand draped protectively over a shoulder. Having not looked through the box of pictures recently, Mrs. Wozeck was startled by how much of her mother's life had a documentary record.

Margaret Flannagan had come from Ireland in her teens, part of an early-twentieth-century migration. The young woman successfully supported herself, cleaning houses, until she married Mike Flannagan. "My mother's parents were dead, and she only had herself to depend on when she got here," Mrs. Wozeck told me. More to the point, she continued to "depend on herself" after her marriage to Mike. Like other women in steel towns of the Mon Valley, she took in boarders: men who worked in the mills and girls who did housecleaning in the houses across the river in middle-class Squirrel Hill.[8] "Keeping boarders had recognized customs, a code of behaviors for landladies and boarders of which no one who lived in the First Ward was ignorant," writes Thomas Bell. "The secret of being a successful boarding missus . . . was to make the boarders understand from the beginning that she was boss."[9]

There were customs and codes for all the work women did. Mrs. Flannagan, her daughter told me, did the same thing as every other woman in a steel town: shopping on Monday, washing on Tuesday, cooking on Wednesday, and so on through the week. These were the "turns" in a woman's work week. By describing women's activities in language that echoed men's work, the women I interviewed accorded domesticity importance. In a reversal that underlined this impulse to link women's and men's labors, a former steelworker assured me: "Making steel is just like making soup. You put in all the ingredients and stir it up."

Mrs. Wozeck came upon a small snapshot of her mother standing in

Two generations, daughter and mother (family collection)

front of a modest house in neighboring Braddock. "When did we live there?" Mrs. Wozeck wondered out loud, and remembered a brief period in the 1920s. She also remembered that the family had moved often: Mrs. Flannagan, it seemed, added to the family resources by buying and renting or selling houses. Mrs. Wozeck told me this hesitantly. "Yes, well, my parents bought another house. They had bought their original home and it was all paid off. I guess things were going well. And mother wanted to— they wanted some type of investment. So they bought another home, which they were going to rent." Revealing my own gender stereotypes, I speculated, "Your father was successful in a sense . . . ?" With my words, Mrs. Wozeck corrected my assumption: "I think in a sense that my mother was very good at buying, good at planning, good at budgeting, and things like that." By now confident in her positive appraisal of her mother's contribution to the household income, she finished her thought: "She managed money very good. Yeah, they bought a number of houses."

Once the portrait of her mother as strong, resilient, and a "genius" at household management emerged, Mrs. Wozeck interpreted further snapshots in this light.[10] In a picture of two girls in fancy party dresses, for instance, she found the seamstress and thrifty buyer of cloth scraps. In another snapshot, there was the "boarding missus" and two of the girls she took off the boat from Ireland. As a married woman, Mrs. Flannagan shared in her husband's income; still, according to her daughter, she maintained the independence she had learned during her first years in the United States.

Mrs. Flannagan's life and Mrs. Wozeck's account of it are typical. The daughters' views and the mothers' work are equally central to the history of Homestead; in personal histories, the heroism of women's activities got passed down from decade to decade. Rarely public or published, these histories complete the portrait of a steel town.

"Just tagging along with the other mothers"

Women in industrial towns worked outside the house as well as in it. Through all the years of the century, women in steel towns had to take jobs—especially African-American women, but also wives or widows in any family that misfortune had struck. Even women who were proud of what their mothers had done at home and boasted of the skills it took to run a household were, regardless of age, reluctant to discuss wage-earning jobs their mothers also sometimes took.

Several daughters described their mothers' work out of the home as an accident or a response to a crisis. The Second World War came up prominently at these points in a narrative, the "real" crisis sending women to work. Accounts of the Depression, by contrast, portrayed women as making do, not going out to work. During the Depression men were supposed to be the breadwinners, not women. But the war was different: "Oh, yes, before World War II there were some ladies there that got a job in the Heinz Company in Pittsburgh, in North Side, across the river from downtown Pittsburgh." Louise at last brought up her mother, explaining why she worked at Heinz: "My mother went with them. She says, 'Well, I'll put my application there too.' Not thinking nothing of it. She's just tagging along with the other mothers there. And she got a job there. They hired her just like that."

Undertaken in a crisis, and almost by accident, the job did not fit the typical Rosie-the-Riveter story. Working at Heinz, a woman was doing female activity: food, cooking, nourishment. Still, the daughter justified her mother's decision in terms of an emergency—an emergency that, however, opened the way to a permanent job. "She worked every day. And she worked there till she was sixty-five years old."

Women's
Activities
and
Men's
Work

100

Like stories of the shop floor for men, stories of women's labor emphasized the bonds formed in a work setting. "She likes it, even now," Louise told me. "She still goes back to Heinz, like every so often [when] they have a luncheon for their retirees." At ninety-two, she still "pushes herself," her daughter told me. "She's an independent person. She wants to do what she wants to do." Then Louise said something that gave me pause: "I guess it [work] makes a better person out of you." No one would have said this about steel work, not in any generation in Homestead.

The idea of self-improvement or betterment was not a part of discussions of men's work. It was often how women talked about their own, their mothers', or even their daughters' work outside the home. Despite the framing device of a crisis or emergency, women's work was treated as a source of personal satisfaction rather than as a source of income. Such an interpretation combines a conservative view of women's work with a modern rhetoric of self-fulfillment. This language kept women's work distinct from men's, appropriate to steel town culture.

In describing her own wartime work, one woman emphasized how "exciting" and "stimulating" it had been. Hers was the Rosie story; she had moved from the Nabisco Baking Company into a local ship-building company—she moved from assembling Oreos into welding steel. The end of her story, however, was a return to hearth and home. To have remained a welder would have been too radical; in her family, to remain at work when her husband earned a good income was also too radical. For the rest of her life this woman, like her mother and grandmother, devoted her energy to running a household. As times changed in a steel town and women left the house for income-earning work, those jobs were still described as "fulfilling" and "improving." The occupations I heard about also tended to be extensions of women's domestic activities: work with food, children, and clothing.

I talked with a woman in her sixties who was a librarian at a local university. She did not have to work, she told me, but she found working a "pleasure." Then she added a justification in terms not of crisis but of personal development: "My mother says, 'you come first, make yourself feel good. And the heck with everybody. You're a good person, do yourself some good.'" It is unlikely that her mother would have made such a statement in an earlier decade, but along with the change in the economy came a change in the culture of Homestead. This woman's husband, however, did not like it that she worked, and he told me she was planning to "retire" soon and take care of their grandchildren. Other women offered

Women's
Activities
and
Men's
Work

101

versions of the "make yourself feel good" reason for taking a job. Even this was all right only as long as the work fit a model for female activities.

As a widow who had to work, Vivian Smith translated the task into pleasure. She worked in a college cafeteria "feeding kids," and she said her job was "fun." But Vivian also used language that recalled the values of work in a steel town: endurance, hardship, and "being called in early one morning to handle a job no one else could handle." Like other women her age, Vivian returned to language describing mill work to convey the importance of her work. Yet her job involved "kids," she repeated, attaching her labor to a familiar domain.

These interpretations of women's work came up regardless of the age of the interviewee, though they were not so prevalent among the few middle-class women I met and did not come up at all in the interviews I did with African-American women. The work a woman did outside the house was described in terms of her role as a woman within the family. She worked either to supplement income in a crisis or to become a "better person." As true economic actors, men retained the upper hand. And some women disguised the work they did, portraying it as just another hobby or activity.

Though I knew her quite well, for a long time I did not realize that Joanna had a job. She talked about her father's work on the railroad and her husband's in the mill, and every now and then mentioned her "music." Gradually, she let on that she was the organist for a number of Homestead churches. Hard work, with demanding "shifts," playing the organ seemed negligible the way Joanna told the story. (Her husband added to this view by interrupting to say it was "how lovely" she looked playing that caused him to fall in love with her.) "I eventually got involved, well, just through the church locally, starting out—with our family growing and everything—in the church. But then I really took on the responsibility of the church choir, well, it's been like thirteen years now that I—," and she trailed off. The next thing she said showed how she distinguished women's "activities" from men's "work": "I studied [music] as a child and I don't even look upon it as work. It's a real—well, not fun, it's just a real fulfillment. It's just a wonderful feeling, you know."

Women's
Activities
and
Men's
Work

102

"My mother's worked all her life"

Some women in Homestead were less subject to the ideology that women's work came in a crisis or was character building. These were women who did not identify strongly with men in the mill, either because the men in their family were not in the mill or because upbringing had given them a different slant on life. Having acknowledged the importance of her mother's real estate skills, Mrs. Wozeck went on to give her own work its proper economic place.

When she married Sam, she effectively became a shopkeeper, standing alongside him in the store hour after hour. "Then I would start working in the store and help out in the store and all. Since we just lived next door, it made it kind of easy. And as the years went by, I worked more and more with the store." After Sam's death, she took over the store completely, and without the slightest hesitation. The store was hers, its customs and customers under her control. Admiring her business capabilities, her own daughters had taken up careers; both went into banking, not into the shop that looked like it might die when Mrs. Wozeck could no longer work the long hours.

The job had come with marriage, not, as in her children's cases, because of training. Another woman of about Mrs. Wozeck's age, from a middle-class family, had a similar tale. Julie had completed college. Yet her job came with her marriage and her move into the Homestead community. One evening soon after the wedding, her husband Terry came home "and he said, 'I bought you a moving company.' And I said, 'you did *what?*'" She considered the gift an odd one, she remembered, from a new husband. "And I didn't know anything at all about vans except that you got in one end and out the other. But I learned in a hurry."

In her intent to persuade me that her work was a lark, Julie failed to mention that the moving company was part of a family-owned transportation business and that her role was that of manager in a corporate organization. She was proud of her work—at one point she called herself an "early feminist"—but not so bold as to ignore Homestead conventions. As she continued, her job at the van company sounded increasingly like housekeeping. She checked on employees, made sure routines were followed, and assured customers that drivers would be on time. "Well, I was into trucks, but also the house and that," Julie said, explaining that she hired one person to take care of the boys at home and one to take care of them when they visited her office "in a trailer." Later in the interview, she talked of "taking care" of the drivers and seeing to their well-being, hinting at the maternal in her managerial style. Perhaps most conventionally, Julie deferred to her son when he was present, asking him to confirm her statements, to remember something for her, and to validate her facts.

Women's
Activities
and
Men's
Work

103

The third generation presented a different version of the balance between moving from a parental generation and obeying steel town conventions. One chilly evening in March 1988, I spent several hours with Rosie, Jane, and Jim, three of the six children in the Sam Wozeck family. Jane and Jim were in their twenties and Rosie was not much past thirty. Unlike the generation before them, they were not shy about describing the influence their mother had had on their lives. She was the main disciplinarian, cook, and housekeeper. She also worked in the store every day. "Well, my mother's worked all her life, day and night," Rosie said. "Day at the store and at night with us." It was her housekeeping, however, not her shopkeeping that impressed them as significant. The three competed in giving me detailed accounts of having to vacuum every speck of dust out of the living room before anyone had company. Sounding more and more like Mrs. Wozeck describing her mother, they talked about laundry day, baking day, cleaning day: all the "turns" in a woman's life.

At the same time, Rosie, Jane, and Jim suggested a transformation in Homestead imagery. Their parents reluctantly told me about women's domestic labors only after steel work had been described. For the younger generation, the drama of steel was more a legend than a reality. Now men's work was in disarray compared to women's activities; now as often as not women upheld a household. In the late twentieth century, men's work did not have either the presence or the glory of the "old days."

Byington's *Homestead* reminds readers that there was always a contrast between women's routine chores and the risk-filled work of men. Men's work took a dramatic toll, as Hine's portraits indicate, while women's tasks went on in quiet dignity. A photograph of laundry day, for example, minimizes the effort it took to clean grimy clothes and shows instead a woman standing sedate at her tub.[11] Even in this book, stories of women's lives are part of an endeavor to document conditions in an industrial town. The mill is always a dark backdrop for the households.

Residents of Homestead did not find women's chores dramatic, and their photograph collections did not isolate women's activities from family celebrations or public rituals. Like professional photographers, few amateurs found housework fascinating enough to document. But when they looked at family albums, they suddenly relished the small details of mundane days. Brodsky granted the details artistic worth in her photographs and, seeing this rendition, residents adjusted town history further toward the domestic. Residents who saw the photographs responded with pleasure, discovering the beauty in ordinary places and poses. Under this tute-

Women's
Activities
and
Men's
Work

104

lage, their own pictures gained value and depth; the incidental, everyday activity became a subject to look at, not simply part of the flowing continuum of life.

A glance at Brodsky's photographs also provides insight into why the hierarchy expressed through a contrast of male *work* with female *activities* persisted for so long: rows of houses, backed by church steeples, do not prompt the awe a heavy, glowering mill can. Work inside such houses did not have the mystique for people that work in front of an open hearth did.[12] Even in the early 1990s, when a person saw Charlee with her camera, he or she would advise photographing a still-working mill rather than "just" a residential street. History meant the history of a steel town, not a family town. That aspect of identity would not be relinquished easily.

Yet when they talked over photographs, women and men recognized the importance of the household in keeping a steel town alive. Through economic depression, a world war, an influx of wealth, and unexpected layoffs, those at home kept crisis at bay and, often, spirits up. Prompted into *seeing*, residents of the town acknowledged two kinds of work in Homestead, while not totally giving up the generations-old perception of the ideal division of labor. Definitions of women's and men's roles remained tied to the past; however much a woman valued her job and (even) equated it with male work, she also learned the distinction between her tasks and a man's work.

"It didn't feel like home when my wife wasn't there"

Men's views of women's work became more important in Homestead after the mill shut down. Faced with early retirement, the loss of a familiar job, and nowhere to go after high school, men of all ages had to reconsider the traditional division of labor. The probability of women working outside the home went hand-in-hand with the possibility of men working in it. Not every man I interviewed was willing to talk about a likely role reversal in town, but when telling their stories they often revealed how daunting such a change would be. Gender stereotypes hung on, a note of stability in a shifting world.

Men in Homestead, like their wives, mothers, and even their daughters, understood that women had to work in a crisis. Several men I met who grew up during the Great Depression were proud of mothers who had "gone out to work" during that period. Ken spent a considerable amount of time describing his young mother's courage. Widowed in 1936 when she

Women's
Activities
and
Men's
Work

105

was in her early thirties, she had two young children to bring up and begged for a position at the local elementary school. At this point, Ken extracted a snapshot from the pile he had brought with him to the interview. It showed a slight-looking woman in a long somber skirt standing in a playground. "Here she is. This is the playground over on Second Avenue. She was a teacher over there."

The second time I talked with Ken he had a larger pile of snapshots and mementos, which he spread out over the table. He wanted to show me more pictures of the "old days," and he searched for snapshots of himself, his brother, and his mother. He found another of the same small woman, still dressed in black, standing in front of a school building. This time he called her a "janitor." In essence, it turned out, his mother supervised playground activities, including cleaning up after the children. The word *janitor,* however, allowed him to emphasize the physical side of her labors: "Oh, she left at seven o'clock, started at seven, and she worked till four. But she had like an hour and a half for lunch." She did her turns. Then, as if to remind me of why she was at work, he pulled out a picture of himself, a bereft-looking little boy. *"Now,"* he asserted, "here's when I was a kid. Look at this, this is when my dad died."

A later photograph revealed something he had not mentioned previously. Out of the pile slid one of his mother standing in front of a Westinghouse plant with a group of workers. When I remarked on her change of job, he admitted, "My mother worked in Westinghouse." He added that it was kind of a family affair: "My father and my uncles all worked in Westinghouse." Then he pushed the Westinghouse photo aside and once again pointed to the two schoolyard ones. They fit the image he was creating in words of a woman struggling to survive against the odds and without much help. "She had it rough. We had it real rough at that time."

The Depression was like a war—it allowed women to do what they ordinarily did not do. Was deindustrialization going to have the same effect, breaking down the stereotypes residents of a steel town had long accepted? For older men, the answer was no. The decline of the mill town did not justify a woman's leaving the house to work; it helped, too, that these men had pensions to support the household. That a woman might *want* to work did not occur to a man in this generation. His mother had to work, his wife did not. The past permitted a tolerance the present did not, and the son granted his mother a leeway the husband could not grant his wife.

Women's
Activities
and
Men's
Work

106

For a man of that generation, the lives of daughters posed a different dilemma. Ambitions for children warred with traditional expectations for women. Prosperous steelworkers had the resources to send kids to college, but not the certainty that that was what a girl ought to do. In describing his daughter's career, one man frequently told me about his grandchildren, *her* children, thus maintaining a semblance of the "old days." More than once I heard a man boast that his wife took care of "all the grandchildren." Like the men interviewed in Mirra Komarovsky's classic study of a working-class community, men in Homestead believed, "It just doesn't seem like home to me when I know that my wife is out working."[13]

Mark, the tavern owner, had a hard time reconciling the work of his mother, his wife, and his daughters: "Well, now, see, my mother-in-law originally started her little deli store in there in 1925," he said, explaining the origin of the building we were sitting in. "She was the tough one," he added admiringly. He described his mother, too, as tough and hardworking. On the other hand, his wife, he told me, had been frail and sickly most of her life. He put the contrast bluntly: "my mother was a workhorse" and "my wife was a bundle of nerves." The descriptions suited his narrative and not, as I observed, his experience. While we talked, his wife served drinks to the customers at the front bar, brought food to diners at the back room tables, and generally managed the business of the evening. She looked pretty tireless to me.

Mark was reluctant to discuss his wife's work. Usually easy in his narrative, these were moments at which he hesitated or changed the subject. A hard worker all her life, she did not fit the image of a wife in a prospering steel town. Even when he talked about the difficulties in 1990s Homestead, Mark presented himself as the main breadwinner in the family, despite the counterevidence right before our eyes. The story was different for his daughters because the economic situation had worsened and Mark wanted me to know he respected new cultural norms. Not only did his daughters have "prestigious" jobs, but, according to Mark, he had encouraged their ambitions all along: "My [attention to] education has paid off for me in this way. I have two daughters. And I'm very proud of them because the one is a vice-principal at Holy Mother High School." He was inordinately pleased with a daughter who had succeeded within the domain of education and religion. The second daughter was working toward an advanced degree at a local university.

Mark took credit for their achievements. He described how he supplemented their schooling, determined that they would get into college: "I think what motivated me was the fact that nobody in my family got a high school diploma except my older sister [and himself]. . . . But out of the five of us, two of us got high school diplomas." He himself had tried college for two years, then left to serve in the Second World War. After that, he married into the tavern family.

His daughters were following a different mill town script. They would be upwardly mobile. Mark did not bring his children into his work world, but he did present himself as a model for their choices: "I know how *I* was, you know, if I knew something that everybody else in the class didn't know, they all came to me. I was like the kingpin, you know. And I know they [the daughters] felt the same way." His pride in his daughters' achievements echoed his descriptions of his mother and mother-in-law, and he felt himself to be the conveyor of these values. Yet he minimized his wife's work. An ability to encourage a woman's ambition existed as long as a man's own performance in the work world was not threatened; as son and as father, Mark admired the working woman. As husband, he did not.

Women of Mark's generation shared his view of gender roles: "Listen to this," the wife of a retired steelworker began her life story. "My Dad died when I was three years old. I had a younger brother. My mother had to work all the time." An emergency drove a woman from her usual role— and not without penalties, said Marie, thinking of the present in Homestead. The children were left alone: "Unless you had somebody like a grandparent or a sister or somebody that would come over all the time. You would never know the experience it is to have a hard time at school and come home and the house is empty. No one to tell it to. Then your mother comes home from work at six o'clock." This was not good for children, she remarked, and only tolerable when there were no other options. "My mother did day work," Marie continued. "She came home at six o'clock. She's so tired, so there isn't anybody to tell your troubles to. And they wonder why kids go bad. I can see why they go bad because it's like nobody cares."

Marie had been a stay-at-home mother and had that luxury because her husband made good money in the mill: "We talked about it. And he says if you want to go out to work, you have to be home when the kids come home from school. Well, at that time it was hard to get that type of job." With her mind on childrearing, Marie agreed. "We had this thing that I stayed home so that the kids would have somebody home all the time and it kept them out of trouble."

Women's
Activities
and
Men's
Work

108

"The wife has to work too"

In the early 1990s, men and women in steel towns throughout western Pennsylvania faced the fact that resources were dwindling and jobs disappearing. Regardless of how many years a family had in the mill, a boy could not expect to work in steel; nor could a girl plan on marrying a steelworker or a shopkeeper who would be prosperous on the income from steel. Seeing the smoke vanish from mill stacks, machine shops close, and bulldozers flatten the land on the riverbanks, a resident of Homestead realized that if one were to survive, ideals about women's and men's roles were equally likely to disappear.

An ex-steelworker, in mid-career when the Homestead Works shut down in 1987, considered the nature of women's activities and men's work. He described a scenario that was becoming familiar to every resident in town, whether articulated or not: "Today, at the rates they pay an hour, the wife has to work, too. You want that house, the two of you have to work." He knew who to blame. "Again, we go back to Reagan. Reagan wants everybody to make $3.35 an hour. When I went to job services one day, I said, 'You can't live on $3.35 an hour,' and there was already somebody there telling me that you can't live on that." He bitterly compared the present with the past. "My last job I was making $9.50 an hour, plus time and a half. Good job. I thought it was going to last until October. Would have been all right. I could have collected unemployment and made about $200 a week." When I interviewed him, he had no job, no unemployment compensation from the corporation, and no prospect of a job. He lived with his mother, who herself worked, and he was looking for a newspaper route.

A man of the same age and sharing the same predicament, Peter had a family to support. When I interviewed him in late 1988, he was still hoping for a steady job. He hated the idea of his wife going out to work and was outraged about leaving his kids without their mother. His mother, whom he described as "really active for seventy," had worked, but only until he came home from school, he remembered. "She worked during the day while I was in school. She was always home. Somebody was always home with me. I wasn't a latchkey."

To raise the fourth generation as latchkey children—kids who let themselves into an empty house—signaled the town's decline for parents in their thirties and forties. In the course of his interview, Peter admitted he stayed home with the kids while his wife cleaned houses in another part

Women's
Activities
and
Men's
Work

109

of the city. Pleased that his children had constant supervision, he momentarily relinquished his macho image as the hardened steelworker. On the other hand, he mourned the loss of a job that had given him not only a solid income but also status and an identity.

Facing a real tragedy, members of families that had been in Homestead for generations began to release their attachment to inherited gender stereotypes and expectations. Looking at the weed-filled lot on the Mon, at the boarded-up stores on Eighth Avenue, and at gangs of adolescents, parents wondered whether the children of a mill town had the resources to handle a future without steel. Observing the growing-up generation, parents wondered what values they should maintain at home and argue for in the school system. How much of the "good old days" did families have to relinquish in order to move into the next phase of life in Homestead?

Women's
Activities
and
Men's
Work

110

AT HOME

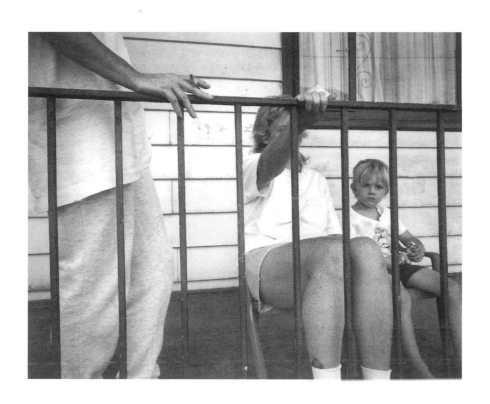

RAISING A NEW GENERATION IN AN EX-STEEL TOWN

Through children, more than through insurance, or savings, or even through home owning, does a workman's household lay claim upon the future. Here both the oldest instincts and new half-formulated ambitions find expression. . . . Here the community has set before itself what it feels to be high standards.

—Margaret Byington, *Homestead: The Households of a Mill Town*

The town of Homestead, with church steeples rising to counteract the visual dominance of the mill, was also once a town full of schools. School buildings were attached to the churches and scattered through the residential areas of the industrial town. A walk through the town in the 1990s revealed a transformation: some schools had been torn down, only a brave set of front steps left standing; others had been converted to other uses, though none were remodeled into apartments a middle-class population might rent. A few schools looked aban-

doned though they were not; budgetary restrictions left playgrounds in disrepair with graffiti on the fences. Day-care facilities sprung up in private homes, reflecting a Homestead with new work and family patterns.

How important schools were to the way residents envisioned Homestead became clear when I brought out old photographs of the town. Squinting and staring, a person would find the school she went to or, failing that, the church where she had suffered through Sunday school. School buildings did not appear frequently in family albums, but formal classroom portraits did. So did school graduations, athletic award ceremonies, and confirmations: all reminded the viewer of a child's passage into adulthood through the educational institutions of a town. Brodsky and I spent a good deal of time looking at school yearbooks with the people we met; those volumes presented a vivid image of Homestead education as it once was. The teachers' appearances changed decade by decade and so did the looks of the students; with different faces, the roles of best dancer, best athlete, best writer, and best community volunteer were always filled.

Comments on old photographs also revealed the significance of parks and playgrounds in the steel town. Once well-kept and well-populated, by the 1990s Homestead's parks looked deserted. Some had been paved over while others were appropriated by strangers, drifters, and drug dealers. Children had to learn the town and their tasks differently from the way their parents and grandparents had. The story of childhood socialization in Homestead, from the first to the third generation, is a story of slow but unmistakable change.

What education meant in Homestead varied like everything else with the fortunes of the United States Steel Corporation. The presence of the mill as an available option, at least for some members of the community, determined the significance of learning for all members of the community. In *Homestead*, Byington devotes one chapter to "The Children of Homestead." In it, she remarks that the mill influenced the way teachers taught kids as well as how priests and parents communicated expectations to the younger generation. Hine's photographs convey the style of learning in a mill town: small children in a courtyard, for example, amuse one another. On another page, two small boys in overalls stare solemnly into the camera, miniatures of the adult male workers who usually dominated Hine's camera.

In the early twentieth century, Byington tells her readers, girls did not have much opportunity for "technical training" or for "domestic service," another form of training. They could, however, marry mill workers and practice domestic science at home. And for the boys, she writes, concentrating on the Anglo residents, the mill was always there:

> The sons may work a little further up than their fathers; a man told me
> with pride that his son, who was a foreman, had secured for him a job

Children at McClure Street, 1913 (Pittsburgh and Lake Erie Railroad)

in the mill, and a mother was eager to relate how her boy had taught the new assistant superintendent the way to do his work. Only rarely, however, do they secure an education that fits them for an entirely different kind of labor.[1]

When the people I interviewed thought back to their childhoods in the 1920s and 1930s, or the 1950s and 1960s, they echoed these sentiments. Until recently, the mill was there for boys and marriage to a mill worker was the choice for girls. Talking with me in the late 1980s and early 1990s, parents wondered whether it would be possible to teach children a new kind of labor.

"Learning to labor" was not altogether school-based in Homestead, not when Margaret Byington did her survey for the Russell Sage Foundation and not when I started asking questions about school, work, education, and plans for the future.[2] Learning to labor occurred at home, in backyards, on the streets of the town, in churches, playgrounds, and community centers. Byington used the phrase *home training*: "The working people of Homestead when talking of their children show a distinct recognition of the value of education and home training, as compared with the immediate money value of wages."[3] Home training meant learning in a domestic and familial setting—if not in the kitchens and parlors of the home, then from mothers, fathers, uncles, and aunts. It meant learning by watching and by being assigned particular tasks—a kind of apprenticeship combined with a definite emphasis on character building.

When asked what they learned growing up in Homestead, almost everyone I interviewed, regardless of age, gender, ethnicity, or race emphasized rules at home. Home meant family, including extended kin, and it also meant religious training—the values transferred from church to domestic hearth. While at home, children of a mill town learned to labor and to live right. Inside the mill, the techniques and the content of learning did not differ. The withdrawal of USX from the town left a big gap and few strategies for filling it. A few schools revised their curriculums and some programs arrived with promises of new skills. These changes, however, barely altered the dominant way in which individuals learned: through close, personal absorption of old values.

"Well, this is where I'm going"

From the early twentieth century until well after the Second World War, a boy growing up in Homestead knew that *men* worked in steel. That knowledge shaped his view of his activities as a child, an adolescent, and an adult; it also shaped the viewpoint of girls growing up in a mill town. Like boys, girls took the measure of their futures against steel, learning to manage a mill household as a part of growing up. A boy who grew up in a mill family could follow easily in the footsteps of his father and uncles, entering the mill with barely a second thought and not much prior training. The pattern for boys and for girls in working-class families seemed familiar and secure.

Familiarity did not erase ambivalence about mill work. From the time the first workers entered Carnegie's industrial empire and began the long walk toward retirement, there were parents who planned so their children might escape the grip of steel. A Homestead resident could not be aware of the grueling, dangerous labor of a daily turn without giving thought to a

Raising
a New
Generation

135

better future for his or her child. Whether a child actually took a new direction varied with opportunity, temperament, and the availability of necessary resources—among those formal schooling.

A child in a mill town traditionally learned by doing, taking on tasks and skills that the older generation demonstrated and dictated. For much of the twentieth century, steel town schools supported this system, maintaining existing social divisions while rewarding those with special initiative or forceful parents. In every decade, a few broke away, and their stories are part of the history of Homestead: a decision to go to college, a rejection of the manual training offered by the local high school, a star performance on a sports team. Until recently, a choice to leave was as linked to the fortunes of the mill as a choice to stay.

Informal and kin-based, home training was a form of apprenticeship that paralleled the workplace. Interviewees claimed they had learned to labor "on the job," whatever the work space. Kin were there to teach the newcomer: "In 1951, of ten thousand male employees at the Homestead Works, more than four thousand were father-and-son combinations."[4] In 1987 when I talked to an appliance store owner, who had taken over the shop from his father, he pointed to his sisters and his sons, clerking along with him in the traditional fashion.

In *Out of This Furnace*, Thomas Bell never tells how young John Dobrejcak learned to labor in the mill so well that he won the respect of his fellow workers. Nor does Bell mention schools, except to remark on John's impatience with being in class at all. If one were going to learn from fathers, mothers, uncles, and aunts, why bother paying attention to a teacher and staying awake in front of a blackboard? One sunny afternoon, sitting on her front steps, a woman who had been married to a steelworker told me in no uncertain terms: "You don't need to be educated to work in a mill." This represented a point of view on schools that persisted into the late twentieth century. I was to hear, expressed in various ways, a deep suspicion of people who concentrated on "book learning."

"There is a general belief that the college trained man, with all his theory, is less expert than the man who has learned the industry through work with his hands," wrote Byington in 1910. "As few men with technical training are at the start familiar with the processes of steel making, the value of their theoretical knowledge cannot overcome the prejudice created among the men by their early blunders."[5] Taking a Progressive stance and as a partisan of workers, Byington offers an opinion of "theoretical knowledge" that hints at a town's contempt for those whose work involved using words. To spend time accumulating literary skills did a resident of Homestead little good. Yet, as individuals I interviewed remarked in hindsight, rejecting those skills also did the town little good.

"The younger people, they just assumed that, you know, when they were in their teens, 'well, this is where I'm going,'" Joanna began her discussion of education in Homestead when she was growing up in the 1950s. "'I'm going to go where Dad was. I don't have to worry about it.'" What she meant was that, in the past, no one had to worry about doing well in school, getting good grades, or taking "college prep" classes. She added, "And they already knew, in dollars and cents, what they were going to start out at" in the mill. Joanna concluded with a cogent remark about education in virtually any working-class community:[6] "At that point, it wasn't their education that was doing anything for them, you know, other than being able to get along, I guess, and not having a personality conflict with the bosses and things like that."

Being able to get along was a primary skill, taught and learned in the schools of Homestead. It allowed a boy or girl to learn on the job and to succeed wherever he or she worked. This view of school put books in their place—as luxuries, not necessities. "Book learning" (or "theory") did not make money in a town like Homestead, and for decades it did not matter much if a child never tried college or dropped out when he or she did. Another view was that a nose in a book could be a danger on the job.

In his memoir *Steeltown,* economist Charles Walker describes his shock at realizing how useless a Yale education was compared to army training: "I watched carefully for a long time, which was a cardinal rule of practice with me on joining up with a new gang. It was best, I thought, to shut up and study for a spell the characters of the men, the movements and knacks of the job," he wrote, attributing his wisdom to participation in a platoon.[7] Only scrupulous watchfulness, he noted, would save his own or another man's life.

Military training and wartime service provided a trope for mill work in interviews I did. One older worker recalled his nightmares about the army; his wife reminded him that his dreams about the mill were "the same." Their conversation referred to the teamwork, alertness, and bravery needed in both domains because of the ever-present fact of death. The analogy between work in steel and fighting at the front glorified labor in steel, lending it the aura that steel town residents gave to participation in war. "The single characteristic they all share is their perception of danger," an observer of steelworkers noted. "This perception produces a set of perspectives around the problem of danger that is rigorously and continuously enforced."[8]

"The shop floor abounds with apocryphal stories about the idiocy of purely theoretical knowledge," writes Paul Willis in a study of British working-class youth. "Practical ability always comes first and is a condition of other kinds of knowledge."[9] Stories of what happened to men who read rather than worked abounded in a steel town; idiots were drummed out of a crew. In Homestead, as in Willis's Hammertown, these stories seeped out of the workplace, influencing the lessons learned at home, in playgrounds, and in schools.

An ex-steelworker I met in Homestead claimed he had "ignored" books all through his school life. The texts offered him by nuns and high school teachers seemed trivial and useless—he knew he would get a job. Jobless in 1988, he realized he had missed something during those years. "Now," he said rather ruefully, "I do a lot of reading." He had been reading since, as he put it, "I got laid off and had time on my hands." He did not say whether he was reading for pleasure or to learn a new way of laboring; he was reading because he was bored and had nothing else to do. The idea that books were impractical, time fillers for those who had time, hung on.

"They did pay good wages"

Until recently, the culture a boy of Homestead inherited was formed by stories of the shop floor, reports of nicknames and jokes, and descriptions of rituals that made men under fire become men. School could not compete: there were no myths surrounding those six hours a day, no tales of risk, and, for members of steelworking families, no genuine conviction that education would get them where they wanted to go.

At the same time, American society has generally viewed education as a route to social mobility and status. In the early twentieth century, Margaret Byington met "English-speaking" parents who spurned mill work and encouraged their sons to try schooling instead. Hunkies did not have the same choice, but, as Thomas Bell wrote about one character, "He wanted to live well, to live in a nice house away from the mill, and to give his boys a good education so they wouldn't have to work with shovel and wheelbarrow like their father. He used to say, what was the use of coming to America if not to live better than we lived in the old country?"[10] But Bell's heroes are the steelworkers who struggled to establish a union and improve conditions in the mill.

I still heard expressions of a point of view that honored social mobility, but these were thrown into critical reflection when it became clear the Works would never reopen. Parents in their fifties and sixties talked about college and the prestige a college degree brought. They talked about salaries replacing wages and white collars replacing blue. They also remembered back ten or twenty or thirty years to when they were planning for a child's future and when the arguments against college were persuasive. Why should a boy leave home and Homestead for an advanced degree when his manhood and his livelihood had been apprenticed to steel? Mrs. Wozeck spoke glowingly of her father, the open hearth worker, and did not find it contradictory that he discouraged his son from following in his footsteps: "My father didn't ever want him to go into the mill, no matter what he would do, anything but that." Nor did she find it strange that her brother quit college after one year. He decided, Mrs. Wozeck told me, to go into steel where he could "make money."

Mrs. Wozeck had ambitions for her own sons when they were young and the Homestead Works was still running. With two uncles in the mill, they could have followed the route of dropping their books and picking up a shovel the day after high school. The two who were old enough did take summer jobs in steel, but Mrs. Wozeck pushed for other things—book learning, to be exact. She was proud of a cousin of hers who had published a novel and brought him up in the context of recalling her lessons to her boys. She won her argument in the end because of the corporation's decisions. By the time her sons were ready for full-time work in the early 1980s, the future of the mill looked dismal. Pay dropped, men left, and shops closed down. Being a steelworker had lost its place in a changing America. The Wozeck boys turned to white-collar work.

Not all third-generation children had the advantages of the Wozecks—resources for a college education and an ambitious mother. Perhaps the fact that Sam Wozeck was not a steelworker helped his children along another path. For children in families with "over two hundred years" in the mill, exposed domestically to the mystique of steel, the choice to change was difficult. The children I interviewed whose fathers worked in the mill had incorporated the rhythms of turns into their interpretations of adulthood. For these children, tasks and gender identities were influenced by the cycle of eight-hour shifts. The pull down the hill, as residents put it, operated through the "blood" as well as through a pragmatic assessment of opportunity. Well into the 1970s, parents in Homestead expressed an ambivalence that kept the mill an attractive option for girls as well as boys.

"There is a fascination about the mill against which even unwilling mothers find themselves helpless to contend."[11]

The dilemma was real, sadly relieved by the demolition of the mill. For generations, fathers and mothers hoped for mobility in their children while recognizing the "lure" and the security of the mill. Book learning represented status, but steel work represented a sure, and often high, income. Moreover, college removed a boy from his father's crew and a girl from her mother's customs. At the same time, as Luther reveals, decisions remained difficult.

He told me he would "break the legs of any kid of mine" who went into the mill. Then he regaled me with stories of controlling an enormous swinging crane, of drinking with the men he had supervised, and of burning up in the summertime mill heat. What I heard, his children undoubtedly heard as well. It was not surprising that his sons took summer jobs in the mill and that his daughters sneaked down to hang around the mill.

Luther's wife Joanna had an opinion about steel work, too. She knew the temptation Luther's stories of being in the mill posed to their children when they were growing up in the 1960s. Recalling the lure of the mill then, she said: "Well, like Luther says, it's hard work, you know, it's very hard work, and they did pay good, they did pay good wages." She also remembered debating the value of high wages when they came at risk to the worker and with a drain on family time: "But he said they expected an awful lot out of you and living through—" the unmentioned "hell" of long turns. "It was," she went on, "the kind of job where it was just like a doctor or people at the hospital. There was no such thing as a holiday. The mill never shut down."

But it was not "just like a doctor," and that fact contributed to a child's ambivalence about choosing mill work. Doctors had a prestige in American culture that steelworkers did not have, no matter how vital to the American economy steel might be. Joanna and Luther told me about their son who had gone to college and then to graduate school in engineering. They spoke proudly of the youngest boy who was attending a private high school in Pittsburgh. Their daughters had also resisted the temptation of the mill, though Kim and Theresa confessed to me the "magnetism" of "down there." Had the Works stayed open they might have joined a labor gang, but as it turned out USX was not hiring in the early 1980s when they graduated from high school. By then, too, any mill job would have been unstable. Moreover, mill work had little to do with the rhythms and routines they had learned from their mothers and grandmothers. Learning for girls in Homestead had its own pattern, carried from generation to generation, just as learning to labor did for boys.

"She'd take the downstairs"

I interviewed the sisters together. Through their intersecting responses, Theresa and Kim composed a story of women's lives like the ones I heard from the generation of their mother and aunts. Women in Homestead, according to the two younger women, learned at home to be housewives. If a boy learned from his father and uncles, a girl received her main lessons from her mother, aunts, and grandmothers.

When I asked what their mother did, Kim responded first: "Housewife." Theresa picked up the theme: "Housewife, housewife, definitely. At that time, in fact, you know, none of my friends that I knew had working mothers." Kim: "Working mothers! They were always at home." Theresa: "They were always at home." Kim: "In fact, a lot of my friends, . . . when we were in high school now, most of my friends, their mothers weren't working." But of course their mothers were working—at the task of instructing daughters who would assume the same labors the women before them had. How to keep house was only the first lesson mothers gave daughters. At home, girls learned proper character and behavior. The counterpart to creating "maleness" through hard labor was creating "femaleness" through the activities that maintained the domestic hearth.

Rules were significant to this training: "We weren't allowed to go out on weekends, like after we were teenagers, to go out with our friends or go on dates unless we had our work done," the sisters told me, constructing an account in tandem. "And we weren't allowed to go out on Friday nights if we didn't have that work done. So we'd do it on Thursday [laughing]." Not surprisingly, Kim and Theresa mastered teamwork that would release them sooner from their household turns. Kim explained: "She'd take the downstairs and I'd take the upstairs." The punishment for failure—being grounded—if not a life-and-death situation, was devastating to an adolescent girl. The punishment also made their mother's values unmistakable. Kim and Theresa accepted their mother's values—and lessons—and treated school mainly as a social arena.

Sam's wife spoke of, and embodied, the ambiguities surrounding education in a mill town family. I asked her about school, and she remembered one nun who had ambitions for her female students: "We had one nun who felt that not everyone was going to go to college, and she got them [the parochial school] to teach typing, shorthand, and bookkeeping. She says, 'a lot of you girls aren't going to go, and you're going to need something. This is much more practical.' So we did have that." This was a lesson from the Depression—to prepare women to help out in an economic crisis and, perhaps, to manage if they never married or were widowed. It was a lesson daughters in a 1980s economy could have used, women for whom divorce increased the possibility of being on their own. Mrs. Wozeck inserted a nostalgic memory of the good old days: "But you still had to have all your other—you had to have your languages and everything else. So they expected you'd all end up with good jobs and things."

Mrs. Wozeck went to college for a year and a half, then left in order to earn money. "I wasn't really interested in being anything particular. I thought being a secretary would be fine. So I got a good secretarial job downtown. I was quite happy that way," she said. Mrs. Wozeck went on to minimize what must have been a significant trip from the familiar context of a steel town to the center of the city, from the lunch boxes and overalls of a mill to the coffee and suits of a business community. She did not say much about her move into the more traditional career of housewife. For, according to her story, it was not long after she began work that she met Sam at a dance. The ensuing rapid courtship ended in her long life as a married woman.

As a housewife, Mrs. Wozeck had much to teach her daughters, including traits she had been taught by her own strong-willed mother. Models for the third generation, these women had expanded the boundaries of "household management"—the grandmother by buying and selling houses and the mother by working in the store all day. Describing their mother to me, Rosie and Jane portrayed a woman who, like the heroines in Byington's book, managed everything: a nearly twenty-four-hour turn. The lessons Rosie and Jane learned were not so much the cooking and cleaning than a generalized coping with whatever came along—a variant of the education girls received in the first half of the twentieth century. Rosie's house was as orderly as her mother's, and, like her mother, Rosie combined household management with a full-time job. Her job, however, was in a downtown bank; some things had changed in a mill town.

Overall, a working-class ethic of hard work and endurance pervaded a girl's education as much as a boy's, regardless of class or race. This was at the heart of the home training Byington described and, as in her account, the staff was multiple and varied. Girls learned not only from their mothers but also from equally insistent grandmothers, aunts, and cousins. The

A
steelworker's
"pride"
(family
collection)

molding of a woman in Homestead was as intense as the molding of a man in the mill. In both instances training was accomplished by a platoon, a group of kin with priorities and an order of command that resulted in the effective transmission of attitudes from one generation to the next.

"Ethnic backgrounds and the traditions"

In her encounter with the households of the mill town, Margaret Byington wondered about the fate of the younger generation. She wrote, somewhat sadly, "The mothers, too, expect that their daughters will eventually marry mill workers. Yet they desire for their children greater ease and culture than they themselves have enjoyed. One woman told me very sweetly of her efforts to teach her children better manners than she had ever learned."[12] For a Progressive like Byington, greater culture and better manners meant assimilation and participation in the process of becoming American. For subsequent generations of children in Homestead, "culture" had mixed meanings, often referring less to Americanization than to "ethnicization." It was the woman's responsibility to transmit the components of ethnic identity in a town where ethnicity was a primary social category.

Theresa and Kim remembered their strict Serbian grandmother who lived next door when they were growing up. "Well, she taught us a lot too. She taught us all our ethnic backgrounds and the traditions and everything. You know, it was pounded into our head." In their typical alternation with one another, Kim and Theresa talked about a particular Sunday soup. Theresa assured me, "You don't want it, it's made out of sauerkraut juice. You don't want any." Kim amended the judgment: "It's not bad." Theresa: "And dry mushrooms. It's nasty." Kim: "It's not bad." Theresa: "Grandma's was bad. Yours isn't like Grandma's. Grandma's soup was black. It was black, it was actually black!"

Anecdotes about food represented ethnicity for men as well as women. In a typical American gesture, food habits were used to claim ethnic distinctiveness. Yet the men's inclination to talk about food may also have resulted from the change in their lives that brought them to an unexpected domesticity. One afternoon, for instance, Luther took me to see the brand-new church his congregation had just built. In Homestead Park, the gleaming white structure contrasted with the dark brick buildings characteristic of Homestead proper, the original location of this church. Luther, however, was less interested in the building than in the bustle of activity inside; we stood in the kitchen for a long time, observing women preparing a huge feast for the next Greek Orthodox holiday. Explaining the foods to me, he asserted his attachment to the ethnic tradition that framed the upcoming celebration. The detailed explanation also announced a benign interpretation of ethnic difference.

Like ethnic festivals, religious practice conventionally fell into the woman's domain: mothers enforced church attendance and girls went. So did boys, but for the girls in a mill town, religion was part and parcel of learning to run a household. The image of "below the tracks" and a version of history in which religion cemented a family and solidified a neighborhood served as a backdrop. The significance of religious training endured, even though Rosie and Jane joked about playing hookey from church: "We would all get up and act like we were going to church when one of us was old enough to drive," Rosie explained. "And one of us would run in and get the bulletin so that we could prove that we went to church. And we'd get McDonald's or something." But they never fooled their mother. According to the story, she always discovered the trick: "Then my mother would go in another car and come down and see that our car wasn't parked anywhere near church, so she knew we weren't inside. I mean, she used to come around and catch us. We got caught a lot of times." Looking forward as well as backward, both Rosie and Jane assured me they would do the same to their children. Religious training, they agreed, preserved the moral life of the town.

Rosie went to parochial school, so church was an extra for her. She could safely skip Mass every now and then. "I didn't have to go so much because I went to a Catholic school. I would send my kids to a Catholic school." I asked why. "The education is good. It's good discipline." Early in the century, Byington noted the importance of parochial schools in steel towns. "Through parochial schools, also, the church exerts a strong influence," she wrote, then went on to criticize these schools for hindering "the work of amalgamation in which public schools are so potent a fac-tor."[13] The tension between maintaining a distinct identity through reli-gious practice and "amalgamating" continued into the late twentieth cen-tury. Rosie and her younger sister Jane debated the virtues of Catholic school versus the virtues of public school. Listening to her older sister de-scribe parochial school, twenty-five-year-old Jane interjected her feelings. She was relieved, she said, that she had not had to do that. "If I went to a Catholic school, I would have never been, you know, never been able to be a majorette in the band and [go to] Disney World. I'm so glad I didn't go to Catholic school. Plus you have to wear uniforms, too."

The choice between parochial and public schools, as Rosie and Jane implied, amounted to a choice between "discipline" and being just like everyone else—not having to wear a special uniform. Going to public school, Jane continued, made her high school experience "normal." As she remembered the trip to Disney World—"good old days" of not more than ten years earlier—she leafed through the albums that were lying on the floor in front of us and found snapshots from the trip. There she was, baton in hand, in an outfit that obviously did not count as a uniform in her eyes since it evoked such a different world from that of the parochial school her older sister had attended.

As I drove over the High-Level Bridge in the early 1990s, Homestead's famous "forty-two steeples" stood out, especially since there was no longer a mill to distract a viewer. From that vantage point, the church buildings looked fine and solid; a closer look showed changes: empty parking lots, slightly tarnished paint, a synagogue turned into a fundamentalist Chris-tian church. Interviews with residents indicated the changes were pain-fully visible to them, along with the fear that they were seeing the last generation to make church a central part of life. Worshipping with a visiting minister or in a suburban church was not easy for families who had known the same neighborhood church for "hundreds" of years. Along with the mill and ethnic lodges, these had seemed the most permanent institutions in the town. By 1990, individuals had to reconsider where to worship and what to teach their children.

In a time of crisis, church attendance and religious training loomed large for the children in a mill town. Peter, for instance, insisted his four and six year old go to bible school every afternoon. This was something he might not have done when the mills were running, his job secure, and his wife home with the kids. Now, he told me, bible education was "good" and the program "took care" of his daughters.

In another manifestation of the same impulse, Ken became the active churchgoer he had not been since childhood. Thoroughly involved, he apparently did not think he had taken on a role traditionally held by women. Rather, he became engaged in activities that provided satisfaction at a time when there was not much else to do. The activities, moreover, had long been central to the continuity of community in a mill town.

"They don't know any other way of life"

Rosie and Jane both went to Steel Valley High School, up the hill near the well-kept neighborhood of Homestead Park. There, perched on several acres of green land, the high school visually represented the beginning of a change in Homestead. A consolidation of local schools in the area, Steel Valley looked different from the old, three-storied brick buildings that once housed high school students. Steel Valley shone in the white concrete of modern architecture, its sweeping driveway reminding an observer that few students walked to school as they had in the good old days. Steel Valley was completed in 1972, replacing public and private high schools in several boroughs. For residents, this "consolidation" symbolized the crisis in their lives.

Thinking back to her childhood, eighty-year-old Mrs. Tennant recalled an abundance of schools. "There were schools all over the place," she assured me. In her narrative, she recreated a picture of children pouring out of their houses, crossing the streets and the railroad tracks to go to schools in various parts of town. Part nostalgia, her anecdotes were also history: school buildings occupied a chunk of the Homestead landscape in the 1920s and 1930s. Mrs. Tennant had photographs to support her memory and yearbooks to jog it further. After we talked, she opened the yearbooks and began leafing through the pages. Not only her own school but schools throughout the area were represented, in photos of sports events, debating clubs, and "raids" on each other's grounds. There, too, was the display of Anglo faces, Slavic faces, and a scattering of dark-skinned Italians and Mexicans.

As she turned the pages, Mrs. Tennant went on to muse: "We had high schools, Catholic schools, public schools. We had a lot of schools. Homestead was bigger then." Homestead *was* bigger, and the events pictured in Mrs. Tennant's high school yearbooks showed that "big" meant not only size but also prominence. High school events drew the attention of a wide public: they were "big" in the minds of Pittsburgh residents and in the headlines of Pittsburgh newspapers. Then, Homestead was on the map not just for its strikes and lock-outs but for its home teams as well.

In going through her yearbooks, Mrs. Tennant recounted the extra-curricular triumphs. Football games, dances, and end-of-year picnics were the arenas in which she and other mill town children learned adult roles and the distinctions crucial in a steel town: who would go where in the future, and why. The significance of ethnic, religious, and racial distinctions came up even more prominently in another interview I did. A decade or so younger than Mrs. Tennant, Ken did not have yearbooks, but he did have class photos, with rows of children's faces illustrating so much about a steel town. Looking over his photos, he pointed out a prosperous shopkeeper, a local beautician, and one school friend who had succeeded in professional sports. He also wondered "how many still lived here." Not many, he answered himself.

In his interpretation of the class photos, he added another dimension, telling me who was Hunky, who Irish, and who, in his term, "colored." And, it seemed to me, he emphasized the success of the Jewish students he came across—he had long before ascertained that I was Jewish. His was also a then-and-now tale, as he described "harmony" in his school years compared with the "harshness" of what his children experienced at Steel Valley High. In the consolidated high school, they encountered strangers, unfamiliar faces, kids with no ties to the neighborhoods of Homestead.

Ken took me on a tour of Homestead that revealed how profoundly the secondary changes consequent on the mill closing affected him. We drove first to his church, Saint Anne's. The physical structure was impressive, standing high on a hill behind West Homestead where it had been rebuilt in 1951, the original building destroyed in the Second World War demolition of Lower Homestead. Characteristically, Ken did not stint on his duties as guide, and we went through the building methodically. He pointed to each replication of components of the original church. The golden oak pews had been moved up, and the beautiful rose window had been reconstructed piece by glass piece for its new home. We stood at the pews and we walked past the altar. Then we went upstairs to see the priest's rooms. From here we had a stunning view of the Monongahela River, the Homestead High-Level Bridge, and, across the river, the crowded neighborhoods of Pittsburgh's East End. Our tour ended with a visit to the elementary school attached to the church.

Two-storied and containing about twenty classrooms, the school reflected the optimism of 1959, the year it opened. In 1988, the classrooms were silent and spotless; the long first-floor corridor, with a familiar feel and smell, was bare of pictures—none of the signs and drawings one associates with an elementary school. We did not go up to the second floor, which was occupied by nuns who had moved in when the school closed. The school, Ken said, had been shut since 1984. The very last place on his tour was the cafeteria kitchen, glimmering stainless steel from top to bottom. No one used the room regularly anymore, and the only disturbances that day were our reflections in the cabinet doors. We spent a lot of time in the room, as Ken expressed his sorrow at the changes so effectively symbolized by the gleaming space.

The tragedy in rust-belt towns like Homestead is that public and private schools begin to decline at exactly the moment education is needed most. Without the mill, parents and children had to reconsider the importance of book learning. In the last five years of the 1980s, it was not smart to sleep through classes or dismiss book learning as "boring." In such towns, too, parents and children had to get used to the idea that schools might no longer be local, in one's own backyard. To go to school outside the borough meant entering another's domain entirely. Even members of the third generation refused to do that, as long as they could.

A woman explained why she had decided not to go to a high school in Squirrel Hill in 1970. "From that school [elementary], I should have went to Alderdice. But it was my choice to go to Boyle," where she was on the academic track. "I really would have got a much better education if I'd gone to Alderdice." She elaborated on her reasons for staying in Homestead: "Alderdice is real scary to a lot of people just because it's such a big school, and you're used to kind of being used to a smaller school. A lot of my really good friends were going there [Boyle], and I went ahead and went there." She added a final touch to her sense of community: "These people I went to high school with, their children now go to school with my children, so I know all my children's [friends'] parents. My kids will come home from school and say, 'so-and-so wants me to come and play,' and they go, 'you went to school with her [mom], it will be OK.'"

A mother of adolescent children said, "But I would say that was probably the biggest disappointment to a lot of the young people, the fact that they no longer had that [the mill] to look forward to, which meant they would have to rely on getting some education in order to get ahead now in the world." The set of mind, she implied, was unfamiliar and upsetting. "I think right now we are in a transition period where these young people, they just feel like, 'well, what am I going to do?' They don't know any other way of life."

"When I was growing up, all adults were strict"

The problem was the same throughout the tri-state area, from western Pennsylvania into West Virginia and Ohio. Kids had to change the ways they learned to labor, and parents had to alter their expectations for a child's career. In a late 1970s study of Youngstown, Ohio, two social scientists reported: "George believes that when his son graduates from high school, he should learn a trade. When asked if he would advise his son to work in the mill, George's answer was a firm 'no.'" Under the prodding of interviewers, George also considered his daughter's education from the perspective of a precarious employment situation. She too, he said, "should develop a marketable skill, something she can 'fall back on,' if necessary." The authors do not dwell on the challenge this posed to traditional gender roles in an American industrial town. "Perhaps because of his own family's experience, George feels that it is important for a woman to be able to step in and provide for a family in the event the husband cannot."[14]

The likelihood of George's scenario working out depended on whether schools in former industrial towns would train girls as well as boys in "marketable skills," skills that fit them for a labor few in their families had performed. In Homestead, it depended on whether parents would send their children across the river to the Pittsburgh city schools when the local schools failed. Above all, it depended on whether the regional job market could expand enough to absorb the marketable skills learned by girls and boys; not everyone in Homestead was ready to move away.

Steel valley kids who finished high school in the late 1970s and early 1980s found they had nothing to do. Faced with a nonhiring mill and a declining town, a high school graduate might well regret having slept through classes. A few made it to local community colleges. More enlisted in the military, got pregnant, or turned to alcohol and drugs in the sad ending of one scene in a postindustrial narrative. Elaine was an African-American woman in her forties. She had grown up in the steel towns of the Mon Valley and had fought her way onto a labor gang in the Homestead Works. After she was laid off, she became active in organizing workers and supervising a soup kitchen. In our conversation, she expressed anger and bitterness about lethargy in the steel towns of the Mon Valley. We met on Eighth Avenue and I asked her about kids in Homestead. She answered curtly, "Look across the street," pointing to the army recruiting station on the corner. "That's where the boys go." "And the girls?" I asked. She responded instantly, "They get pregnant."

As early as 1983, in a series of articles on the death of American steel, the *Wall Street Journal* had reported on the availability of the military as a solution to unemployment in Mon Valley towns. "This year's male graduates, who were raised to inherit steelworker jobs ('We are iron men,' they chanted at school football games) must find a new future. So must the females, who expected to take clerical and sales jobs at neighborhood stores, if not become steelworkers themselves." The newspaper reporter saw a phenomenon that Elaine did not mention: "In Homestead, recruiters are receiving inquiries not just from high-school seniors but also from men in their twenties," the article continued, mentioning older men who confronted a forced retirement. "'Three or five years ago when you tried to get them to sign up, they said they were going into the mill to earn money,' says Air Force Sgt. Bruce Fox, a recruiter here. 'It's a different story today.'"[15]

The article described a situation that intensified over the next ten years but did not speculate on the economic or social impact of increased enlistment. What about the iron men who chose this path? Would the military provide training for a better civilian job? Did joining the army mean leaving friends, family, and the customs of a mill town forever? Metaphorical connections between the army and the shop floor apart, for a Homestead boy basic training was not like apprenticing in the mill. In the army, there were no fathers or uncles to ease him into the setting, to joke him into learning his tasks, and to take him out for a relaxing beer at the end of a day of hard labor.

Yet boys enlisted and so did girls. Military service was a job, with promotions and status, not the dead end of a job training program. And if

Graduation:
Three
generations
(family
collection)

learning to use a machine gun seemed useless in a civilian world, so, according to men I interviewed, were the skills taught in job training programs. Cynicism about these programs was rampant in Homestead, and not unreasonably.[16] Walking into the Homestead Area Recruiting Station might be the best option anyone had—anyone who was young and in good health. The military did not absorb everyone who needed work in Homestead, and parents were not sure that was the route they wanted their children to follow; it was not the traditional way to learn to labor in a steel town.

The fact was that few children in Homestead had been prepared for lives that were substantially different from those of their parents. A boy might take a higher position in the mill, a girl become a secretary rather than a salesperson or a housewife; a married couple might own a house sooner than their parents had, but in broad contours, it was the same story. When the mills collapsed, parents and children revealed the conservatism in their expectations, and parents did not always change to meet new circumstances. Like George in Buss and Redburn's study of Youngstown,

Homestead parents hoped their children would learn "marketable skills." Like their own parents before them, Homesteaders in the 1980s and 1990s also hoped their kids could stay home and "sell" those skills nearby. And the kids I interviewed, the third generation, shared the viewpoint to a surprising degree. They lived next door to their parents or in the same house and claimed they would "never leave town," whether they had a good job or no job at all. These "stayers"—a word used by the press—valued family connections and the benefits of home training, and they said so.

"Bad kids"

In the face of economic disaster, the meaning of home training shifted from skills and "the traditions" to strictness and good character. When individuals discussed the decline in town, they talked in the same breath about the lack of discipline parents exerted over children. A theme in memories of childhood, the importance of strictness became more prominent with a consideration of the current state of Homestead. Children now, I heard, were disobedient and wild, a contrast with children in the old days. Unspoken was the thought that maybe keeping a reign on kids could improve the town's fate.

Mark, the owner of the Millhunk Tavern, had much to say about the past and the present in his town. Standing in his doorway one day, he remarked on how "different" the blocks around his tavern looked, with the crowds of teenagers wandering "aimlessly." "When I was growing up," he said, "all adults were strict." Moreover, he added nostalgically, every adult watched out for every child, regardless of religion, ethnicity, or race. The memory was a critical comment on kids in Homestead today. As if to confirm his viewpoint, the next time we visited his tavern, Charlee spent time photographing teenagers who seemed to have nothing to do except hang around and pose.

Posing was better than what Mark and others had in mind. The opposite result of a strict upbringing was, in his account, "bad kids." From his point of view, they were all over the place, dominating the sidewalks with their swaggering walks and Sony Walkmen. Worse, no one even knew whose "kids" they were. Sitting on the front porch of a row house, a baby in her lap, Flora complained about the same thing. While keeping her eye on two toddlers, Flora extolled the virtues of a "strict upbringing, especially in these days." Her own mother, she recalled, had been a stern disciplinarian, and she had brought up her sons the same way. "I guess it comes just from my mother. You know, just the way that she brought me up. I mean, she wasn't totally strict, but when she had to be, she laid the law down. You knew what you could do and you knew what you couldn't do." Both her sons were successful, one a cook in a fine restaurant and the other a skilled craftsman and Little League coach. (Neither had ever worked for USX.) As if to illustrate the right childrearing methods, periodically she would reprimand or whack one of the children for misbehaving. In the middle of the interview, one child spilled orange soda all over the porch. "Go get water from the kitchen," Flora yelled, "and watch what you do next time!"

These were little children. Flora expressed more concern about the teenagers she saw "around the town." Her descriptions resonated with my own observations. By the time I interviewed Flora in 1991, Charlee and I were cautious about where we went in Homestead and how late we stayed. Teenagers on Eighth Avenue were not, as Flora noted, sauntering in and out of shops, but standing in small clusters on street corners. Flora painted a vivid picture of "bunches of kids" with time on their hands and nothing but trouble in their heads.[17]

Comments on kids without jobs, and on the groups of males and females who dominated the corners of Eighth Avenue, crossed the boundaries of generation, race, and ethnicity. A white woman, twenty years older than Flora and a longtime resident of Homestead, told me she rarely went "down street." It was "not safe to go there," she said, even in the daytime. Like Flora and Mark, this woman attributed what she saw to the disappearance of family discipline and, she added, the greed and materialism of the present generation. Back then, she noted, "We weren't selfish and greedy, like children nowadays. The more they have, the more they want. They always say, I want this, I want that. We didn't hear anybody say 'I want this,' or I would never used to say, 'I want this or I want that.' Whatever I got, that was OK, or whatever I had, it was OK with me." In other words, the youngest generation was *spoiled,* a classic term used to indicate the decline in family values. Furthermore, these were spoiled brats whose next step was the pickpocketing, petty thievery, and burglaries being reported in local newspapers in the early 1990s. The increasing use of drugs and alcohol, visible to all residents, contributed to the sense of despair.

With her nineteen-year-old daughter and three-year-old grandson, Linda had moved to Homestead in 1988 because she heard the town was "friendly and homey." At the same time, she admitted her neighborhood was not perfectly safe, and she planned to be "very strict" with her grandson. "I think I would have raised my daughter more strict than what I did. I was very lenient with her because my father was so strict with me." Linda had not followed in her parents' footsteps and in retrospect she wished she had. "I don't know, it was just such a strict upbringing. Your homework was real, real strict. Your parents were stricter then. Parents today aren't as strict as what my parents were." Her father, she added, was just as stern as her mother: "He was so old-fashioned and so strict." Then, perhaps fearing she had given away too much, she assured me, "I mean, he never had to beat us or whip us or anything. Our punishment was to stay in your room, without the radio or TV on. That was the biggest punishment we have ever had."

Pregnant in high school, Linda's daughter fit the stereotype Elaine had constructed in her conversation with me. At the time I met her, Linda was trying to make up for her leniency and discipline her daughter now as she had not in the past. Unexpectedly pregnant herself at sixteen, Linda remembered bitterly her own punishment: her father had abruptly taken her out of school, and she never went back. In that respect, she was not going to follow in her parents' footsteps. Linda insisted her daughter finish high school and go to the local community college. The rule held despite her daughter's protests. "She was like, 'No, mom, I don't think I'm going to go back there.' And I was like, 'Oh, but I think you are.' You know, and all of a sudden part of my dad just came out"—meaning she realized this was a moment for strictness. "I was like, 'Oh, but you *are*. You're going to go, and you're going to make the dean's list this year. You came close to it last year, and you will make the dean's list this year. And you will struggle and you will fight. And you will get good grades. Because I take on the responsibility of your son while you're at work, I mean, while you're at school." In repeating the interchange to me, Linda concluded with the real point: "I said to her, 'You're not going to be sitting around here in Homestead not doing anything.'"

Linda's slip from "school" to "work" recalls the traditional view of education in Homestead, as a training ground for work and not an activity pursued in and of itself. School was a preparation for doing something, not just sitting around. The trouble, as Linda knew, was that Homestead did not offer a lot of opportunities. She was unemployed, partly because of a back injury, and her sister, discouraged, had turned to drugs and alcohol. Her daughter confronted a bleak situation as well—kin could not walk her into a job or provide the contacts that in a steel town had once helped every child to find work. Education was the new source of possibility, the certification that would replace the word of an aunt, an uncle, or a close neighbor. Linda's daughter went to college, reluctantly and under the strict eye of her mother. Her dreams were to go to Los Angeles. Both of them also knew she might end up at the corner recruiting station, enlisting in the army. But neither of them was enthusiastic about the army option. Neither was ready to relinquish the three-generation household they had established. If the mill town was collapsing, then the households of the mill town ought to preserve a semblance of community. And family members were still able to offer support, if not access to labor.

A sense of despair at what the youngest generation "is coming to" is not unique to Homestead or to rust-belt communities. But the emphasis on strictness and discipline as the keys to a good upbringing takes on a wistful quality in the context of boarded-up stores, For Sale signs, and abandoned schools. Home training, in which traits of character and habits of work are passed down from one generation to the next, does little good when the supporting institutions vanish. Yet a number of people I met in Homestead clung to the old ways of learning to labor and to get jobs.

Until the disaster of the 1980s, these ways worked. In the late 1960s, a student of labor relations wrote, "Personal, informal methods that place a premium on individual self-reliance seemed to be both effective and held in high regard by these job seekers."[18] Twenty years later, an anthropologist tried to find out how effective these techniques were for laid-off tire company workers. Living in Barberton, Ohio, after the Sieberling Plant closed, Gregory Pappas traveled with workers on their job searches. "We drove to three factories on the first day. He had been to two of them before and had applications in but now wanted to follow them up. The plants were in widely separated areas around Akron, and the traveling took up most of the day." At the end of this unsuccessful day, Pappas and Mark talked about whether Mark should shave off his beard to avoid giving the impression of being an irresponsible "hippie type."[19]

In Homestead, Peter did not worry about his beard; he worried about his ability to prepare a resume. He had gotten his first job the way his father and grandfather before him had, through family connections. In a steel town, the techniques for getting a job were transmitted over generations as thoroughly as were the techniques for using a blowtorch or for sweeping a porch to remove every speck of glittering yellow sulfur. By 1990, when Linda insisted her daughter go to college, and Kim and Theresa learned how to file insurance claims, the techniques were obsolete, discarded by the wider forces of changing capital investment. Demonstration of character, of persistence, and of an "ability to take the heat" did little good when a man or a woman stood waiting hour after hour to apply for a job in a place he or she had never seen before and knew nothing about.

A deeper break had occurred as well. The closing of the mill ripped apart the harmonious community recalled by members of each generation. The town lost its "homeyness" when it lost its mill, and the households of the mill town seemed fated to give up the home training that had formerly carried them through decades of development and of decline. Visually, decrepit houses corresponded with the crumbling mill, and devastation was written on the landscape from river bank to hilltop. In between, and unmistakably, Eighth Avenue began to take on a bombed-out look—the look that Homestead residents, seeing it occur in neighboring steel towns, had long dreaded would be theirs.

The wives of steelworkers and merchants and funeral parlor own-ers—the wives in their fifties and sixties I interviewed—told me they re-fused to shop "down street" anymore. They drove themselves or asked their husbands to take them to the suburban malls. Their daughters and sons, too, found comfort and company at the malls, not on an avenue that seemed increasingly "foreign" to these old-time families, white and black. Noth-ing "down street" looked or felt familiar anymore. Individuals I interviewed referred to violence and to "young people with nothing to do." They talked of petty crime and of the closing of yet another store. And they talked of "strangers," people who came to Homestead neither to work nor to shop. Occasionally, in a quiet voice, they speculated on what these newcomers *did* come for.

Homestead had had newcomers before and periods of uneasy accom-modation. Now, interviews revealed, newcomers were perceived as having no interest in establishing continuity over generations or participating in a community. For those who had lived in Homestead all their lives, it appeared that these newcomers lacked the "ethnic backgrounds and tradi-tions" crucial to the good upbringing of children. To such observers, the newcomers did not demonstrate the signs of ethnicity and of religious prac-tice that ordinarily positioned a person in the steel town. If the word *diver-sity* came up at all, it was to distinguish past from present. "Below the tracks" had been diverse, while the present mixture in Homestead was divisive.

HARMONY AND DISCORD

6

Interpretations of Ethnicity and Religion in a Steel Town

The section where the Slavs live is in itself gloomy. The level ground in the Second Ward cut off from the river by the mill and from the country by the steep hill behind, forms a pocket where the smoke settles heavily. There are oases in these wards, sections of street with yards and trees, but for the most part here on the original site of the town, garden plots as well as alleys have been utilized on which to build small frame houses till the blocks are all but covered.

—Margaret Byington, *Homestead: The Households of a Mill Town*

I met Sam while looking at photographs from the *Homestead Daily Messenger* that the librarian at the Carnegie Library of Homestead had given me—her way of introducing me to the town. Public events such as parades and political speeches, the opening of a new area in the mill, or a new restaurant on Eighth Avenue dominated the collection; they were news photos, after all. Some pictures came from before the Second World War, when the neighborhood around the mill flourished despite the economy of the Great Depression. Others were of wartime Homestead, including views of the progressive razing of the mill neighborhood. A few photos were more recent, before the gloom of deindustrialization set in and the *Messenger* folded.[1] Sam, however, was not interested in the photographs depicting his town after the Second World War. His attention was gripped by the scenes in the 1930s, in the neighborhood he referred to as "below the tracks." This was the mill neighborhood, the Lower Ward, crowded with people who could not afford to move to the more desirable housing on the hillsides.

Sam introduced himself by reaching across the table for one of the photos and offering to interpret it for me. He had been looking at the newspaper clippings along with me the whole time, not seeming to mind that his view was upside down. "That," he told me, pointing to a figure in a scene of a celebrating crowd, "is the Gypsy King. He played at all our weddings." Behind Sam's short statement lay a long story he began to tell me that day, and would continue to tell for the three years I knew him. He died in 1990.

The story was about the mill neighborhood and about the solidarity demonstrated by its residents, all of whom, Sam assured me, would participate in the musical celebrations accompanying a wedding. His story was also about diversity and about various ethnic groups, each of which demonstrated distinctiveness in such public events. Differences, according to him, were perfectly tolerated. Looking carefully at the photos, I could catch a glimpse of that diversity in facial features, items of clothing, an object here or there. It was not as easy to see the harmony Sam described or to appreciate the fellowship he claimed existed "below the tracks."

Those celebrations and ritual events were the oases in Homestead life, the spots that constituted relief from labor, whether that labor was in the mill, in a shop on Eighth Avenue, behind a desk, or over a stove. The pictures Sam and I looked at were a small sample of the moments of color in a gray world, of joy in a life of tiring daily routine. Not only weddings but also shared meals after Sunday Mass, an ethnic festival at Kennywood Park, and the childish leap into the water of an open hydrant on a hot day were signs of freedom from the pressures of outside forces. The photos I saw of such moments were pictures of a life that had nothing to do with steel, the state, or the federal government.

When Sam insisted that "everyone" participated in a neighborhood wedding in the old days, he introduced a more complicated text about inclusion and exclusion, about exactly who "everyone" was and how shared celebrations accorded with the famous diversity (for Sam was not the only one to use that concept) in the town. Repeatedly, regardless of age or background, individuals would emphasize the distinctiveness of groups in Homestead and, equally, the blurring of boundaries in daily interactions. "Below the tracks" was the prime symbol of difference with tolerance, even for those who had never lived there and were too young to have seen its shops and houses. The important differences in Homestead were ethnicity, reli-

Expert on Homestead history (family collection)

gious affiliation, and, of course, race. The first two bore an intricate relation to one another; the third, race, deserves a chapter of its own.

"Below the tracks" was the site of nostalgia. This nostalgia was a commentary on ethnicity and religion that persisted over at least three generations. Nostalgia also, I discovered, influenced the accounts of individuals
who moved to Homestead in the 1970s and 1980s, when the town had lost
many of the features associated with its past. Nostalgia was a powerful
sentiment precisely because it represented the genuine qualities in a community. In *Yearning for Yesterday,* sociologist Fred Davis writes: "What is
most evident [about nostalgia] . . . is the warm glow the speaker, despite
occasional qualifications and asides, imparts to some past era: the celebration of now ostensibly lost values, the sense of some ineffable spirit of
worth or goodness having escaped time, the conviction that, no matter
how far advanced the present may be . . . , it is in some deeper sense meaner
and baser [than the past]."[2] In Homestead, as people looked out their windows and watched the mill being torn down, or walked by boarded-up

stores on Eighth Avenue, lost values and a spirit of worth or goodness provided an attractive blueprint for the future.

A "spirit of worth or goodness" is an abstract concept, vague until embedded in a specific story, a concrete episode in a longer verbal narrative. Sam's memories of the Gypsy King leading "everyone" down the middle of Eighth Avenue, another person's recollection of the fruit dealer's half-English, half-Hungarian shouts, a young woman's outline of different parochial school uniforms communicated the harmony and diversity Sam mentioned the first day I met him. These were memories of childhood, but they were also evocations of a community and suggested the significance of community in an American steel town. As Sam filled in the sense and meaning of *community*, a word that has been much bandied about, he painted a picture of diversity that did not lead to divisiveness and of harmony that did not mean homogenization.

A notion of choice emerged from Sam's anecdotes and from his interpretations of photographs. He implied that in the past Homestead residents had a measure of control over their social interactions—who they invited to a wedding, shared a meal with, and helped through a crisis. What choice really meant, I learned, was that things could be worked out by individuals in one-to-one contact. That situation existed in neighborhoods, social clubs, and churches; it existed in the mill when a labor crew got along especially well.

Other residents shared this version of community, accentuating one-to-one contact and minimizing the importance of outsiders like politicians or company bosses. In the old days, history maintained, people *chose* where to live and how to have fun, if not where and how to work. In this perspective, choice was based on common values and customs, and change was marked by the disappearance of a way of life attached to ethnic traditions and religious beliefs. The importance of these elements also served to separate a Homestead way of life from surrounding economic and political forces. So, as in the remembered years of "below the tracks," in the present years of an emptying mill lot, acting on individual values might sustain the town.

Snapshots of family outings, pictures of christenings and weddings, a studio portrait of a confirmation or a sixth grade graduation all vividly represented this way of life. Photographs did not focus on the diversity and harmony people said were characteristic of Homestead culture, but visual representations showed an interviewee the town he or she conjured up in words. As Richard Chalfen points out in his book on Japanese-American family albums, individuals rarely take camera to eye with the deliberate intention of picturing cooperation or "getting along."[3] But the sentiment comes out.

Pictures of relatives and friends display striking similarities of face, feature, and posture. Candid shots or posed studio portraits, the bodies and heads of subjects constitute "one big family." Such collections also revealed a strong association between religious and ethnic ceremonies and the joyous moments in a steel town. In displaying happiness and, in recent albums, raucousness, family albums contrast with Hine's portrait of Homestead. His pictures of relaxation have a somber and dark cast; children look like small adults rather than playful kids.

The *Homestead Daily Messenger* played its part by featuring ethnic and religious ceremonies on the front page in photos and human interest stories. Pictures of Slovak Day at Kennywood or of a Columbus Day parade down Eighth Avenue reminded townspeople of the mainsprings of their "real" life.[4] Public relations brochures emphasized the importance of religion by highlighting the steeples and onion domes of Homestead churches. Brodsky added documentation of the storefront churches established by recent newcomers. Her photographic images, like those in the newspaper and in family snapshot collections, counteract the visual dominance of the Homestead Works and highlight the domestic theme in Homestead history. Looking at published photos, along with their own collections, individuals in Homestead recast history so that it was not just steel, not just labor, and not just impersonal institutions.

"We all got along"

"You didn't even have to lock your door," Sam told me. "You were safe. And like I said, you had blacks, Slovaks, Russians, Hungarians, Mexicans—all lived in those apartments." This was another day, and Sam had thoroughly warmed to his role of amateur historian for the project. He was describing "below the tracks," a central setting in Homestead history. For him it clearly epitomized the "ineffable spirit" of community. In concentrating on where and how people lived, Sam shifted his narrative away from the corporation and toward the ways people made "lives of their own."[5]

Though he did not have visual material to jog his memory—neither snapshots nor existing buildings—Sam managed to recreate the vision of a crowded, lively neighborhood. By all accounts the mill neighborhood was, as he suggested, a jumbled melting pot, populated by the waves of immigrants who came to work in the mills. At the time Sam was growing up in the 1920s, most residents of "below" were Eastern European, Catholic, and white; early immigrants from the British Isles had moved up the hill to greener and more spacious residential blocks.[6] Blacks appeared in Sam's quick list of ethnic groups, but he did not again refer to that group when he extolled the virtues of neighborliness. He mainly wanted me to know how "everyone got along in those days," with respect and reciprocity despite noticeable differences in habits and appearances. Quarrels, Sam claimed, occurred only behind doors, not in the middle of a street or courtyard. "There were," he remarked, "some domestic quarrels."

One afternoon Sam took me on a tour of the town. "Below the tracks" as he knew it was gone, but Sam stood on Sixth Avenue and reminisced about his routes through those blocks when they had been full of houses. Safe and harmonious though the area might have been, Sam still had to negotiate a path through blocks that—though he did not put it this way—obviously had boundaries around them and dangers attached to them. He walked on Fourth Avenue, he said, because he did not like Sixth Avenue, which was filled with "vice." Sam was describing what historian John Bodnar called "enclaves," which "emerged wherever industrial workers and their kin congregated. They grew up around such bases as race, ethnicity, skill, or shared economic status."[7]

An enclave was more than a residential arrangement and more than a network of kin. It was a society, with shared values, amusements, celebrations, and responses to the work world. Cooperation across front porches, over backyard fences, and in shops constituted "integration." From this point of view residents stuck together because they wanted to and not because they were forced into one place and excluded from others. They mapped the town in a way that flowed in and out of administrative units, depending on circumstances and the remembered event.

Sam's version contradicts interpretations of social enclaves as conservative—keeping immigrants unassimilated, according to Margaret Byington, or vulnerable and isolated, according to novelist Thomas Bell. Bodnar claimed enclaves stood in the way of political activism.[8] Sam wanted me to see now, as he did in looking back, the spring of vitality that characterized the areas lying under the smoke and shadow of the Homestead Works. Louise, his age peer, made the same point, drawing on her memories of the liveliness of "below" in the 1920s and 1930s to show that her parents' generation had not been victims of industrialization, but actors in a spirited community.

She started off with a sentimental return to the "good old days": "When we grew up together, we were all the same kind of people, I guess." Like Sam's, Louise's map consisted of religiously and ethnically distinct blocks. "We were all friendly, we all knew each other. We grew together, the children, we played together, we went to school together, we went to church together, we knew each other real well." Familiarity bred safety: "We were able to walk to school, to walk to church. At that time, we didn't have cars like now. And that was so nice, because while you're walking, you see different things on the way to school or to church, and you're walking with your neighbors, with your friends, whoever you live nearby. And that was a real—that time it was more happy times."

The significance of "we were all the same kind of people" became more apparent as Louise continued reminiscing. "Where we lived, we had a variety of different nationalities—Slovaks, Russian people, Hungarian— I noticed everything but Italians. I really don't know what the Italian people—are you Italian?" "No," I answered. "'Cause I wanted to watch myself," she laughed, "so I don't say anything against it. Well, I don't have nothing against Italians."

With this last remark, Louise indicated that the distinctions in Homestead were not neutral and certainly not all equal. "But where we lived, we didn't have any Italian people. I didn't recognize them until later on, when I was in high school, and I met a couple of Italian girls." Caught up in her narrative, she evoked the feelings she had had as an adolescent: "It was, 'oh, gee, they're so different. They're dark, dark hair, dark complexion,' and they had a different personality, like." Italians were strange, her repeated "darks" conveyed. They had, she told me, their own customs and ways of living. Louise brought up the unfamiliarity of Italians several times during the interview. "I noticed Italian people, or the girlfriends that we had in our class, that they were, like, not one of us."

Louise was not the only person I interviewed who mentioned Italians in order to portray a substantial difference between groups. "I remember the Italians were having problems—see, I wanted to tell you this," a woman twenty years older than Louise confided to me, "—problems among themselves," she repeated. Even then, and even in glowing accounts of childhood, some people did not fit in. "Italian" stood for dark and exotic, in much the way blacks would in other episodes and other chronological periods of a person's narrative.

Significantly, in the old days, Italians did not "mix." They lived down the Monongahela River in a separate community called Hays. It was, and is, a typical western Pennsylvania "hollow" town of about forty houses in between hills and, by the 1960s, bordered by a parkway. "We used to call Hays 'Little Italy' down there," a businessman in his early fifties explained, the day we talked in his Eighth Avenue store. "And there's still a lot of Italian families living there. I used to do service calls down there, and I never failed to come to one of them on my way home, there was always one of them would—I'd end up with a Seagram's Seven whiskey bottle full of wine."

Food and wine, domestic quarrels and loud behavior were innocent markers of difference; there was nothing dangerous in such signs of diversity. Mention of these features disguised the hostility and bitterness that greeted each new wave of immigrants in a steel town—and Homestead was no exception. In any decade, newcomers were competitors for jobs, housing, and classroom desks; moreover, they did not look like already-established residents. Louise did not discuss the economic and political aspects of diversity, but her anecdotes about "exotic" Italians reveal the substantial and persistent exclusionary patterns of her hometown.

Most residents described ethnic and religious differences in terms of food, customs, and celebrations—a typical American reading of diversity, but, in light of Homestead's history, a particularly slanted one. Such a perception contrasted with that of bosses and bankers, who determined positions and benefits in terms of ethnic group status. An emphasis on customs might also have been a reaction to pressures toward assimilation that were as much a part of Homestead history as that of any American industrial town. In the light of the loss of the mill, residents turned to nonmill activities in their interviews, detailing for me the songs, dances, and parties remembered from childhood. In doing so, they gave the impression that what sounded like stereotype to an outsider was central to identity for insiders. Thus, Maria's account of growing up in Hays constitutes a nice response to Louise's view of Italians.

Maria had grown up in a family of bootleggers and home brewers. She went on to buy a bar herself, she told me. Working in a bar, she added, came naturally. "Well," she began, "my family was—I think I told you we were Italians." She paused, then continued: "And when I was about her age [pointing to a teenager sitting on a bench outside the bar], my family were bootleggers." She explained to me, "they make their own moonshine. . . . So really I was raised in a family of bars. But my family was hard workers. You know, not always legal, but hard workers." When liquor became legal, she said, "then they [her family] took over that Italian Club." Her remark reveals another component of ethnicity in Homestead: the establishment and patronage of institutions along ethnic lines. Clubs were the most obviously exclusive, but so were supermarkets, clothing stores, and bakeries.

Mrs. Burton talked about shopping in Homestead in the 1920s and the 1930s, when she came to town as a young wife. Eighty years old when I met her, she had spent her childhood in the small mining towns of central Pennsylvania. Somewhere along the way she met a steelworker from Pittsburgh, married him, and came to Homestead to live. The steel town looked like a "big city" to her, she remembered, crowded, mixed up, and smoky. She soon learned her way around, acquiring the coping skills Byington had documented twenty years earlier. Her story, like Byington's, related household management to ethnic traditions and consequently revealed ethnic separations.

The Burtons lived in Homestead Park, politically a Pittsburgh neighborhood and socially a white ethnic enclave. Mrs. Burton shopped carefully: "there was Kobolinski's for the Poles and Pianelli's for the Italians." Down the hill, there was Wozeck's for the Slovaks and George's Bakery for the Greeks. "But you know," she continued, there was a "struggle between them, because you're going to go to the Italians because everybody went to their own. So then, and like I say, they shut Pianelli's and A & P was a company already—." The disputes over shopping were radically altered by the arrival of the Great Atlantic and Pacific Tea Company, a supermarket that could cater to and please anyone's tastes.

Ethnic differences did not disappear with the arrival of a national grocery chain nor did the importance of ethnic food became less vital for maintaining identity. An apparently good-natured woman, Mrs. Burton bragged about her cooking skills, which, she added, she did not share with anyone outside her "family." Her skills, she told me, were a gift from her female relatives and from God. Foods appeared in special glory during holiday celebrations and these, many of my interviewees implied, were the most exclusive occasions of all in Homestead, inasmuch as they presented the most important evidence of difference. Maria, for example, insisted that Italians "really" celebrated Christmas in August. "And on the 15th of August, which for Catholic people," she explained, "is the Blessed Mother's birthday." She meant, of course, *Italian* Catholics. "And we always felt as though the Blessed Mother, we were always taught that she was Italian. So you have a big celebration on that day. That's the day for Italians, as big as Christmas."

Harmony
and
Discord

165

"They celebrated the same way we did"

In the ward, Louise reminded me, "we were like all one big happy family."
In Louise's memory, the unity was manifested in the celebrations held by
ethnic lodges. Lodges appeared when the first group of immigrants arrived
in Mon Valley steel towns in the late nineteenth century.[9] Throughout
those towns, ethnic clubs held a central place, culturally and sometimes
geographically. In Homestead, the Slovak Club was built just off Eighth
Avenue, a monument to the past that has lasted into the 1990s. Lodges
carried members through various life crises, from births through weddings
to deaths. Lodges in Homestead also served as alternative recreational spots,
a place a worker could go to for an after-work drink if he or she wished to
avoid the hodgepodge of an "occupational tavern."[10] Ethnic lodges were
supportive, exclusive, and, some outsiders argued, conservative and anti-
American.

Margaret Byington had mixed feelings about the lodges scattered
throughout the town. In *Homestead,* she recognizes their value: at least
they provided amusement and joy to men and women living an otherwise
"gloomy" life. At best, they saw a couple into their new life as wife and
husband or a man into the grave. In *Out of This Furnace,* Thomas Bell
emphasizes the importance of the lodge's function in a town filled with
work accidents and deaths: "Mike's lodge paid a five-hundred-dollar death
benefit, all of which went for funeral expenses, masses for the dead and a
four-grave plot excellently situated (near the chapel) in a newly opened
section of the cemetery."[11]

For Byington, the ethnic lodge, despite its good services, kept immigrants from becoming Americans. Isolation was a consequence of the very
services the lodges provided: "The fellow members of a lodge become nurses
who care for the sick or injured during nights of suffering, and friends who
give comfort in times of bereavement." According to Byington, self-
sufficiency slowed down assimilation: "The Slavic lodges are usually limited to the members of one nationality, Slovak, Hungarian, Polish, and in
so far as they tend to perpetuate racial and religious feuds, miss their opportunity to amalgamate the immigrant colony."[12]

No one I interviewed made the same point. Looking back from 1990,
most Homestead residents valued any institution that brought individuals
together, allowed them to share limited resources, and gave them an opportunity to have fun. Above all, lodges turned a personal identification
into a public moment—rendering positive the designations that had a

negative cast in the mouths of foremen and, often, of friendly investigators. For historian John Bodnar, ethnic identification led to enclaves that were "circumscribed, cut off from social and political influences, from those of higher social rank and even from other workers."[13] People helped one another through a crisis but did not consider themselves a class with interests in common. Pursuing a similar line of thought, two labor economists argue that ethnic chauvinism explains the apparent passivity of steel towns in the face of shutdowns.[14] And in his portrayal of Homestead's tragedy, journalist William Serrin suggests that strong identification with an ethnic group results in withdrawal from political action:

> For years there were more than fifty lodges in Homestead, and today there are still the Russian Club, the Slavic Club, the Ancient Order of Hibernians, the Moose, the Elks, and, at West Street and Eighth Avenue, the major intersection, the Owls, where, year after year, in the windows of the club are the gray or bald heads of the old-timers who sit and play card games by the hour and watch the passersby on Eighth Avenue.[15]

Bell's semiautobiographical novel insists on the value of lodges as a compensation for continual discrimination in the mill. At one point, the hero bemoans to his wife, "And I've been working in those furnaces over twenty years. I know my job, Marcha. I could take over that furnace tomorrow and make as good iron as Keogh ever did. But I'm a Hunky and they don't give good jobs to Hunkies."[16] The lodge was a contrast. There, the term *Hunky* bound families together instead of placing a man on the low rungs of an employment ladder. For most decades of the century, inside the mill, *Hunky* meant limited positions; outside the mill, *Hunky* could mean who you were and how you chose to live. So, in 1992, Jackie told me without any hesitation that she lived in Hunky Hollow with people who "are like me." Within such "Hunkeyvilles," the legacy of ethnic lodges endured.[17] Jackie was petitioning Homestead City Council to establish a community center at the end of the hollow. If not a traditional lodge, the place would recapture some of the features of that old institution.

Individuals in Homestead readily distinguished one group from another in their interviews. Ignoring the past job discrimination and housing segregation, residents described differences in food habits, celebrations, and character traits. For over three generations in Homestead, individuals learned to attribute characteristics to members of ethnic and religious groups as if their observation were neutral. With the disappearance of the steel industry, it was even safer to emphasize character traits, since stereotypes no longer related to employment.

One afternoon, Mrs. Wozeck remarked rather off-handedly, "A lot of the Slav people are extremely jealous of one another." She did not pause before adding another ethnic stereotype: "Where I don't know how true this is, but years ago you would hear about Jewish people sticking together and everybody would prosper. Slavs are very, very jealous of one another." Sam, too, thought nothing of offering me the information that "there were mostly Jewish people that owned all these businesses," hinting at a "typical" Jewish trait. Looking at me and then at a picture of the Katz siblings in his yearbook, Ken told me that "Jews owned the best jewelry store in town."[18]

My interactions with Homesteaders reveal another aspect of the idealized picture of ethnic differences. As long as the situation in which differences arose was personal, one-on-one, face-to-face, no harm could be done by recognizing the strangeness of others. With her usual predictive perspicacity, Byington recorded this aspect of diversity in the steel town: "As I went into one woman's kitchen one day, she showed me a half bushel basket full of fine, large potatoes scrubbed clean and ready for baking," which she was giving to a hospital. "'My husband,' she explained, 'isn't in a dangerous place in the mill, but I am glad to help even if most of the injured are Hunkies.'"[19]

Eighty years later, Sam gave me another version of the same theme. We were sitting in the Millhunk Tavern, and Sam was going over what life had been like in the past. Sometime after the Second World War and the destruction of the mill neighborhood, Sam's father decided to rebuild the store up the hill from Eighth Avenue. It turned out to be a cooperative endeavor: the house and store were constructed "together by me and my father and Andy Allen, who is a Scotsman and he hated Hunkies—," and he interrupted to explain: "You know that term, that's the term you [people in general] used." Then he continued his tale of prejudice overcome. "But he [Andy] loved my father, who was a Hungarian. But my dad built that [house] with Andy Allen and a guy named Adolph."

An image of Homestead filters out of these accounts of ethnicity which makes the place seem much less like a teeming industrial town than like a country village. With the mill gone, individuals turned from the industry that had shaped their lives to memorialize a town based on neighbors, not workers. The vision of a country village had a stunning embodiment in Brodsky's photographs of the Monongahela River, undisturbed by a mill and leafy in spring foliage. The sense of community and of a natural rather than an industrial landscape wove through nostalgic memories. The references were to neighborly, not work-related, interactions; to ethnicity and religion, not position as primary identifying traits. This was, for many Homesteaders, a better world than even a prosperous world of "steel." Embracing an ethnic identity, maintaining customs so that every Hunky girl knew how to make *halushki*, and laughing about the "jealous" Slavs was invigorating and perhaps the basis of a revived community.[20] In this regard, wedding celebrations stood out, a demonstration of custom and of the rules that were important in a steel town.

"They celebrated like for a whole week"

There are no pictures of weddings in *Homestead: The Households of a Mill Town*. Concentrating on work, and on depicting leisure activities that compensated for the struggles in life, Hine did not present the occasions of optimism and joy that weddings in Homestead represented. His photograph, "Saturday Night at the Saloon," for instance, suggests a group of people solemnly trying to amuse themselves; in another photo, the women "gathered for a bit of gossip" look stern-faced and worn. Byington, on the other hand, appreciated the significance of life-cycle ceremonies: "On most of these occasions, whether weddings, christenings or funerals, joy and grief and religious ceremony are alike forgotten in a riotous and good time. The weddings are the gayest affairs in the life of the community. After the morning service at the church, all return home if the house is big enough, and if not, they go to a hall, and there the dancing begins."[21]

Charlee did not take pictures at weddings, but photographs of weddings filled the family albums we looked at. Often, in fact, wedding pictures were the first things a person showed me when I explained that we were interested in visual material.[22] Most households in this mill town had several generations of formally posed bride-and-groom portraits displayed on mantelpiece and walls. But even before pictures came out, verbal accounts of weddings occupied a person's narrative of Homestead history. As Byington documented, these ceremonies marked phases of life apart from work and other compulsory tasks. Weddings also represented the genuine culture of a steel town—Sam, after all, had introduced himself by pulling out a picture of the Gypsy King. For him, the scene incorporated both the diversity and the unity of the town: gypsy music and gypsy costumes made "everyone" follow in the wake of this peculiar Pied Piper.

Like Sam, Thomas Bell stresses the pleasure weddings held for people in a steel town. Old man Kracha tells his grandchildren about life in the early 1900s: "And every Sunday two or three weddings. . . . Every Sunday without fail. All you had to do was walk along the street until you heard the gypsies playing and there was your wedding."[23] Members of the first generation in Homestead remembered weddings as the best times and a sign of a past that had long disappeared. The evening Sam and I had dinner at the Millhunk, he told me weddings were the "happiest times" of his childhood. "But I do remember quite well the dances, the weddings." He explained further: "The weddings, everybody pitched in, there was no such thing as a caterer. Everybody baked and made cakes and things like that." Then he qualified his sweeping statement: "If you lived in the neighborhood, you went to the place, you were invited."

Here, evidently, was a rule: "if you lived in the neighborhood." For a man like Sam, the neighborhood *was* everyone. To back up his version, he told me to "see it in *The Deerhunter*." The opening shots, he said, contain "a great wedding scene which is reminiscent of the weddings they had in the thirties down "below the tracks," the weddings with the babushkas and the singing and dancing and polka bands. You should rent it." The film begins with a mill town wedding, everyone costumed and uproarious—the picture Sam wanted me to have of the good old days.

"Our entertainment was, well, we used to sit out in the evening, the mothers, the parents, and everybody would come out, to sit around and mingle together—just talk about anything that was on our mind. We'd dream about things," a woman in Sam's generation recalled, "just use our imagination." Her point was that then, in the 1920s and 1930s, people did not need a lot of things to enjoy themselves. The "best times," she added emphatically, were the weddings. At these ceremonies, crowds of people gathered, making it easy to have fun. She, too, implied that no one was left out of these celebrations: "Every time there was a church dance or weddings, even if we weren't invited, as little children we'd hear that music, and we'd go to the hall, and we'd go in, which nobody objected—the children'd come in and dance. Everybody was welcome. Long as everybody was having a good time, that was the main important thing."

Eventually, as she continued to probe her memory, the parameters around "everybody" emerged. "At that time they had big weddings in the [Russian] Hall. And they had, like, Slovak music and English music. In the one building—there was a Russian Hall there—[they] would have two floors. Downstairs would be for the Slovak, or Slovak music, and the upstairs would be the English, English music." Harmony was not perfect: the festival hall was divided, separating one group from another by musical taste, perhaps by degree of assimilation, and almost surely by generation. For just as weddings gathered crowds together, they also made distinctions clear.

These separations accentuated the negative aspect of ethnic diversity in Homestead and perpetuated the stereotypes that one group used against another throughout the town's history. Occasionally a conflict erupted around a wedding, and the celebration become a moment for outright hostility between groups. In the early part of the century, it was not unusual for cops to quiet down an "ethnic" wedding. "The *Presbyterian Banner*, for instance, a local publication, applauded the use of constables in breaking up what it regarded as unruly immigrant wedding celebrations."[24] In *Out of This Furnace*, Bell reminds his readers that wedding celebrations took place in the shadow of the mill and could be broken up by another feature of the steel town environment: At Mike and Mary's wedding, "there were times when the music of the gipsies' beribboned fiddles was drowned out by the riveters' iron clamor."[25]

Echoing the narratives of their parents' generation, Kim and Theresa described the wild weddings of their contemporaries—the noise and drunkenness and carousing that might well have led to police intervention in the 1980s as it had in the 1910s and 1920s. "Everybody was bombed. You should see the videotape," they both chortled, like Sam assuming that pictures on film were better than words and, possibly, better than the formal wedding portraits that were once the conventional documentary of such celebrations. Their albums, however, were jammed with candids, which they editorialized: "And it was like three, four o'clock in the morning, and there was people still going past our house tooting!"

Whether thinking back to the early half of the century or to more recent decades, Homestead residents treated weddings as the break in a routine that was mainly tedious work. Weddings were removed from the mill and the economic institutions it sustained, and that too made them happy moments in a narrative: "'Cause when they had weddings over there ["below the tracks"], they didn't celebrate one day," a middle-aged woman assured me. "They celebrated like for a whole week, and they wanted everybody to come and, you know, be happy with them. And they had a lot of food, a lot of drinks."

Finally, in the text that was hidden beneath the surface, weddings

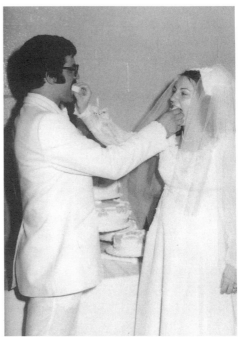

Wedding (family collection)

were a time of choice: the chosen spouse and the chosen guests. But choice was not unlimited, and at weddings the rules of whom to marry showed up as clearly as the red garter we saw in one wedding snapshot.

"Ours was a mixed marriage"

Rosie Wozeck, thirty-two years old, had five full albums from various phases of her life. She took out the wedding album and talked about a marriage that had recently ended in divorce. The album included an array of the usual subjects—studio portraits of bride and groom and of the families, candid photos done by the professional photographer, amateur snapshots with the awkward composition and color that comes from a Polaroid camera. There were two newspaper clippings: Rosie's wedding picture had been in both the *Homestead Daily Messenger* and the *Pittsburgh Post-Gazette*, a reminder that weddings mark changes in a social setting as well as in an individual life. The Wozecks were prominent enough to make the society pages of the local and the city paper. Rosie laughed at this—and she laughed about specific shots in the album: a cousin pinning a rose to a garter on her thigh, her brother falling over himself on the dance floor, a particularly solemn view of her mother.

Joke as she might, however, the wedding album contained an important piece of information, one that Rosie was well aware of in the interview. Her name, she noted, changed at marriage from the ethnically discordant "Rosie Wozeck" to the ethnically harmonious "Rosie Malloy." The daughter of a mixed marriage between an Irish Flannagan and a Croatian Wozeck, she had returned to her mother's Irish roots when she married a Malloy. Rosie missed the mixture she had embraced as her own identity, she told me, finding the euphonious ring of her married name odd. Rosie could be playful about mixed ethnicities not only because by the time I interviewed her she had returned to her original name, but also because her parents' mixed marriage had lasted for fifty years.

When her parents talked of their marriage, the difficulties became clear. The two had crossed several lines and ethnicity was the least of the problems. In Homestead, religious divisions carried even more weight than ethnic differences, and marrying "out of faith" was a much worse sin than marrying someone whose food habits, customs, and Christmas celebrations were strange. It turned out that the third generation—Rosie's—shared this perspective with the second and first generations, who would never have divorced with the ease she did. In Homestead, the depth of attachment to religious identity was great, exceeded only by racial identity. Marrying into another church was just barely acceptable, under certain circumstances; in the view of many steel valley residents, no circumstances justified marrying a person of another race.

Sam's story about religious difference casts light on the ethnic mixing his daughter relished. A self-defined Hunky, Sam told me with some pride that he had married "an Irish girl." But ethnic background was not the only difference between them. Sam, a member of an Eastern Orthodox Church, had married a Roman Catholic. Initially emphasizing the Slav-Irish mixture, Sam avoided what really caused the problem—that he was marrying outside his church. The rest of his autobiographical reminiscences showed how strenuous a violation of norms that was in the 1920s.

Sam described his courtship of the daughter of Mike Flannagan, an Irish immigrant steelworker. He met Margaret in the late 1920s at a dance and was instantly smitten with her. He pursued her assiduously, taking her out and introducing her to his family. I asked how his parents felt about the fact that he had fallen in love with a girl from such a different background. "That really had them worried, to be honest with you," he responded, "because they always talked to me about marrying somebody with our background." What he meant by "background" emerged as he went on with his story. It was not her Irish background, which was what I had meant, but her membership in the Roman Catholic Church that distressed his parents. Her Irish personality, he recalled, appealed to his parents as much as it had to him: "My mother and father loved her right off the bat."

In her interview, Mrs. Wozeck also commented on Sam's purposeful courtship and the subsequent negotiation of their diverse backgrounds. As in his story, so in hers personality played a crucial part in bridging the gap between ethnicities, between the Slavic and the Irish. Upon meeting him, her parents, she said, "*loved* Sammy. He was very easy to get along with, and they liked him." When I asked how significant his background actually was to her parents, she replied honestly, if awkwardly: "I'm sure they'd have been happy had we—when we were, like, teenagers and things like that, yeah, they would sometimes with their friends' sons or daughters— 'Oh, hey, he's kinda cute,' or things like that." The truth was her parents would have preferred her to marry a Roman Catholic. "They didn't mind if they [potential spouse] were a different nationality. They did—ah, the religious thing was a big thing in those days. They did want them to be Catholic. Which, fortunately, it all turned out. They were all Catholic. And there wasn't any problem there." But Sam had found a problem she had either forgotten or did not want to mention. In Pittsburgh and the Monongahela Valley, there was no such thing as an overarching "Catholic" designation.

With the rise of immigration, historian Linda Pritchard notes, "between 1904 and 1921, a new church was founded every thirty days." Moreover, she adds, "between 1880 and 1920, Pittsburgh developed one of the largest aggregations of non-Roman Catholic parishes in the country."[26] That there were Catholics who were non-Roman caused a problem for Sam and Margaret; each sect had its own fierce loyalties. The priest in Sam's Eastern Orthodox Church refused to hold a ceremony for a Roman Catholic. Sam and Margaret had a hard time finding a church that *would* marry them. The parents might have been swayed by appealing personalities, but the priests were not. "That was my biggest worry," Sam said. "Then the church she had, she was supposed to get married in my church." But Margaret had a different idea. "She said, 'I want to get married in my own church.'" Her determination posed a problem for Sam; his church was not happy about the choice. "The church," he admitted, "ruled against us." I did not understand what he meant until he went on to say that he had had to "confess" to his priest that he was getting married outside the church: "I went to the monsignor at our church. I said, 'I have a beautiful girl, she wants to get married in the Latin rite church.' 'Well, I'll tell you this, Sammy,' he says, 'I won't help you but I won't stop you.' So we got this Irish priest. We had to get a dispensation from an apostolic delegate. For her to get married in her church." The intolerance, he claimed, was not his own but that of other people. "I said, 'It's all Catholic to me, baby.'"

The Wozeck children experienced the consequences. They complained, laughing, about Sundays when they were stuffed alternately with pierogies and Irish stew. But they did not laugh about their religious upbringing. "We always went to Roman Catholic mass," the trio of voices told me. Margaret Wozeck prevailed in that regard, and there was no slipping between religious affiliations as there could be between ethnic identifications. Religion was essential, while ethnicity was a social category.

The night we looked over her wedding album, Rosie talked about a future marriage. She was dating a man, she said, who was Jewish. She also insisted that her parents "would not mind" if she ended up marrying him. But I noticed that she slipped into referring to him as "of German background" rather than Jewish. Then the difference was ethnicity and not religion; thus redefining him, she might pull one over on her parents—

though given her view of her mother's acuity, probably not. Her speculation led Jim, her younger brother, to bring up his own dilemma. He had a fiancée whom everyone in the family liked. He had not, however, told his parents that she was Presbyterian. In the Mon Valley, the distance from Catholicism to Presbyterianism was vast, a distance of religious practice and of class. Presbyterians were the elite, historically in control of the mills and the finances of the city. Presbyterians were the "old" immigrants, Catholics the "new." Presbyterians had called in the constables to break up the wild weddings of their Catholic neighbors. What was Jim to do? Rosie tried to convince him to tell; there was more tolerance at home these days, she said. She claimed, without perfect certainty, "I think it's not as bad as she used to"—trailing off, but meaning to suggest that their mother was not as demanding about shared religious affiliation as she used to be. Jim encouraged himself with an alternative thought: "If she [fiancée] was a Muslim or something, yes. Or Buddhist, she might. You know, if we had to bow down to Mecca. If we have to bow to Mecca five times a day, you know, we're going to have a problem."

As they continued talking, it was evident that neither Rosie nor Jim was absolutely sure *what* their mother would approve of. Marrying a Presbyterian might still not be acceptable, which explains Jim's hesitation about bringing up the subject. Imagining the unlikely scenario of marrying a Muslim woman, Jim revealed his lurking suspicion of the trouble a Presbyterian would cause at home. The youngest sibling, Jane, cut through the ambiguities both Rosie and Jim expressed. She knew her mother's opinions: "If I tell her about this guy that I just met or something, if I say, 'Oh, he's Irish Catholic,' she'll say, 'Oh, I like him.' Right away, 'Oh, I like him.'"

Jim continued to mull over his dilemma, as if rehearsing for an encounter with his mother. Not surprisingly, a major issue was whether his children would be raised Catholic or Presbyterian. Jim ended up with a strategy that was not likely to solve anything: "I would give my kids completely free choice." He immediately qualified his own position, saying he would teach his children the religion he had learned until "they were old enough to understand it. Then say, 'Well, now you know what religion is,' and if it's not their religion, you know, 'you can make a choice. And whatever you say is fine with me.'" But, carrying on family tradition, his children would have gone to Catholic Mass in their formative years.

In a changing town, religion was an unchanging element in people's interpretations of its role in their lives and in the way it divided the town.

Though a few individuals I met claimed "choice" of religious affiliation, choice did not seem actually to happen. "She was Roman Catholic," a young woman said. "She's a Roman Catholic so—." Her sister finished the sentence: "So we, you know, he wanted us—, we were raised in the Greek Catholic Church." One parent or the other determined where the children went to church. Jim's ideal was not practical in a Mon Valley mill town.

Mrs. Tennant, a woman in her early sixties, described her marriage: "See, our marriage was a mixed marriage. I was Catholic, he was a Protestant." The problems between them came after the children were born. "He didn't want to go to my church, and I didn't want to be at his church. So we never got the kids baptized." Her memory was that therefore they gave the children "free choice" about which church to attend. "We let the kids pick their own religions." She was immediately interrupted by her daughter, who was at the interview with us: "Three out of four of us were Catholic," she reminded her mother. For the Tennant children to take their mother's religion fit the patterns in a steel town; church tended to be the domain of women.

The pattern persisted. In her mid-thirties and upwardly mobile, Olivia repeated the dicta of her parents' generation. She began her narrative about growing up in Homestead with a reference to her parents' marriage; they had been married just before the Second World War. "My father is Hungarian and my mother is, like, Irish and English and Pennsylvania Dutch." I asked, "Do you know how your grandparents felt about the marriage?" and she answered, "I think that was a problem." Child of the mill town, she meant the problem of religious not of ethnic difference. "My mother was Presbyterian. I think it was more the religious back then than the ethnic [that made a difference]." The problem seemed easily solved: "And so she went ahead and turned Catholic." But in the next minute, Olivia recalled that things had not been easy at all. Her parents could not find a church to marry them. "In fact, when they got married, she wasn't even allowed to have a ceremony because she wasn't Catholic. They just stood at the front of the church and that was their wedding."

Olivia demonstrated greater caution than her parents, having the luck to fall in love with an "appropriate" man. She married within the church and inside a church, with a large wedding that marked the comfortable match of Roman Catholic and Roman Catholic. Religious similarity overcame the fact that her husband was Italian and, in the culture of Homestead, alien from both the Eastern European and the Northern European of her own ethnic background. But Olivia, like others in her generation and in the generations of her parents and grandparents, put ethnic differences in terms of food and holiday customs; a matter of taste, such items could be tried out and learned.

A commemorative book about Homestead published in 1980 boasted about its ethnic amalgamation and, equally, about its continuing religious diversity: "It speaks well of these people that the wide cleavage between these [ethnically different] groups amalgamated into a working whole," and, "historically the tri-boroughs and the surrounding environs have supported forty-two churches and one cathedral whose members encompass many denominations and nationality groups."[27] Photographs support this view: churches get a page to themselves, while culture is crowded into pictures of neighborhoods, memorials, and schools.

Separation on Sunday and amalgamation on weekdays—for decades that was how residents envisioned their town. The churches stood apart from one another in appearance, organization, and practice. By contrast, the signs of ethnicity were fluid and alterable, the right ingredients for mixing. A major indication of collapse in Homestead after USX left was a breakdown in these orderly mixtures.

"They don't even pay attention anymore"

Eighth Avenue was a stage for the changes that were occurring in Homestead in the 1980s and 1990s. Looking out the window of his small shop, Julio wondered "what Homestead was coming to." What Julio saw was visible to shopkeepers and pedestrians on other blocks of the downtown area: a "mix" that had the quality of disorder rather than amalgamation. "So it's all mixed up," John, another middle-aged, white businessman said to me, resignedly. Though he did not explain, it seemed evident he did not mean a melting pot but the confusion and chaos "all mixed up" conveys. "That's the way it is around here, though" he repeated, with an air of fatalism. Then he referred back to the old days to evoke the order, understood and respected by residents, that had once existed. "Now, years ago they used to worry, 'Oh he's Catholic, she's Protestant. They'll never get along, they'll never get married. They don't even pay any attention to that hardly any more," he concluded, regretful at the disappearance of rules.

We moved through his store to the front window and looked out. Rather than pointing to the "mess," or recoiling from what he saw as Julio had, John pointed to the array of church steeples visible from his shop.

Harmony
and
Discord

178

Ranging from the blue-and-gold onion domes of Eastern Orthodoxy to the narrow white steeples of Protestantism, these church tops represented the kind of diversity he respected. "You stand here and look up that hill, and you'll see up to Ann Street. You'll see one [church] on that corner, one on that corner." He paused, then added, "You'll see a lot of churches in Homestead."

But this, too, seemed to be changing right before his eyes. Not only had USX abandoned the town, but churches seemed to be leaving as well. Whether or not it was their choice or that of the diocese, congregations were moving to the suburbs where population was growing not declining. "Some of them have now moved out into, I think it was the areas of Munhall, West Mifflin, and those areas, and built new churches," John explained. Warming to his theme, he went on: "But, boy, there was a lot of churches around here. They were like ethnic churches. There was a German Church, there was—it was all separated."

The visible distinctions among churches maintained the social and cultural categories crucial to Homestead's development. Through churches, and the homogeneous neighborhoods around them, Homesteaders represented "below the tracks" and a "good" community of respect for differences. Like the celebrations that distinguished ethnic groups and the ceremonies that separated religious groups, the streets that divided residential groups struck residents as natural, the way life ought to be. I was taken on several tours of the town, and it was not unusual for my guide to point out: there's Hunky Hollow, there's where the colored lived, here is where we lived, and so on up and down the hills of the steel town. Sam's performance as a guide was typical, in that he emphasized the role of churches in defining neighborhoods and indicated that an individual could be in the wrong place at the wrong time.

"This is Seventh Avenue, this is Sixth Avenue," he announced, plunging into rapid-fire commentary. He remembered back to his childhood when those blocks were the heart of the ward, home to small but thriving commercial establishments. "I'd cut down here and I'd get a real eerie feeling, like coming into the Twilight Zone—," alien territory, in other words, before the familiar loomed into sight: "And I'd look down there, and I was born on Fourth Avenue. I get chills right now even thinking about it because I used to cross these tracks."

As we walked further, he filled in the details of these journeys through the ward: "And then [I'd] walk up to a church, and your life—everybody's life revolved around their church. You had Saint Peter, Saint Anne's—

Slavic church, Saint John's—Russian church. At Christmas the ladies would bake like crazy and we'd go around and we'd wish them a merry Christmas in Russian and they'd respond by giving us a quarter or something." Like Sam, Homesteaders gave me tours because they recognized the history written into the physical landscape and the jog to memory that came from visualizing the places of the past. Having looked at archival photographs, they went one step further to show me commemorations in street corners, old doorways, and abandoned railroad tracks.

Sam talked, too, of how the familiar features had faded and once-clear boundaries had broken down in the last ten years. As we stood in front of an ornate, Gothic-style cathedral, Sam said, "Here's the Irish church. It's not Irish so much anymore. One time it was strictly Irish; it was called Saint Mary Magdalene. Now you have all kinds of nationalities going right there." His phrase, "all kinds of nationalities," was accompanied by a frown of distaste; he did not like the "mixed-upness" of recent times. By 1990, the majority of individuals I interviewed gave the impression that pulling the mill out had pulled out the stopper on the controls townspeople had once enforced. Much as some residents hated the mill and what it stood for, steel had been the anchor for a way of life vividly pictured in those steeples every few blocks.

But a number of residents also saw the beginning of the downfall occurring before U.S. Steel made its move. They were the women and men who talked of the changes civil rights legislation brought, "mixing up" whites and blacks. Antidiscrimination laws in housing ended the easy homogeneity of neighborhoods Sam remembered and Byington had described in 1910:

> Neither in lodge nor in church, nor, with a few exceptions, in school do the two [white and Slav] mingle. Even their living places are separated; the Second Ward, except for those who owned homes there in earlier years, has been largely abandoned to the newer immigrants. This sharp division, while partly due to the barrier which differences in language and custom create, is intensified by a feeling of scorn for the newcomers on the part of the older residents.[28]

Though discrimination was officially illegal, the scorn for newcomers whose language and customs were different did not disappear. The struggle to maintain a sense of order and keep up parameters continued into the 1970s and 1980s. No law forbid a person from ignoring a neighbor, refusing to lend a cup of sugar, and shunning all conversational interactions. No law forbid someone from searching until she found a house or apartment where she "felt comfortable."

As late as 1989, the three boroughs were still described in much the way the first generation described "below the tracks." According to Theresa, "if they asked Kim, Kim says, 'They live on Hunky Hill.' This is called Hunky Hill and down below, on Ravine, it's Hunky Hollow." Although neighborhoods retained a positive aura, nicknames did not: "But this is— like, there's all old—you'd never say to an old person 'Hunky,' because they're highly offended, and they'll tell you right to your face, 'I'm not a Hunky, only Hungarians from Hungary are Hunky.'"

Thirty year olds joked about Hunky Hollow as men and women in their sixties and seventies could not. "Rampant discrimination against all 'hunkies' enforced the segregated working and living patterns," historian John Hoerr writes.[29] In 1990, no mill existed to enforce labor or living patterns. Under those circumstances, "Hunky" was OK, and enclaves were a sign of solidarity.

In her thirties, Jackie had grown up in a family of mill workers. After a "druggie" time in high school, she told me, she enlisted in the army and did a tour abroad. Along the way, she had three children and then, "getting my act together," came back to Homestead to live. She moved into Hunky Hollow, the small, winding roadway of her childhood years. In her conversation with me, she saw nothing odd either about her choice or about the existence of such a segregated area in the late 1980s. "It is a wonderful place to bring up children," she said, and then, echoing an older generation: "It's like family here."

Hunky Hollow was not just Eastern European. It was also white. My account of Homestead has so far left out a major aspect of steel town history: race. Blacks have lived in Homestead since the turn of the century, present in the work force, the neighborhoods, the schools, and the recreational spaces of a steel town. How blacks were seen by whites changed over the course of the century, and these changes in perception constitute a barometer of other changes in Homestead.

FACES

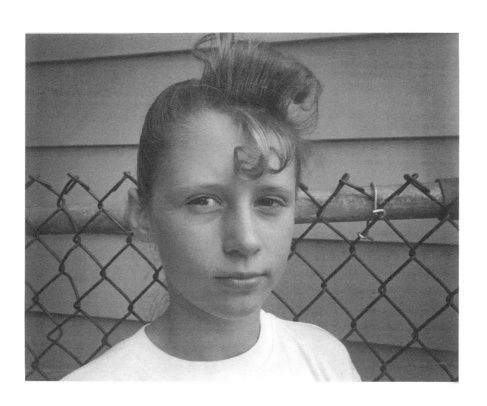

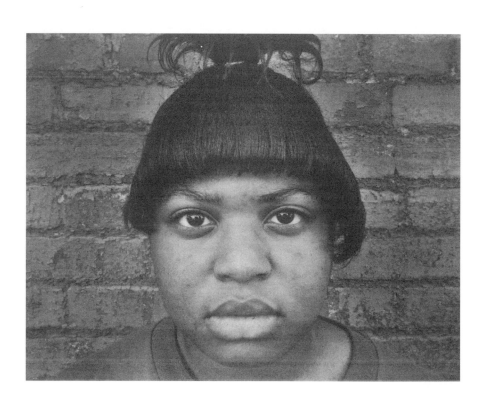

STEEL AND SEGREGATION

Race Relations in Homestead

A white woman who had been for many years a resident of Homestead was especially vexed because a nearby house had been sold to a Negro. Some weeks later I visited the wife of this colored property owner, who had been ill, and she told me feelingly how good her white neighbors had been to her. She spoke especially of this older resident who had complained to me, and mentioned how she had brought dainties and finally helped persuade her to go to the hospital. Thus, though social distinctions still exist and the colored people have their own lodges and churches, the more prosperous among them are winning respect.

—Margaret Byington, *Homestead: The Households of a Mill Town*

ouise described the Italians who lived two miles down the Monongahela River in Hays as "dark, different, and strange." When she thought back to her childhood, she did not mention a group that may have seemed even "stranger," the blacks who lived in the Lower Ward along with the Slovaks, Russians, and Hungarians she did mention. African Americans in Homestead were part of Homestead history for whites, but a complicated part; these fellow workers and neighbors did not fit smoothly into nostalgic memories of the good old days.

Holding a distinct place in the stories whites told of their childhoods and of the changes in the town between the Depression and deindustrialization, blacks in Homestead were also given a special space in the social and economic landscape of a steel town. The "colored people," as Byington put it, had their "own lodges and churches," their own apartments, street corners, stores, bars, and positions in the vast structure of the Homestead Works. Separation lasted into the 1980s, despite federal legislation against discrimination.

Interactions between whites and blacks in Homestead obeyed informal norms and customs which were guided by a pervasive myth expressed in terms of "harmony" and "we all got along." In interviews with me, and with other investigators over the years, white residents of Homestead were likely to place "race relations" under the umbrella of "ethnic relations." This meant, in effect, that they seemed to view blacks as just another group, part of the melting pot of a steel town and incorporated into the diverse community epitomized by "below the tracks." That this viewpoint has been persuasive to generations of outside observers tells something about the role Homestead plays in the American imagination. Portrayed as an ideal working-class community, Homestead is not usually described as discriminatory or racist; economic conflicts take precedence in the literature, overshadowing the conflicts among racial, ethnic, and religious groups that are also a part of Homestead history.

In my interviews, white and black residents painted a complex portrait of race relations in the steel town. When an individual remembered a past in which *everyone* got along, this reflected a present in which no one seemed to get along; the informal norms once so powerful for residents were breaking down piece by piece, just as the mill was. Whites had a story in which race was sometimes ignored, sometimes equated with ethnicity, and sometimes evidently difficult to discuss. Blacks had an entirely different story to tell, though that was not always apparent in the early stages of an interview. Sam's version typified what I would hear from other white residents of his generation: down there, he said, "you had blacks, Slovaks, Russians, Hungarians, Mexicans," as though there were no differences. But in the several versions of history he subsequently provided, he did not mention blacks (or Mexicans) again. His life revolved around the whites of Homestead.

Thirty years old, Sam's daughter also remembered a past that was harmonious. During her "good old days" in the 1950s, she said, "everyone got along." And for the same reasons they always had: neighbors knew each other and kids played together. Sam and his daughter expressed the dominant white view of race relations in Homestead. I did not hear a very different account from long-time black residents until somewhat far along into an interview.

While the official text provided by most whites in all three generations was of harmony, there were "hidden texts" within their statements as well.[1] "Getting along" had distinct limits, and the characterization of groups had distinct connotations; the lay of the racial landscape was not smooth for any of the decades during which Homestead was under the shadow of the mill. That it seemed so is another aspect of the story of the mill's collapse. Black residents initially claimed the same version of history as whites when they were interviewed, suggesting the power of a town's self-representation. The steel town was not without discrimination or racial hostilities in any period, as the blacks I interviewed eventually revealed in the anecdotes they slipped into an "official" account. Hiring practices perpetuated by U.S. Steel had a good deal to do with black and white relations outside the mill walls.

"Now it's the Hunkies looking down on the niggers"

Like whites, black residents used "below the tracks" to present a picture of harmony in practice. Like whites, blacks also portrayed "below" as a neighborhood of households whose diversity contrasted with the discriminatory policies imposed by the steel corporation. In these accounts, the impenetrable structure of the mill formed a backdrop for lively, on-the-street interactions—conversations shared by small groups of people: two couples leaning against a wall, their arms thrown around each other's shoulders, as in one of Brodsky's photos; a bunch of kids leaning over their bicycles in another. Posing for the camera, these subjects underlined a story their parents and grandparents "posed" for the tape recorder: once, we all got along.

The mill neighborhood was a melting pot of sorts, the first stop for black immigrants

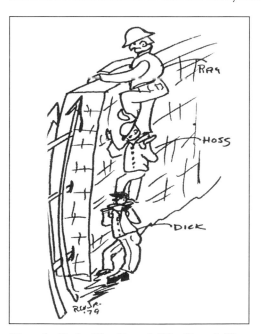

"From the Desk of Ray Hornak Who Doesn't Want to Forget How He Got Where He Is"
(R. Wurtz collection)

from the American South, just as it had been for the English and German immigrants who ran the mills and then for men and women from Eastern Europe who kept the mills running. Blacks, like whites, came in the late nineteenth century because there were jobs in steel. African-American men of this first migration tended to hold skilled positions and to work side by side with white workers. But this form of integration did not last. As the twentieth century began, changes in the steel industry and in the factors leading to black migration altered the look and the composition of arriving immigrants.[2]

After the First World War, a large number of blacks entered western Pennsylvania as well as other industrial towns in the north.[3] They were unskilled laborers, men and women competing for jobs at the bottom of the ladder and often facing hostility from the individuals they worked with and lived near. The situation worsened in the 1930s with a growth in the black population. In a depressed economy whites, as Bell points out, re-write their own history: "But I was just thinking that once it was the Irish looking down on the Hunkies and now it's the Hunkies looking down on the niggers. The very things the Irish used to say about the Hunkies the Hunkies now say about the niggers."[4]

Throughout its tenure in western Pennsylvania, the U.S. Steel Cor-poration (in all its guises) organized a work force without full racial inte-gration. The hierarchy of jobs and the ideologies of practice on the shop floor influenced living arrangements and social interactions outside the mill. Residents of Homestead told their stories around a visible and persis-tent distinction between blacks and whites on a crew, in a bar, in a school-room, and on the street.

The experience of blacks in the steel town constituted a distinct so-cial geography. Blacks might "see" the three boroughs as unified, the way whites did, but they could not travel the boroughs in the same way whites could. A Hunky might live separately from an Anglo, but a black could not choose to live side by side with either, especially if he or she decided to move out of Homestead proper and into West Homestead or Munhall—and Munhall was out of bounds for an African American for most of the twentieth century. In the 1990s, whites added a chapter to their version of race relations in Homestead by pointing to the "darkness" spreading through town, particularly evident on Eighth Avenue. The change in the popula-tion "down street" was visible.

In their accounts, whites compared blacks in the past with blacks today, much as they compared a 1930s "below" to a 1990s collapsing community. At the same time, whites drew from a generations-old point of view: newcomers always look stranger than those who have been there awhile. Yet in Homestead, the new, incoming blacks of any era were not assimilated as readily as new, incoming whites. Blacks initially arrived as strikebreakers, in the legend of the steel town, and without the recognizable ethnic and religious customs that quickly categorized Eastern European immigrants. In interviews with me, white residents revived an earlier view that blacks brought "trouble," had peculiar customs, and "talked funny."

The breakdown of an economic system and the disappearance of its main structure framed this version of race relations. Without a mill to absorb newcomers—no ladder whose bottom rungs could be safely occupied by blacks—relations turned bitter. Without steel, the niches for newcomers disappeared. In 1990, a white woman said, "Homestead is turning dark." For black as well as white residents, the town was darkened by the collapse of the mill. Familiar patterns of interaction fell before the wrecking ball as definitively as did the heavy girders of the Homestead Works. What also collapsed, though less abruptly, was an effort to maintain an image of Homestead as racially harmonious.

"White and black was raised together"

Whites I met established and communicated the official text about race relations in Homestead. The text, however, was not consistent or unchanging, from year to year, person to person, or, even, moment to moment in one person's account. The metaphors and phrases that conveyed *black* and *white* also shifted, carrying different interpretations. Blacks who started out with the official text ended up providing me with another.

Mark, the tavern owner, narrated perfectly the white myth of good relationships "below the tracks." He relished his role as spokesperson for the history of Homestead from the Great Depression to the equally great deindustrialization. His reminiscences about the "golden days" before the Second World War did not omit race. As far as blacks were concerned, he said, "they were no different from us. . . . We went to school together. We fought together, we played together. They used to come to our house and eat, [we'd go to] their house and eat." Then, to impress upon me how close a family the neighborhood really was, Mark told a classic anecdote: "If there was a tragedy struck your house, on your street, the whole street came and helped. We had a colored family, matter of fact, he owns the funeral home here, Mr. Frederick. He had a brother who was in the hospital, who needed blood. And at that time blood transfusions were—things were shaky, they didn't process the blood, I think they gave it to you directly. I'm not sure, I don't know, I was just a youngster. This was about 1934 or '35. But all the kids on the street went to give blood for him. And he was a colored fella, we were all white."

Taking a fine lens to Mark's account, however, can reveal its hidden text. As he conveys integration in his hometown, Mark makes it the domain of children: children ran from house to house; children (or adolescents) shared blood in an emergency. Even allowing for the fact that he is remembering his own childhood and adolescence, the incidents he cites suggest a more general truth. Mark does not, for example, talk either about neighbor women borrowing cups of sugar or neighbor men strolling to work together. There were limits on who shared what with whom.

Children played a large part in the arguments some black residents made that a principle of live-and-let-live guided practice as well as belief in Homestead. Three black men in unison, in conversation with an interviewer, recreated a "below" that sounded like Mark's. In their sixties as well, Scribble, Gene, and Duke had grown up in Homestead and were aware of the town's official text on race. Their interview occurred on Eighth Avenue. Standing around looking at archival pictures—Homestead in the 1910s and in the years of their childhoods—they began to construct the same story I heard from other residents: a thriving, harmonious, happy community: "the best place to live in," one of them asserted while the others nodded vigorous agreement. Pointing to a spot on one of the photos, Duke started the ball rolling: "I can remember when we went to school down there." Gene put his finger on the same spot: "School was right there, wasn't it? Where the projects are." Scribble: "Yeah, the school was there."

Then, with a deft backhanded move, Gene slid into the risky arena of social interactions: "I remember all the Czechoslovakians there [in the ward]. They're fighting over in Czechoslovakia now." What was really on his mind came up quickly: "When they lived down there, man, we ate in their houses. They come to our houses and eat." One might imagine that Gene restrained himself from saying "Hunky" to a white stranger, using the term *Czechoslovakian* instead. Warming to his subject, he took on the language Mark had used: "Sure, [we were] like one big family," he assured the interviewer. Duke concluded: "They didn't know nothing about no black and white." Still, these perceptions were based not only on a memory of childhood but also on the world as seen through a child's eyes—running

from house to house at dinnertime. And they were the views of men looking back, men who as boys had the run of the streets and had sports to
unify their activities.

An interview with a black man in his fifties, a different generation
and background from Duke, Gene, and Scribble, shows how slight the
integration in sports actually was. Thomas Johnson was the son of a prominent businessman who grew up on the "upper" side of Homestead. Like
almost everyone else I interviewed, Thomas greeted the visiting anthropologist with the official town history. Homestead had been integrated
and harmonious, a good town in the past, he assured me. Like most of the
townspeople I interviewed, Thomas brought up weddings to indicate how
spirited and cooperative the town had been. During celebrations, he said
in the voice of his community, "everyone came together." Later in the
interview, he described the congregation of his father's church, and it was
evident that no more than there were black faces at Hunky weddings were
there white faces at black weddings.

Thomas's story of integration looked back to his own childhood and
to the experiences children had in a steel town. It began on the note I
heard often: "We got along fairly good back then with the white children
coming up, the youngsters, you know." He remembered other aspects of
life in Homestead: "But we'd have our own ball clubs and we'd have our
street basketball, and we'd have three or four whites and four or five blacks
together, playing and doing—." His efforts to portray an ease of interaction were not entirely successful. That Thomas had never played on the
same Little League team as the white children was part of his story as well.[5]
Perhaps because he had not grown up in the ward or perhaps because his
position in town required a more critical outlook, Thomas did not draw
forward a vision of "below" to emphasize Homestead's harmony as strenuously as, say, Gene, Scribble, and Duke did. Moreover, the ward for him
was a "twilight zone," and he did not venture down there; his father had
forbidden him to go "beneath" Sixth Avenue.

The Lower Ward was a separate world, bounded by the railroad tracks
and in visible contrast to hillside households.[6] A curious visitor to the
ward had to cross Eighth Avenue and the railroad tracks on Sixth Avenue
before entering a domain of small wooden houses and shops closely packed
amid residences. Before its demolition during World War II, the mill neighborhood was a social if not an administrative unit; as a distinct place, the
ward maintained rules about racial mixing (and sharing) that were not
customary elsewhere in the three boroughs.

Scribble fell into a nostalgic tone about the security and comfort of the good old days: "Everybody loved everybody and shared. No burglarizing your neighbor." Duke expanded: "We didn't have that racial problem. We had our own congregation down there. We had our own little world down there." Asked to explain why racism ever developed in Homestead, Scribble began, "When they tore the ward down—," only to be interrupted by Gene, who said impatiently, "I'm talking now, today, 1992, dude." He added, apparently to illuminate Duke's explanation: "*He* says it's an economic thing, man. *He's* talking about one section of the United States. *She's* talking about all over, man."

But Duke returned to his own interpretation of why racism had not been present in Homestead in the 1930s: the isolation of the Lower Ward. "What we did down there, nobody knew how we lived down there," he claimed. "Nobody in the world knew how we lived. Nobody knew 'cause we never ventured out"—the last said with some irony. Gene agreed with his friend: "It's a microcosm compared to what's happening in reality. The only real tight white dude you know now are the ones that grew up with us." Scribble: "The steelworkers." Gene: "Yeah, that's what I'm saying." Scribble: "They're all older guys now." Gene: "Yeah, they're older, but they still got the same bond as they had when they was little." The implication was that as long as no one looked, life went on in the ward according to each individual's best sense of proper sociability. If children were the only ones who ate in each other's houses, then that was the way integration worked. Like their white age peers, the black residents conveyed a notion of "natural integration," a state of affairs deeply associated with and significantly characterizing the mill neighborhood.

Residents conveyed a state of affairs in which people interacted or ignored each other by choice, and outside observers such as social workers gave it a legitimacy. The phrase *natural integration* became a way of talking about practices that were, in the last analysis, "live-and-let-live" only for individuals who had economic and social leverage—primarily the white residents of the steel town. Nevertheless, as a characterization, "live-and-let-live" expressed an understanding of community in which local control and a countrylike quality of knowing one's neighbors predominated. It was in opposition to a life dependent on the mill, regardless of one's workplace, and in opposition to the intensifying intervention of the federal government during the 1960s, 1970s, and 1980s. For Gene, Scribble, and Duke, who had experienced discrimination in the labor and the housing market, the nostalgic phrase announced the worsening of conditions in the present.

"Live-and-let-live" was also an interpretation of the strategies of survival adopted by African Americans in this Mon Valley steel town; the phrase suggested tolerance of an array of economic activities. Blacks in steel towns made their way despite low income, bad housing, and bias in the school system. But when blacks used the phrase "live-and-let-live," they did so with a hint of sarcasm that revealed the racism they had experienced. Interviews with me, in fact, carried forward a style of self-presentation long practiced by blacks in steel towns like Homestead. Black residents accepted the dominant ideology in most eras and most situations. A national civil rights movement, however, provided legitimation for more active protest, as well as a rhetoric for the kind of criticism I eventually heard.

Until then, an outsider could be forgiven for seeing integration where it did not exist and for designating as "natural" boundaries that were the result of class, ethnic, and racial discrimination.[7] The boat that no one rocked had as an anchor the premise that "people want to be with those who are like them," who celebrate the same holidays, eat the same foods, and speak the same language. Such interpretations of Homestead's diversity lasted for nearly three decades after the World War II razing of the mill neighborhood, until the mill closings along the Monongahela River threw the status quo into chaos.

Duke knew why blacks as well as whites in Homestead had been able to accept the idea of integration while living with segregation, discrimination, and a clear-cut social hierarchy. Blacks were at the bottom, but others had their rungs as well. In Duke's sharp analysis there was a reason a rigid hierarchy was manageable: "See, the money and stuff came from the steel mill, and the money was right there." As long as the money flowed, norms and customs regulating social interactions were tolerable. Even during the Great Depression and through intermittent periods of downturn, the steady hum of the works was reassuring, promising security to all residents. For those who worked in the mill, as long as there was smoke, jobs were waiting. For those who did not work in the mill, persistent production provided a cushion for the swings in their own enterprises. As theories of racism hold, a sense of comfort in the "ecological niche" cuts down on the most virulent expressions of hostility and allows people to accept an official text that does not portray their own experiences.[8]

A number of people assured me that behind those hot, heavy walls, "everyone" worked together regardless of skin color, beliefs, or food habits. On the shop floor, all workers were equal—or at least equally necessary to the safe completion of a task. The idealized image of a work crew was almost as powerful as the one of "below," and it spread through the community, influencing women and men, children and grandchildren who had never entered the mill and now never would.

"We never went by, 'He's black'"

In giving a history of the town, people often used mill work to represent the virtues of a mill community. These virtues included, along with endurance and stamina, a tolerance for those whose traits and dialects were unfamiliar. And the assumption I heard, in interviews with residents of various backgrounds, was that these virtues spread out from the mill to affect interactions in the town. The assumption was not unreasonable: a solidarity created at work bound individuals together in ways that moved from a shop floor to local bars, churches, and parks. At any rate, that was one interpretation of mill and community relations.

That interpretation is offered by sociologist William Kornblum, who studied a mill neighborhood in South Chicago in the early 1970s: "When white and black steelworkers labor together over long careers in the mill, they no longer must rely in their dealings with each other on the stereotypes which govern relations between whites and blacks outside the mill. Men from interracial work groups routinely share wakes, funerals, retirement parties, weddings, and a host of family activities over the course of their lives in the mill."[9]

In Homestead, the notion that men worked together side by side without regard for color hung on forcefully, generation after generation. So, too, did the perspective Kornblum took, that getting along inside implied sharing activities outside. But, like any interpretation, this one was geared to an agenda, an aspect of nostalgia about "better days" when an industry flourished in a one-industry town. Was the Homestead mill really "interracial"? Did men and women troop outside and into the bars along Sixth and Eighth Avenues without regard to race or, for that matter, ethnicity? For most of its history in the town, the Homestead Works was not fully integrated; work crews might mix men of different ethnic backgrounds but rarely mixed blacks with whites.

Mark described the situation to me one evening in his Millhunk Tav-

Office worker (R. Wurtz collection)

ern. He had never worked in the mill, but he had heard hundreds of mill stories as he poured drinks for the workers. On the shop floor, he told me, "things" went smoothly. "They would just tell you, 'all you Hunkies get over here. All you niggers get over there. John, you're gonna be the pusher today. You take them five niggers and you get down the checkers. Andy, you take your five or ten men and you go down the cinder pits.' . . . That's the way they approached it. Nobody thought anything of it."

This anecdote is complex. On the one hand, Mark suggests that life on the shop floor was fine, distinctions accepted. On the other hand, he conveys the harshness of conditions, as well as the enforced discrimination that characterized work arrangements in every era of mill history. For it was the "niggers" who reported to the checkers and the whites who were "men." For Mark, that's just the way things were. "Nobody thought anything of it" was a form of live-and-let-live.

Other men and women I interviewed mentioned the integration of a work crew to illustrate how much better life was in the past and, like Mark, to imply a diffusion of harmony from shop floor to town sidewalks. A businessman on Eighth Avenue, like Mark a white, longtime resident, had an explanation for the (presumed) harmony on a crew: "It's like being in the army then. You had to work with them and rely on them for their safety or your own." From his point of view, somewhat more realistic than Mark's, the danger and risks of a job in steel drove men to work together without thought for individual distinctions. Heavy equipment, for instance, swung precariously over the heads of those wandering below. "You've got cranemen in cranes and guys walking below."

The army reference explains the behavior and, perhaps more than this man intended, distinguished what went on in the mill from what went on outside the mill. Men worked together because a man could lose his life if he did not watch out for his fellow workers. But these same men did not necessarily drink, pray, or visit together, despite what Mark wanted me to believe. The wife of an older steelworker told me one day that her husband never brought men from the mill home. In Homestead, a crew might take an after-work drink together, but the interaction ended after that.

The notion that black men and white men worked together on a crew in itself represents a nostalgic view of the past. Depending on the era of U.S. Steel history, the story of blacks in the mill varied. From the incorporation of a few skilled laborers to the reception of a large number of unskilled workers, the tale is tortured and does not end with the Second World War boom, the federal laws of the 1960s and 1970s, or the slow, frightening decline of the early 1980s.

The peaceful period of black acceptance in the mill town was short. The earliest migrants were skilled workers. "These men," Margaret Byington wrote, "have in the main come to adopt the same standards as their white neighbors, and are usually treated with genuine respect by the latter."[10] By the time of the First World War, however, new blacks had come into Homestead. These men were not skilled workers and they found it difficult to get jobs in the steel mills of the Mon Valley.[11] Their best times of employment came during strikes, when the mill owners brought them in in large numbers to cross picket lines. Though the most dramatic influx came during the strike of 1919, the pattern had been set before. Byington writes: "Of those who are now in the mills, some came in the first instance as strike breakers and have advanced to well-paid positions."[12]

This legacy was devastating in a working-class community. Regardless of individual interactions, and the rare occasions of shared work spaces, the sense that blacks had once been strikebreakers lingered on in the history of the town. African-American workers could prosper and move up the hill, but their role in breaking strikes never quite left the memory of whites who worked in the mill. Though not the cause of racism, the arrival of blacks during strikes certainly did not encourage good fellowship between them and white workers. The most egregious instance of this was the 1919 strike. "Perhaps the largest single importation of strikebreakers occurred during the Great Steel Strike of 1919 when Blacks and Mexicans were brought into Pittsburgh and many of the mill towns along the Monongahela River," writes a historian. Black and white workers, he notes, were "pitted" against one another.[13] Labor journalist William Serrin claims the "thirty thousand black workers, many brought by bus and railroad from the South," allowed the industry to crush the strike.[14]

I did not interview anyone who remembered the 1919 strike first-hand. Still, the post–World War I strike was a crucial event in individual histories of Homestead, a strike that, like the famous 1892 worker protest, shaped the understandings of virtually everyone in the town. And, like the earlier strike, the 1919 strike was remembered in glowing terms of heroic action, endurance, and solidarity in the face of oppressive work conditions. No one I met mentioned the impact on race relations that a company decision to encourage one group of workers to break the strike of another would engender. According to novelist Thomas Bell, in newspapers the strike of 1919 was portrayed as the work of radical, anti-American Bolsheviks. The accusation not only let the company off the hook but also utilized patriotic sentiments to damn efforts at unionization.[15] Bell does not mention the recruitment of black workers to break the strike.

At the end of the 1980s in Homestead, black as well as white residents described past strikes as moments of solidarity, not as times of exacerbated racial hostility. Thomas Bell's story of a steady move toward unionization and collective bargaining is more attractive in late-twentieth-century Homestead than an account like Dickerson's of the continual struggles a black worker faced. A few older, white ex-steelworkers recalled that blacks did not attend union meetings or sign petitions against management policy. "What happened was we had an awful time trying to convince the black brothers to join. It wasn't a matter of trust. It was a matter that the company had put the fear of God in these people," a steelworker told historian John Bodnar.[16] A white craneman I talked to mentioned that black workers he knew in the 1960s and 1970s were more loyal to *their* political organizations" than to the USW. Such perceptions made it hard for a white worker to feel solidarity with a black worker beyond the demands of the tasks at hand.

Yet from the craneman's point of view, relations between blacks and whites were better then than now. Recalling his bird's-eye view over the floor, Luther talked about blacks in the mill. "We had guys on the shears, and they were black, but we never went by 'he's black' or 'he's a nigger.' We never—it wasn't even in the vocabulary." He also added another side to the story, referring obliquely to the civil rights movement: "They were the type of guys—now, we had a guy who was on the shears, he was a nice guy, but he belonged to the NAACP all right. The head chairman, he'd say, he'd tell all the guys, 'Hey, today's payday, we got to pitch in for the NAACP.' So they'd go over to the shear, and they'd get two pennies and cut it in half and say, 'You get the next half next payday.'"

The attitude revealed by this anecdote was typical of older white steelworkers I met in Homestead: a joking discomfort with the efforts blacks made to redress grievances in the mill and in the town. Luther's anecdote also hid the real threat some white workers felt when blacks became more public in their protests. Interviewed in the 1970s as part of a labor relations study of Homestead, one white worker remembered the days before civil rights, when "*they* were too busy working to go out parading and carrying on trying to destroy the system."[17] From the point of view of white workers, blacks should have accepted the system, just as whites thought they themselves had.

"It was better thirty years ago"

The civil rights movement exposed the racial antagonism that had existed in the mill all along, despite memories of cooperation, harmony, and solidarity on the shop floor. For some white residents I interviewed, the public protests a national movement encouraged in the 1950s constituted the first step in the downfall of a live-and-let-live arrangement in which everyone knew, and accepted, his or her place. From this point of view, no Homestead resident had expected to cross racial lines at work any more than engage in a mixed-race marriage. "Civil rights had done the town in," one businessman told me. In his history, race relations had been better before the civil rights movement than they were after it. "Well, you talk about improving racial relations in a particular area. I thought it was better thirty years ago than it is now. You'd see fellows walking together. It didn't matter what color they were, going into the mill, working next to each other. It didn't matter."

His vague phrase, "improving racial relations," almost certainly refers to the federal antidiscrimination legislation of the 1960s. Like others I met in Homestead, he was of the opinion that "things" worked better when they worked naturally: "fellows walking together." A civil rights movement not only broke down the familiar accommodations in the town but also precipitated a loss of local control, the effects of which were still being felt. The notion that one-on-one contact eased interaction reflected the tendency of whites in Homestead to portray race relations in the same terms as ethnic relations, as if the problem and the solution were the same. The civil rights movement showed unmistakably that the situations differed; race received special treatment as ethnicity had not. The intrusion of civil rights law also made it difficult to maintain an image of Homestead as a community where issues could be resolved by good neighborliness.

Thinking back, white residents complained that civil rights activists persuaded blacks to turn outside for help, thus violating a principle of behavior in the steel town. And just as harmony was conveyed through shop floor anecdotes, so *dis*integration was described through accounts of mill policies. The climax came with the 1974 Consent Decree, generally mentioned in a heated tone of voice. The decree, residents told me, messed up shop floor integration by "forcing it."[18] This was not just an opinion in hindsight. One union official put bluntly what others would state more subtly: "I've never heard such racist comments in all the years I've been attached to it [the USW] until we got involved in the Consent Decree, and then it became open."[19]

On a summer day in 1987, Dick Wurtz spread his cartoons and drawings on his kitchen table and offered me an account of race relations in the mill. A white man in his mid-sixties, Dick had been a clerk in the Homestead Works all his adult life. Since he was in charge of recording work hours and job assignments, he knew where people were and when; he put together a social analysis of relationships on the floor. Dick kept track of the comings and goings of workers not just in the official records his job required, but also in the endless stream of drawings he made about life in the mill. He interpreted the sketches for me.

"See, a lot of this is just stuff that was done real fast," he began, as if to persuade me of the accuracy of what was done spontaneously. Then using the drawings to confirm his memory, he talked about the mixtures in the mill. "And I had an Italian boss and I teased him a lot, see? You got to face it. Down in the mill you have all kinds of people. They're black, they're white, they're Slovak, they're Polish, they're German, they're Dutch, they're English, they're Jewish. You name it, you got it. And if you can't handle it, you don't want to go work in the mill." Those, it became clear, were the

"Haw, Haw, Haw" (R. Wurtz collection)

good old days. Dick slid into a story of change by referring to a time when the mutual respect and mutual teasing disappeared. A new "breed" of people came in, not all of them workers. "Now if you're raised in an environment where everybody goes to work, that's it. Here [by contrast], you're sitting around the front porch, you're on welfare, you're not doing it. . . . You're not raised in that environment [of hard work]."

Perhaps reassured by the documentation lying in front of us, Dick went on to say exactly what he thought. "So, some of these black guys, they just come in, and they didn't realize that when you've got the job, you've also got to work. And it was tough for some of the foremen who had responsibility—this had to be done, that had to be done—to get a black guy to do it." Moreover, he blamed the federal government for the increased presence of "some of these black guys" in the mill. He called the Consent Decree "the compliances" because of the provision that the companies "comply" with fair employment practices. "Now, the compliances," he said, "see, this stuff was back when they had to hire women, they had to hire blacks. And a lot of blacks, I guess they just weren't raised in a working environment." He may have minded the presence of women in the mill, but he assumed they knew how to work (or he was being polite in front of me and his wife). His real complaint was about federal legislation, not a group of people. Without government interference, he assumed, the "right men" would be hired in the mill, as had historically been the case.

Angry at the government's intrusion into the world they knew, men in their sixties and seventies talked as if the Consent Decree had radically transformed the steel industry. But perceptions of what happened on the shop floor did not reflect the reality of a decree that was continually modified by the men and the women who walked through the mill's gates. Informal segregation continued to exist, and white steelworkers still defined black steelworkers as a different kind of worker. A white steelworker in his late thirties who entered the mill when the decree was in effect saw the limits of its provisions.

"Oh, blacks were already in the mill," Peter told me about his early years in the mill. "But my shop, it was really closed. We were white all the way from the janitor to the general foreman. Nobody got in crafts—it was tough for a black person to be a craftsman. Now, production, they could get that job. But I don't know, just seemed like they didn't get into the crafts situation. When bids came up, they didn't get them. Certain people got them." He went on to explain how the system worked: "And they [managers] can make life pretty tough on you. I mean, they can make life *really* tough on you if they wanted to. I seen a lot of people get weeded out. And I seen some people, they tried to weed them out, and they were tough enough to withstand it. And after they finally made their mark, then they'd hide them in some backlog. Like they'd assign them to the tar plant. Where you might never see—the crew only comes in the shop maybe once every blue moon just to get some more nails to go back to work." Peter's interview uncovers the flaw in white accounts of integration in the mill, before and after the Consent Decree. Just like the live-and-let-live philosophy outside the mill walls referred to one-on-one interactions, "working together" inside the mill came down to job-by-job and location-by-location arrangements. Boundaries existed, evident to black steelworkers when they attempted a lateral move and more so when they requested a promotion. Then, as often as not, a door slammed shut.

In his seventies and black, Otis had been in the Homestead Works most of his adult life, and he knew the terrain well. He made the same extension from "inside" to "outside" that other people I interviewed did, only his account had a different slant to it. Otis claimed he had never experienced a tolerant Homestead, no matter where or when he was there. Though he had been fortunate enough to hold a job in the mill for forty years, he also experienced numerous constraints on his activities inside the mill. Moreover, he said, it had not been easy to get the job in the first place. As he thought back over his time in the town, Otis likened Homestead of the 1940s to the deep South, "behind the cotton curtain," where he had served in World War II. He recalled with some amazement that "to work in an area where the same thing prevailed, it really taken me back. You couldn't go into bars, you couldn't go into shows, it was really something. . . . They were in another time capsule in Homestead at that time."

Throughout the interview, Otis refused to take seriously the notion that there had been "real" integration in the mill anymore than in the town. His positions and his mobility (or lack thereof) told him otherwise. The account he gave a white interviewer revealed his awareness that the increased integration he witnessed in the late 1950s resulted from state and federal mandates, not from tolerance by whites. And he knew how slowly those mandates affected what managers and foremen decided. Through the efforts of civil rights activists, he said, discrimination "kinda broke down, slow but sure." Among the consequences of change in mill policies, Otis said, were the small shifts outside the mill: "By the 1960s, it was really something to go to the movie, pay the same price, and not to have to go upstairs."

It was a slow tide, both in the mill and in the neighborhoods and theaters of Homestead. Not a resident of the community, Otis was more willing than residents I met to expose the flaws in a myth that claimed that tolerance spread from mill to town. He knew the limits of interaction in both domains. However, even he oscillated in his interview from condemning practices that made his entry into the mill difficult and his rise there virtually impossible, to appreciating the breakdown in discrimination that happened after government intervention.

A younger black man showed the same ambivalence about his career in the mill. I met Randy at a car wash, where he was holding the only job he could get after being laid off from the Homestead Works. In his mid-thirties, Randy appreciated the fact that he had gotten a job in the mill given the odds against employment of an unskilled black man. He had been, he reported, happy to make a move from a department store loading dock. Not only did U.S. Steel pay better, but he also found a fellowship with men inside the mill that was missing at the large retail store. Continuing on this nostalgic note, Randy told me he had been promoted in the mill "from laborer to jamb cutter." His job was to clean tar off the oven doors: "It was a good job."[20] And he met his wife in the Works, an African-American woman holding one of the positions the Consent Decree had made possible.

Randy's narrative meandered on, a pleasant set of memories, until we were interrupted by a white co-worker who sat down and asked what we were doing. It turned out that he too had been a steelworker, in his case since the day he left high school. Bobby was about five years older and somewhat seedier-looking than Randy but, like his younger black friend, eager to reminisce about his days in the mill. The afternoon's conversation was evidently a relief from the job he now held: wiping down windshields was neither challenging nor well compensated. Bobby had had a relatively prestigious position in the mill; he had been a craneman when they laid him off: "I got there in five years," he announced. Randy was visibly startled and responded sharply: "Did you do bids, too"?[21] "Yeah," Bobby said, "crane's what I always wanted and it's what I got. Took me five years to get it."

The interchange is interesting. Randy could not have been in the mill for ten years without being aware of the discriminatory hiring and promotion policies; fond as his expressed memories were, he must have known that jamb cutter was not a high-prestige job. Yet, when Bobby made his blunt statement of his own fast rise, it seemed to be a rude awakening from the nostalgia Randy had been enjoying. Once again, the compromises a black man had to make in order to stay in the mill are evident. Working in steel was a good job, there was no doubt about that, and like Eastern European laborers, some blacks simply accepted the rung on which they were placed. But in the 1990s, Randy had a different perspective, and the news of Bobby's rise was evidently not easy to swallow.

Yet the two men had a lot in common when they remembered their days in the mill. The joy each took in recalling incidents of danger and the crises in which "all pulled together" reveals not only how important this kind of work was to a man in Homestead, regardless of color, but also the shared sensibility that could be translated into "fellowship" despite obvious discrimination. In the car wash that afternoon, Randy and Bobby demonstrated a fellowship; sitting around on rickety chairs, bemoaning the griefs of the present and yearning for the comforts of the past, they could have been two friends in a bar.

In *Blue Collar Community* (1974), sociologist William Kornblum remarks on the ease with which a group of workers wandered into a bar after a hot and heavy shift. The bars, he continues, were close to the mill— what he calls "occupational taverns" since they could well have been an extension of the mill itself, abutting on its edges as they did. A similar recreational arrangement appeared in Homestead. Bars located across the street from the Works opened their doors to workers exhausted after a turn. The sirens brought teams of men in for their shot and a beer, men who likely went elsewhere after a few restful drinks. Up the hill from the mill were other bars, secluded in residential neighborhoods and subjected to the rules that guided these spaces. These were rules of exclusion and inclusion that preserved the racial differences patterning the households of a mill town throughout its history. Walking off a heavy turn, black workers and white workers shared the relief of a drink, and bars near the mill supported that tradition. In areas distant from the mill, the work culture faded, and a culture of rules, regulations, customs, and classifications set the terms of interaction. There, blacks drank in "black" bars and whites in "white" bars.

What happened to race relations in "private" space is a variation on the story of segregation in the steel industry. Race in Homestead can only be fully understood by venturing beyond the mill walls.

NEIGHBORHOODS

OUTSIDE THE MILL

Recreation and Residence in Homestead

From the cinder path beside one of the railroads that crosses the level part of Homestead, you enter an alley, bordered on one side by stables and on the other by a row of shabby two-story frame houses. The doors of the houses are closed, but dishpans and old clothes decorating their exterior mark them as inhabited. Turning from the alley through a narrow passage-way you find yourself in a small court, on three sides of which are smoke-grimed houses, and on the fourth low stables. The open space teems with life and movement.

—Margaret Byington, *Homestead: The Households of a Mill Town*

The mill was not the only institution in Homestead to come under federal surveillance and be forced to change its policies and (presumably) its practices regarding race. By 1960 much had changed in Homestead, and most residents were aware of the significance of those changes. Moreover, a number of the people I interviewed claimed the changes came about because of "outsiders," strangers who fixed what was not broken. When people recalled their experiences of the civil rights movement, they expressed nostalgia for the time prior to it. If people drank in separate bars, it was "only natural." If a Roman Catholic priest refused to marry a Greek Orthodox man to a Roman Catholic woman, who could be surprised when a Slovak bartender refused to serve a drink to an Italian, a black, or a non-Homesteader?

Yet some residents noticed the persistent racial discrimination and did not define segregation as voluntary or natural. They were the men and women who, in the 1960s, formed committees to make changes and who accepted outsiders as crucial to the process. In the 1990s, they interrupted their own nostalgic visions of the past to paint another version of a steel town, one that kept enclaves intact and "exotic" individuals out of workplaces, schoolrooms, neighborhoods, and local parks. Extending from the mill into the town, race relations constitute another thread in the history of Homestead, an aspect of both its households and its recreational spaces. Otis's view of the town in which he worked but did not live is penetrating, critical, and self-conscious. His view also links the past of Homestead to the present and future of a rust-belt town.

"Oh no, no, no, you didn't go in there"

At one point in his interview, Otis described going to after-work bars with white co-workers. He painted a picture of sweaty men pouring out of the mill gates and into the nearest drinking place. There, obedient to the bartender's line-up of glasses, black men rubbed elbows with white. Like whites, blacks also had to be obedient to the distinct norms of social interaction in a bar. The penalty for breaking a rule, however, was far more severe for a black than for a white patron.

"Occupational taverns" performed functions other than serving drinks to exhausted workers. A bartender might cash a check, report a piece of gossip about the mayor, or play umpire in quarrels over mill politics. These establishments lacked the intimacy of bars in residential neighborhoods or lounges in the ethnic clubs, but they seemed to represent the kind of integration whites, at least, prided themselves on when they talked to me about Homestead history.

Otis echoed that when he discussed the after-work bar, but he presented a different version later in his interview. An occupational tavern was the only place he could drink with whites. He did not venture beyond Eighth Avenue: "I don't go up the hill no kinda way. . . . When you get off the main drag, forget it." Bars scattered among the residences of Homestead were closed to African Americans through all the decades Otis could remember. "Oh no, no, no, you didn't go in there," he noted about neighborhood bars. And on Eighth Avenue itself, a black was refused a drink if he walked into the Slovak Club and was served reluctantly in the dimly lit Steel Bar up the block. Bars resembled private clubs and the clientele was restricted. Otis concluded with a bitter observation about the town he had worked in all his life: "It's really something to know you are living in a society that you have to know your parameters where you can operate."

Parameters existed for every resident of a steel town, but some groups and some individuals had more range than others, and this did not change with laws against segregation: the norms were too powerful and too much a part of the texture of everyone's life. When the doors of a bar or a classroom had to be opened legally, the glances shot at a stranger still made the lines of division clear. In residential neighborhoods, real estate agents and residents cooperated in maintaining boundaries.

Bar by bar and block by block, segregation was a feature of the landscape. As in any American town, the racial patterns were crosscut by class: a prosperous African American, shut out of Munhall, could buy a house in a "good" section of West Homestead. Homestead itself remained the most integrated of the three boroughs. On one integrated block in West Homestead, I interviewed a middle-aged black couple; their neighbor, a white woman of their generation, sat with us and occasionally joined in.

Thomas and Lydia Johnson were in their sixties. He had lived in Homestead all his life, and she had moved in when they got married just before the Second World War. They began the interview by describing the tolerance and harmony of the community. Over the course of the afternoon, however, other aspects of life in Homestead emerged from their complementary accounts. Like others I met, black and white, the Johnsons linked the harmony of the old days to prosperity. When Eighth Avenue was teeming with wall-to-wall shoppers and money "flowed" from the mill to the town, there could be "integration." To support this view, they ran through the list of flourishing establishments in the past: five five-and-tens, three movie theaters, sumptuous restaurants frequented by "big shots" from out of town. In describing what it was like to grow up in such a place, Thomas stopped short in the midst of his narrative. Going to the movies on a Saturday afternoon was not a simple business, he remembered, re-experiencing the pain of being sent "upstairs." "And uh, the uh—the movies were segregated. We had three movies at one time here in Homestead. The Leona Theatre and the Stahl Theatre, and there was one more for awhile. And all of them were segregated. You could only sit in the balcony if you were black. Couldn't sit down in the first floor."[1]

Once started on this train of thought, Thomas had a lot more to say. He shifted from the movie theaters to other places of recreation. "All the bars, white owned, were segregated," Thomas said, this time without hesitation. "You couldn't buy a drink in a white bar." Or if you did, another black man, twenty years older than Thomas told me, "they would break the glass." Tim remembered that he frequented white bars in the 1930s, mainly to bring in what he called "contraband goods." He knew what he could supply to the white drinkers but if by chance he also had a drink, he knew what the upshot would be—the glass would be smashed against the bar when he left. If apocryphal, the anecdote represented a truth: Homestead bars were ruled by racial discrimination. Excluded from white bars, Thomas recalled resignedly, "we opened our own."

The most famous black bar in Homestead belonged to Rufus "Sonnyman" Jackson and opened in the 1930s. The son of a religious father, Thomas may not have frequented the establishment, but he knew its importance in the history of Homestead. "Sonnyman Jackson had one of the biggest bar and grill restaurants in Homestead, called the Skyrocket," he added to his account of the businesses blacks created for themselves. Located in the mill neighborhood, the Skyrocket Lounge attracted a large clientele from all over Pittsburgh; it lasted through booms and busts in the steel industry until the 1986 debacle knocked the foundation out from under even this solid institution.

In addition to the Skyrocket, other black-owned bars and taverns flourished in Homestead between the Depression and the years of deindustrialization. They had to exist since, as William Serrin points out, even the most prestigious blacks in town could not drink in a white bar:

> Cumberland Posey, for years the town's leading black sports entrepreneur, who owned the Homestead Grays, the famous Negro League baseball team, could buy a round for the men at Straka's the bar and restaurant on Ann Street. But Posey, highly respected, a member of the school board, an educated man, could not drink at the bar even when the men at the bar were drinking on his money, and he had to come and go by the side door.[2]

An African-American man I interviewed had an explanation for Posey's appointment to the school board—and it wasn't because he was highly respected. "Mostly because he looked like he was a white man. Very high-colored white man, with good hair and everything. And he fell right into the system. Somebody complained, 'Well, we don't have any colored people [on the board],' they said. 'Well, there's Cum Posey, what's Cum doing?'" And so he was appointed to the board, but he was still not allowed to drink where white men drank.

Bars continued to be homogeneous, despite antidiscrimination laws and altered cultural attitudes. In a steel town, blacks, like whites, valued the spaces they could make their own, and bars certainly occupied that territory: if anywhere, that was the place a person should be able to choose his or her companions. Bars were considered private or, in the words of one historian "semi-public," to be governed by those inside.[3] Given the huge number of bars in Homestead, no one was deprived of a drink or sociability. A black person did not have to define this as racism to himself or others until, like Otis, the boundaries above Eighth Avenue stared him in the face or, like Tim, someone smashed a glass. When in the 1960s blacks (and some whites) battled against segregation in swimming pools, dance halls, and housing projects, the rules in bars received a wink.[4]

The further away from the commercial district it was, the more private a bar could be. Tucked away in residential neighborhoods, bars imposed whatever rules patron deemed appropriate, and bar owners expressed confidence that no one would check on their compliance with federal law. To do so would be like policing someone's parlor. Neighborhood bars, in fact, often resembled the houses around them; it took a sharp eye to detect the door into a drinking establishment since it looked exactly like nearby two-story frame houses. The night I had a drink with Sam in the Millhunk Tavern, he asked me to take him "somewhere else" later. We drove through quiet residential streets until he asked me to let him out at a place I never would have recognized as a bar.

The best witness to the privacy of bars was Maria, who for years owned her own bar in Homestead. The B & J stood on the corner of a street that by 1990 was visibly changing from white to black. The day I interviewed Maria, I saw only white faces at her establishment, though some were old, some young, some male, and some female. It was early afternoon, and the benches around her bar were occupied by an adolescent mother with a baby carriage, a boy who hung around for awhile, and an older man, resting on his way into the bar. The atmosphere was casual—a resident might say "homey." Maria and I stood outside on the corner while she watched the passers-by. She began with her life story. She moved from Hays when she married a Homestead steelworker, decided to open a bar, then (briefly) took over another; at the moment, she was contemplating retirement while someone else tended bar for her. But the B & J was unmistakably hers, and she told me proudly that she had always imposed regulations with a firm hand. "Well, it was kind of a controlled bar when I run it. Control in them days—, and I didn't wanna mix colors in them days, but I'm friends with so many across the street." The last sentence, suggesting she was friends with the blacks she would not serve, was a typical Homestead accommodation. To be a good *business* person, Maria had to exclude blacks; to be a good *person*, she had to interact with her neighbors.

Blacks never drank inside her bar, she said, but she did have business dealings with them. She sold take-out food and beer to black customers: "They really supported me with take-outs. They would come in, Thursdays and Fridays, fish and shrimp. Always gave 'em a fair price. And they'd buy their beers. You make money on take-out. You make money, you have no problem 'cause they're gone." From Maria's point of view, this was pragmatic, not discriminatory. Her tolerance was proven, she felt, by an accomplishment she boasted of: the B & J sponsored a trophy-winning basketball team in the 1960s and 1970s. The players were black. "We had beautiful uniforms, I had everything for them—not only just tops, they had their shorts and shoes and socks and towels and everything." She gave the "boys" everything except access to her bar. "But no, those boys who play basketball are interested in sports, not drinks," she said, her rationalization the only hint I got that she was not entirely comfortable with her policies. "But I took them on parties and had steak dinners for them on Sundays when the bar was closed. I took 'em, we went over to Schenley Park a lot of times, had a big steak cookout, so they were good boys. Believe me, to this day they protect me. All good boys."

Maria's interview reveals the kind of exclusion that did not strike residents I met as racism. Though she called the blacks on her team "boys," not men, Maria wholeheartedly supported their efforts. Though she did not welcome them into her bar, she did sit with them in Schenley Park, in public. Maria's actions reflected the dominant white ethos I heard expressed time and again: as long as everyone followed the rules, life went on fine. Like others I interviewed, Maria claimed an appreciation of *difference*. As we stood on the corner, she waved at and identified several black men who passed by. "See, there's one of the boys. Billy, now that's the fireman. That's—the big guy driving the car is the one that used to be my star player." A second or two later a horn honked. "Hey, how you doin' babe?" she called out, and then explained, "There's another one, see what I mean?"

Closer to Eighth Avenue, another bar owner had to finesse the rules more carefully than Maria did. A white man, Barton was in his forties and his bar was catty-corner from the mill site. Down there he could not bluntly impose rules of access, but he made his own curious accommodation to race relations in Homestead. In the early 1970s he sold half of the bar space to an African-American man. When I interviewed Barton in 1988, the place had two bars, back to back, with a common dance floor behind them. At one bar, in the middle of the afternoon, sat a scattered group of white men and women, eating and drinking. At the other bar sat mainly black men. That side of the space, I noticed, was far more mobile than the other side; men drifted in and out, seeming to spend equal time at the office of the jitney service next door.[5]

Barton explained the accommodation he had made to the "natural fact" that blacks and whites did not drink together in Homestead. A side-by-side arrangement, according to him, discriminated against no one, and he was evidently pleased that he had achieved co-ownership with a black man. Together, he told me, they maintained the proper context of sociability in the Corner Tavern, making decisions about the dance bands, the supplies, and the upkeep of the place. Somewhat self-promoting, Barton's account shows the deeply rooted distinctions in place in the post–civil rights era. His black partner was less eager to be interviewed; he chuckled about the two-bars, one-dance-floor space but did not say much about how the partnership worked out for him. It was a living, and a good living, and as a resident of Homestead he kept his counsel in front of a white interviewer.

Residents I interviewed, black or white, did not condemn compromises like the one Barton and his partner made. Side by side was sensible and, anyway, bars were like homes—the inhabitants knew what to do. This version of live-and-let-live was apparent when an individual talked about Sonnyman Jackson's Skyrocket Lounge, which, forced into existence by segregation, was described as a "star" Homestead achievement. Likewise, the Homestead Grays team, created in reaction to racism in American baseball, was described in interviews in glorious terms.

A live-and-let-live philosophy did not erase the divisions in the recreational landscape: the Grays were part of the Negro League, and the Skyrocket was in the black section of town. Happily reminisce as he might, Thomas Johnson came upon the unavoidable fact that he had been relegated to balconies all the years of his young, movie-going life. When race was the subject, there was always another side to the story of Homestead in the twentieth century.

"The town was wide open!"

Racism created a number of alternative domains in Homestead, including the red-light district below Sixth Avenue many whites and blacks referred to nostalgically. African Americans who were not as lucky or as enterprising as Sonnyman Jackson had other services to provide, and during the 1930s, semilegal and illegal businesses thrived despite a generally depressed economy. These businesses, some said, not only thrived but benefited from the support of a U.S. Steel Corporation intent on avoiding the consequences of its own racist practices.

One black man told me all about this one afternoon in a local tavern. In his eighties when I met him, Tim had come to Homestead in the 1920s. As a young adult, he had been pushed out of an impoverished Southern town to try his luck in a northern city. The ensuing story of his life in Homestead was one part teasing, one part truth, flavored with a wealth of provocative detail. Fact or fiction, his choice of scenes and of characters provided substantial insight into race relations in the town.

Tim did not say whether he had come to the steel valley hoping for a job in a mill; at any rate, he did not get one and had made his living in several other ways. He chuckled about this career, claiming that when he arrived, "the town was wide open" and "anything was possible." Despite the Depression, which he mentioned, and the racism, which he did not, an enterprising person could make a good buck. Tim described the mill neighborhood as a virtual marketplace for "under the table" goods. "Below the tracks," he said, "no matter who you were, you could get anything you wanted," and, his narrative implied, he entered the market with full enthusiasm. His primary venues were the taverns that blanketed the ward, into which he brought goods that others wanted, including, he bragged, illegal drugs and available women.

Tim recounted these achievements with a mixture of defensiveness and nostalgia that conveyed the difficulties of being black in a Mon Valley steel town. He had to respect the boundaries, inside and outside of bars, and use his wits when he could not depend upon an easy welcome. That he could not drink inside those places did not prevent him from "working" them. Gradually over the course of the interview, Tim's nostalgic portrait broke down. As a black man, he had had to deal with racism through most of his years in Homestead, and he ultimately revealed this in his narrative. He told me the broken-glass story as if it had happened to him, and it did not matter to his point whether it had or not. He recognized his opportunities were limited and that working "contraband" was a consequence of not being able to work in other places. Yet he also continued to joke about the situation, teasing me about "those ladies of the night," narcotics hidden in dry-cleaning packages, and the fame of Homestead's red-light district.

The story of Homestead's red-light district ran through most of my interviews. Like descriptions of the households and of women's work, accounts of the red-light district formed a counterpoint to an emphasis on steel, a phenomenon that struck people as being more under their control than the fortunes of steel. But for the black migrants to Homestead in the 1920s and 1930s, the district had a special importance. As one historian writes, "For a handful of the [black] recent arrivals, the expanding vice economy provided opportunities for advancement not always available . . . in the mill. Some, like Rufus 'Sonnyman' Jackson, carved out their own niches in the burgeoning vice industry of prostitution, gambling, and illegal liquor sales. Others managed houses of 'ill-repute' on Sixth Avenue."[6]

Vice was an opportunity, but older black residents I interviewed recognized it was an opportunity because other prospects were so roundly denied them. Joking made illegal economic activity seem OK, part of a lively tale, but the undercurrent was a serious comment on discrimination—the "parameters" about which Otis complained. In discussing the red-light district, Scribble, Gene, and Duke adopted the teasing, self-mocking tone Tim had also used with me, a disguise for the bitter memory of discrimination.

Scribble began: "The ward had everything. . . . We had grocery stores, we had pawn shops, state store." Duke added the crucial piece of information: "Gambling joints, gambling joints," and Gene finished tersely: "Red-light district." If not as famous as the mill, Homestead's red-light district was well known throughout western Pennsylvania, a favorite spot for anyone looking for quick winnings and easy pleasure. Scribble, Duke, and Gene did not stress the role of blacks in these illegal businesses, as Tim had. And they did not come as close as he did to noting the racism that pushed adult men out of the town's central industry. None of them speculated about the perpetuation of a stereotype that came from attributing vice—even successful vice—to the blacks of the community. But that was the gist of the stories they, and their white neighbors, told.

On the surface, accounts of black-run vice had a benign air. Reminiscing about growing up in Homestead, Thomas Johnson recalled being warned by his father not to go into "that district," but he did not refer to the racism upon which the district rested. "Oh, everything was hustle and bustle in Homestead. Now up here—," he paused, then continued, "we used to call it 'up on the hill' and 'down below the tracks.' Now, down below the tracks is where all the gambling houses, the prostitution houses—. Most people down there—well, there was whites down there, too, but the majority of people were black." Judging from what he said, Thomas did not spend much time in the ward; the world of blacks was as divided by class as the world of Homestead was divided by race.[7] Thomas was taught the "evil" of the ward by a strict father, but Thomas mainly portrayed the sites of sin as harmless. He did not comment on the success of black illegitimate activities in particular, a consequence of a discriminatory job market and segregated recreational spaces. For Thomas, like others I met, even a vice district represented better times in a town that now had virtually no "fun" to offer residents.

In the past, vice had geographical, social, ethnic, and racial boundaries. The visible parameters made it safe, and that marked the difference between disorder *then* and crime *now*. Everyone then knew the boundaries, it was said, as clearly as if they had been drawn on a map. Black-run vice dominated Sixth Avenue, and next to it, according to Homestead's pattern, was the white vice district. Selective memory and biased interpretations made black vice prominent in personal histories of Homestead, though one or two interviewees did describe the "Chicago mobsters" who frequented establishments on Third and Dixon—the location of white-run gambling and prostitution. This hints of another distinction: white vice was depicted as an isolated activity, limited either to after-hours or to those powerful enough to afford constant "leisure." By contrast, in many interviews black vice was presented either as a necessity—the only way to earn a living—or as an uncontrollable distraction from "real work."

A white woman in her seventies voiced the distinction in an anecdote about black employees of a small company. Blacks, she implied, had "real" jobs, but they risked losing them by spending time in the district: "We used to have to go down and tell them, 'Hey, you have to be out tomorrow,' or something—," meaning she had to remind black employees of their schedules. *"Those,"* she continued, evoking much with one pronoun, "you had to check on." She explained what "they" did instead of reporting to work: "You could go in the door on Sixth Avenue—and a lot of it was on Sixth, on the other side of the track. And you could come out seven doors up the other side, on the same side. They all had ways to go from one to the other, because they had brothels. And if someone was going to come after them or something, they could have got up and out the other way."

Her suggestion of a network connecting all the brothels "down there," reveals how threatening the vice district could be. Not only did vice take money away from other enterprises, it also kept black employees away from stable jobs. Here Julie provided the standard Homestead text: gambling, prostitution, and drinking were acceptable at the right time and in the right places. She also was a self-critical narrator and did not want me to think she had a negative stereotype of blacks. So she went on, telling me about a black employee she had had "in those days," the young woman who took care of Julie's sons. "And we used to have this black—," she paused, then continued, "and I finally had to tell her she had to quit. Because she was going to have a baby. Mary." In her continuing effort to show her open-mindedness, she turned to her son and asked rhetorically, "She was great, wasn't she, Frank?" He nodded, and his mother finished the anecdote: "She also brought her baby out here afterwards, didn't she, for a time? And Frank would be walking beside the buggy, and there she has her baby in the buggy, and they had the dog."

Her two stories underline the separation of blacks from "everyone else"; blacks did not fit the image of upstanding, hardworking citizen that pervaded the Mon Valley region. Julio, a white man in his sixties, reiterated the ambiguities that a then-and-now view gave to race relations. He talked about the "old" red-light district and then about the changes in the blocks surrounding his business now.

Superficially the same as other accounts I heard, Julio's narrative emphasized the responsibility of the steel corporation for the patterns of vice in the town. In the past, he said, U.S. Steel had "poured money" into "black vice," closing corporate eyes to the drunken brawls and suspicious interactions taking place outside the mill. He implied, too, that the steel corporation encouraged gambling and houses of prostitution in order to maintain the status quo. This story had another cast when Julio remarked on the present disorder, caused as well by the corporation. For in leaving the town, USX left nothing behind or, more accurately, left the town wide open for "uncontrolled vice." Mainly, it was clear, Julio worried about the rising crime rate in Homestead.

Running a small business on a block near the mill site, on which there were few other businesses, Julio expressed a sense of isolation and vulnerability. Glancing down the street at young black men pushing their chairs outside the bar, Julio let out his anger at a corporation for "ruining" a town. From his perspective, USX had played fast and loose with the work force and with the fragile interactions in a mill community. Though young black men never found jobs in the mill in great numbers, a prospering economy offered other routes, all of which were denied them now. From this perspective, in the past black vice protected rather than threatened the division of labor and of households in the town.

Mark, whose tavern was not far from Julio's shop, gave a similar history of black and white vice. "Well," he said, pointing out his window, "this all was a red-light district, all along Sixth Avenue, the whole of Sixth Avenue. From this red brick building down." As we wandered outside to stand in front of his bar, he continued the account of men dropping in on "those establishments" after work. It was bad business for white taverns like his own. "My father-in-law decided it's time to get rid of them because the men would come out of the mill gate, they would come by there, they would get propositioned on the way here. And some of the women called up and told my father-in-law, 'I don't want my husband going down to your place' for that reason. So he decided to do something about it and he did. He bought four of those buildings down there and tore them down."[8] Why "those buildings" should have been torn down and not others was obvious to Mark. "Most of 'em were black. This area here was all black. Now down on Dixon Street, they had white girls there." The real problem, Mark's narrative suggests, was that *white men* (his patrons) were being propositioned by *black girls*. The real problem was the crossing of racial boundaries. In terms of vice as of everything else, in the eyes of white Homesteaders as long as parameters were respected, things worked out. Furthermore, maintaining these boundaries seemed especially desirable to merchants, whose wary glances up and down the street revealed more than a search for customers or strolling neighbors. Julio kept his eye on the black bar patrons, whose chairs spread out over the sidewalk. Mark approached the subject of danger in 1990s Homestead more bluntly, if somewhat metaphorically. The "black-owned bars around here," he said, had to be shut down because "they were all matchboxes for the fire trucks." They were not "safe." The possibility of things blowing up once again loomed before his eyes. "You can see one of them still exists here. Bad place. As far as safety is concerned."

Bars have always been a central institution in American industrial towns, and the steel towns of the Mon Valley were no exception. In the early nineteenth century, a traveler noted that Pittsburgh had more taverns than churches, and the same could be said about Homestead for the whole of its history.[9] Making a prominent dent on the visual landscape, vying with Homestead's famous "forty-two steeples" and even more famous Works, bars were the prime symbol of nonwork life in the accounts I collected. Through the subject of bars, individuals delineated the ethnic, religious, class, and racial differences that constituted the town. In discussing the taverns, Homestead residents charted the changes in their town, juxtaposing present "crime" with past "vice." Going into a bar reminded residents that informal rules strictly regulated the terms of entry and of welcome in all domains of Homestead life. The difference was that bars stood for fun, and the rules did not have the severe consequences they had in the mill or when a newcomer bought a house.

"Especially living next door to them"

When I showed photographs at the end of an interview, visual images prompted memories of leisure, either at home or in the parks and playing fields of the town. Because the photographs were both historical and contemporary, they elicited comments about change—the loss of spaces which "in the old days" meant freedom from economic toil. The loss and nostalgia that are intrinsic to photographs suited the mood of most of my interviews; residents saw Homestead becoming a shadow of its former self. Perhaps because the photographs represented someone else's vision, individuals were franker in their discussions of divisions that were not pictured. With photographs in front of us, I heard more about the tensions of the past than I did when a person simply talked.

An eighty-year-old woman looked in amazement at the archival photographs that showed the town in the 1920s, when she had first arrived as a young bride beginning a new life. Pictures recalled the segregation she had not mentioned in the earlier part of her narrative. One photo of "below the tracks" led her to say, "I think more colored people lived down there. They were the ones who would get out and dance. They didn't have the inhibitions, maybe, that some of us who lived in a different area had."

Her reference to "a different area" emphasized the existence of residential segregation, an arrangement that persisted well past the razing of the Lower Ward, the Second World War, and federal mandates. Even if not apparent in census reports, the color of tracts was always clear to residents.[10] Through most of its history, Homestead maintained block-by-block segregation—what social scientists and social workers called a "checkerboard pattern," as if, like residents, they thought it fair. A view of the town itself might prompt the same reading as a view of photographs, which was the case when I interviewed a white shopkeeper on Eighth Avenue; we both looked out the window as he talked. He explained steel town housing to me, echoing the "it's natural to live with those with whom you feel comfortable" phrase I was to hear from others. "Over the years," he ventured, housing has "always been sort of a segregated thing. I don't know how they [segregated neighborhoods] come about, but it has been [true] in Homestead." After a pause he answered his own question: "I guess, through where people rented to them, to various groups, it was why it ended up like that." Underlining his sense that segregation just happened, he concluded: "That's *not* a thing that you get over with in thirty years. It takes hundreds."

Whatever the myth of everyone working together, outside the mill things changed. If a man shared one or two drinks with a co-worker after a turn, for the rest of his recreational evening he probably sat with those who looked, talked, and gestured the same way he did. Hine's posed portrait of five mustachioed "Slav Laborers" might be any line-up at a Slovak bar in the 1990s.[11] His photographs also show the residential segregation that lasted for a hundred years in Homestead. In one view after another, Hine portrays the residential environment, from the "better type" of housing in Munhall to the unpaved alleys around the mill. The boroughs would look much the same in front of Brodsky's camera nearly eighty years later.

After the mill neighborhood was torn down in 1941, new housing maintained old residential separations. Relocation officers in the 1940s, like real estate agents in the 1960s, made the same decisions the townspeople did, ignoring the fair-housing policies established by legislators. Housing patterns affirmed racial and ethnic distinctions that could be overlooked on the shop floor. In his description of a steel community in South Chicago in the 1970s, William Kornblum presents a similar disjunction between cooperation at work and customs at home: the "degree to which common work experiences provide the basis for primary group formation transcending communal cleavages is problematic."[12] In Homestead, communal cleavages are evident in the housing landscape through virtually all its history.[13]

Like looking at photographs, driving around town revealed how precisely residents in the 1980s knew the parameters of neighborhoods and the places where the lines had changed. Ken provided the most detailed map of the three boroughs I received. He had lived in Homestead all his life, and he guided me through the social relations as well as the geographical boundaries he had come to know like the palm of his hand. As we got into the visibly middle-class and well-kept borough of Munhall, Ken remarked, "Well, Munhall didn't have no colored people. In fact, they still don't have colored people."[14]

Alert to his "town of churches," Ken identified each church we passed, underlining the segregated quality of the three boroughs every time he did so. "This is a colored church right here. . . . A fellow went to school with me, he's a preacher." Then, after a pause, he continued, "A lot of colored people started to move into this area. A lot of white started to move out, the last ten, twelve years." As we drove further, he reminded himself, "Yeah, this is nothing but colored people. I never called them 'black' or 'Negro.' I just called them colored [as if that were the neutral term]. We always did call them—, we never called them Negroes or blacks."

African-American residents saw the same boundaries and the same signs of where to live and where not to live. The blacks I interviewed who had lived in Homestead most of their lives described it in much the way the whites did—except that for a black man or woman the rules of exclusion were narrower and more stringent than they were for a white person. Ultimately, it was clear that living in a steel town for even prosperous and stable black families was a different experience from dwelling there as a white family. As the Eastern Europeans moved up geographically and socially, blacks occupied the neighborhoods whites had abandoned. The parameters for a black could be impermeable and occasionally were violently enforced.

When I talked with Lydia and Thomas in West Homestead, they at first gave me the impression that the mixed neighborhood had no problems. Lydia took the lead, recalling her perceptions when she first came to the community in the 1950s: "First I thought it was prosperous and a real nice place to live," she said. "It's all ethnic people. And a lot of blacks and a lot of just everybody. But they all seem to get along real well, I'd say." This memory broke down as Lydia turned to her white neighbor Corinne, who was sitting in the living room with us. Suddenly Lydia remembered the coldness and suspicion that surrounded her arrival in town. "*She* was about the only one that was just a little nice," Lydia admitted, revising her initial story. "That just shows the prejudice some people have." Her husband Thomas did not want to let the tale of integration go and interrupted to soften his wife's remark: "Lot of people weren't used to blacks at that time. Especially living next door to them, you know."

But the comment jogged his memory and altered his story that the move into West Homestead had been easy. For him the experience had been one of hypocrisy and of the pretense about eating and drinking together. "Oh, he greeted me so nice when I moved over here," he said about a white neighbor. "He took me over his house, and I had a drink with him, and he treated me so good." He paused, then finished the story: "You know, he was the first one that sold out up here. When I moved in over there. I was the first black family to move on this row, you know. And he was the first one to pull out." Once started, Thomas explored his perceptions of discrimination. "But that—[mumbling] . . . how nice he was in my face and how he [claimed], 'Oh, I grew up with black people'—well, at that time, they called them colored people. Wasn't blacks then," he explained to me. Then he continued to quote the man: "'I tend bar where all these colored people would come in, and I've been knowing them so long and me and you are gonna be all right,' and all that. And three to six months later he had his house up for sale. He was moving!" Compressed into one incident, the racism of his fellow townspeople burst out, the truth of Thomas's experience in his hometown.

He recognized, too, that the truth of black experiences in a steel town had come into public view, especially after a national civil rights movement. And though Thomas did not reveal his part in civil rights protests, he did refer to one of the heroes in the local African-American community: "And I know you've heard of Melvin Good. The big network broadcaster. Well, he's about to retire now. He was one of the greatest fighters for civil rights in this area. He grew up in Homestead. . . . Started here in Homestead, and he used to make it his business to, if he seen something wrong, if he'd go in a bar and they turned him out, he'd go right down to the police. If necessary, he would get the mayor." Thomas did not talk about the changes civil rights laws made in Homestead. From the point of view of blacks as well as whites, desegregation orders did not necessarily improve the Monongahela Valley towns. Imposed from the outside, antidiscrimination orders for housing, schools, and recreational places were seen as intruding on the familiar contexts of social interaction. For some residents, civil rights legislation was another proof of the evils of government, politicians, and outsiders.

My conversation with Lydia, Thomas, and Corinne indicated that, in fact, informal practices of segregation continued in Homestead, as if the townspeople still controlled the rules for "mixing." In Munhall, as Ken told me, whites did not sell houses to blacks; up the hill, Homestead Park opened its doors to Eastern Europeans and closed them to African Americans. The nearby suburbs were almost entirely white. Overall in the steel valley, blacks and whites did not visit each other's living rooms anymore in the 1990s than they had in earlier decades.

From his vantage point, elbows on his bar, Mark told me, "I didn't notice too much discrimination until Washington started." Before that interference, he remarked, "Black families, I'll tell you, up until the sixties, they were treated just like us. We went to school together, we fought together, we played together." Older African Americans, like their white neighbors, wondered whether the federal government had done more harm than good in imposing patterns of behaviors on communities grown used to following their own norms. In the interests of peace and harmony, racism could be coded as "natural sociability"—as Thomas and Lydia tried to explain. Life's realities did intrude, and no black really shared the experiences of a white in Homestead.

Members of the younger generation talked about race relations the way their parents did. Individuals in their twenties and thirties offered me the familiar explanation: Federal legislation, they said, blew up the existing consensus. These were the individuals who had experienced school integration by being thrown into the huge melting pot of Steel Valley High.[15] In the consolidated high school, the parameters were no longer clear, and strangers could be threatening. "Growing up," one woman told me, "you know, I was never really worried about somebody hurting me. I grew up in the town and I knew a lot of people. I have white friends and black friends, 'cause after we left parochial school—." After parochial school, in the 1970s and 1980s, she confronted a different world: "At first it was kind of strange."

Like her parents' generation, she at first insisted there were no problems once a stranger became a friend. "It was like you never saw the color. I don't see it today still, you know." She also mentioned that some people in the area were "prejudiced" and objected to the integration enforced at Steel Valley High. "Well, that's when the racial fighting started, 'cause it was—." After a silence, the cause came out: "Munhall didn't want to be bothered."

The fighting in schoolyards in the 1970s was the tip of the iceberg of tension that spread through the town during that era. Another white woman in her thirties remembered the opening of Steel Valley High as a sign of "bad times" in the river towns. "There was—I don't know if I should tell you this or not," she said, laughing nervously, "There was a lot of people that lived out in Munhall all their lives who had a real hard problem sending their kids to school at Steel Valley, when there was going to be blacks from Homestead there. There became a real big racial thing there, and fortunately I was not brought up that way and from living in Homestead and knowing all the families and that, I never had any problems. I mean, there'd be girls fighting all the time, guys fighting back and forth. It was really kind of bad the first couple years until everybody got adjusted." She also returned to the notion of harmony I heard throughout my interviews. Eventually, she implied, "everybody got along" and "helped each other out." From this perspective, fighting in the schoolyard did not mean racism but was simply the way kids behaved until they got to know each other.

Another woman in her thirties, who chose to raise her children in a white neighborhood, refused to blame race for everything that had happened at Steel Valley High. She remarked that mixing a bunch of adolescents who had experienced diverse upbringings was a prescription for fighting, no matter what color they were. "Kids *always* fight," she concluded.

Yet the persistent economic and social discrimination against blacks was worsening in the decade the new high school opened. Fighting in the schoolyard was not an isolated incident but linked to a series of events that revealed the "tinder box" right below the surface of harmony. One woman reported a growing fear of blacks in the 1970s and 1980s: "I guess it was in '72 that we had a racial riot," she began. At the time, she had her own troubles. "I was pregnant that year. And my dad just made me not go to school anymore. That was it. He was done. He wasn't going to take on the responsibility of something happening to me or anything. So he was like, 'You're done.'" She was in tenth grade and, to her expressed regret, never went back to school. The story ended: "That was a bad year. That was when all the blacks and the whites were just like, I don't know, it was like, *integrating*. I don't know what was happening, but it was a real bad year." She used *integrating* as if it were a bad word.

"I went to eighth grade with no blacks," a woman told me, adding that ninth and tenth were "the same way." But like everyone else her age, she spent her last years of high school at Steel Valley. "We were the first kids at Steel Valley. It was all black and white going there." There were fights, she admitted. "*They* [probably the media] called it racial, but it wasn't. It was just ordinary anger and irritation. They said it was race, but race had nothing to do with it." She also did not pretend that everything flowed smoothly; having rarely been in the same place with a black person before, she had to learn to cope: "It was hard for us because we weren't used to them. They had different kind of hair. They can't wash their hair as much as we do. They had all those tight curls. We thought it was dirty." Then she repeated, "there was fighting, but it wasn't racial." For her, as for her parents' generation, the past was better than the present. When she came to talk about a 1990s Homestead, she admitted she sent her children to the all-white elementary school near Hunky Hollow, and that she would never let them go to Homestead schools. "The Homestead schools suck. That's all there is to it."

She came as close as anyone I interviewed to blaming blacks for the alarming state of the Homestead schools. In her view, the blacks at Homestead "ruined" her sister's kids. Her nieces and nephews, she said, had a "bad attitude." "My sister's kids could give a shit about school. The attitude up there is different," and, she added, there was a "stigma" attached to that "lice-infested school." A "stigma," she repeated, to impress upon me the full import of being "at Homestead." She tried to help out by taking her sister's kids in. After school, "my sister sends her kids down here. Down here is a totally different world. Up there [in Homestead], they talk like blacks; down here, they're normal."

With the closing of the mill and the decline in the town, the word *mixing* increasingly referred to the breakdown of racial divisions, no longer to the problems of "mixed" religious marriages. Racial mixing was not normal; fights erupted and children talked "shit." With the decline, once-disguised racism in employment, education, and housing was unmasked, no longer contained by a "flow of money." Live-and-let-live faded as a philosophy for life, and "below the tracks" took on a complex meaning. Observing the town now, individuals revised the story of the past. If they were white, they emphasized the harmony *then*, and if they were black they also recalled the moments of discrimination that had always provided a discordant note.

Block by block, checkerboard housing arrangements collapsed when house prices plummeted and rents hit rock bottom; a new group of residents arrived. The differences among schools grew as the population changed. The town lacked funds for educational improvements or for repairing run-down school buildings. It was easier to close and consolidate, crowding kids together. Passivity plagued the school board, which lost the ability and perhaps the will to hire teachers to match the racial diversity of the student body. Hiring black teachers had proceeded slowly in Allegheny County,[16] and in the steel valley after 1980 it crawled to a stop.

I heard a bit of this history from an older black resident, who, despite wanting to paint his town in the best light, realized how unjust schooling in Homestead had been to black children. He began nostalgically: "Like I say, the teachers were all fair. There wasn't any prejudice, so to speak, in the school system as far as the students were concerned." But his conclusion was another matter: "Now, as far as teachers—, you didn't see any black teachers back in that time, not in Homestead." Today, someone else told me, virtually all the teachers are white, "which was a real shame for the black kids."

The notion that race relations, like ethnic and religious differences, were a matter of individual accommodation hung on for a long time. The image of harmony marked Homestead chauvinism, a characteristic that stood apart from its fame as a town of steel. When steel left the town, interactions and institutions collapsed as well, and the customs and conventions portrayed in terms of "below the tracks" came under threat. The sentiments expressed as "we all got along" and endured together the swings of industry fortune were hard memories to cling to in the face of a vanishing economic and social structure.

RESPONSES IN THE VALLEY

9

The Aftermath
of the Closing

The story of that morning, as it is retold among the people of Homestead, suggests vividly the ride of Paul Revere to rouse other insurgents more than a century earlier. Men and women hurried to the mill, weapons were hunted up and barricades erected. . . . In the meantime the life of the town went on, changed but little by the industrial conflict. The local papers tell of weddings, of picnics, of church suppers and of the casual comings and going of the townspeople, while in the mill below was being contested, though in a waiting game, the issue which was to determine in many respects the future of the village.

—Margaret Byington, *Homestead: The Households of a Mill Town*

In Margaret Byington's description of the 1892 strike, the most famous incident in Homestead history, she remarked on the solidarity of the townspeople, rushing to the riverbank in support of their workers, and also on their determination to maintain the ordinary rhythms of life at home. A century later the people of Homestead faced a crisis of equivalent proportions in an apparently opposite fashion. Very few rushed to the barricades, figuratively or literally, after USX finally shut down the Homestead Works. At the same time, rather than preserving its familiar rhythms, daily life began to crumble around the edges. Over the six years of our visits to the town, these facts of life became increasingly prominent in people's accounts of the closing and in our perceptions of the place.

With militant strikes behind them, why a century later did the majority of residents seem to retreat from battle with the forces destroying their lives? Initially, in the early 1980s, there had been organized protests, the details of which were vividly shown on local and national news programs. But over the course of the decade, pictures of women and men marching in front of Mellon Bank to protest lending rates, or in front of a church to defend an activist minister, vanished from TV and from newspapers. By 1990, such images were no longer presented to those who lived in the steel valley or to outside observers who had occasion to think again about the Great Homestead Strike. As the twentieth century drew to a close, residents of Mon Valley towns seemed to grow tired of protests and to turn instead to the domestic concerns of their towns and households. Were the battles over, the town resigned?

The first symptoms of the closing were the pink layoff slips, scattered like confetti through the mill town. Such slips were familiar, not usually warning of a tragedy to come. Gradually, further signs of disaster appeared: the closing of one shop after another, the stationing of guards at mill gates to keep observers out, and the desolation that spread over empty hulks of buildings no longer occupied by a work force. Signs appeared in nonmill areas as well. Hand painted on cardboard, For Rent signs showed up in apartment windows and For Lease in store windows on Eighth Avenue. The gates of the great Homestead Works did not so much slam shut as squeak to a sad and definite close over the course of five years.

At first no one quite believed it. How could one of the most famous industrial plants in the United States simply stop running? Beyond the reference to Homestead history, workers also noted the secrecy with which management made its decisions. Like other industrial workers in the United States, Mon Valley steelworkers had not been warned of the permanency of the closing. News came slowly and ambiguously. Individuals harbored the hope that the corporation would bend, would change its route, would reopen the plant. Steelworkers, their wives, priests, and friends looked at the enormous structure along the riverbank and concluded that no company "in its right mind" was going to sell it for scrap.

Then the wreckers came. The new decade, the last in the twentieth century, opened with a scene of hard hats, cranes, jackhammers, and crews lined up with their lunch boxes. These workers, with their familiar paraphernalia, worked for the Park Corporation, and they had been hired to demolish the Homestead Works. Residents observed, listened to, and smelled the signs of destruction. Incredible as it was, the huge plant was going down, piece by piece, right in front of the eyes of any person who cared to look. Driving over the High-Level Bridge into Homestead, in

"Come on You Guys—Palmer Ain't Gonna Wait" (R. Wurtz collection)

fact, a person *had* to look; off to the left, mill structures fell slowly and relentlessly, until by 1994 the space was virtually empty.

My interviews show the slow evolution of the town's response to the greatest crisis it ever faced, despite a century-old history of layoffs, strikes, wars, migrations, and floods. The town was undergoing a transformation that was economic, demographic, cultural, and social, and individuals reconstructed history around that fact. Residents had albums that documented the past. Views from their windows pictured the present, but visions of the future were hard to come by. Brodsky's photographs of backyards, children on bicycles, a quiet street evoked the stories of "below the tracks" that were an important aspect of the town's self-commemoration while seeming discordant with the landscape of the 1990s. But they were not really discordant, for it was as householders that Homesteaders now lived their lives, beyond the shadow of the mill entirely. The empty lot dominated the scene and the oppressive brown field was enough to daunt even the most committed activist and urban planner. But few had marshaled to protest the USX decision or the entry of the Park Corporation or anything that pushed Homestead away from a running mill to a "steel heritage."

"Pretty soon there's not going to be anything there, and it's just going to be land." The remark was made in 1991 by a woman whose back windows opened onto the mill site. Whatever role the mill had played in her, or anyone's life, that was the bottom line: just land where a large industrial plant had been. Every day, she said, she watched the men come in and tear down the smokestacks, furnaces, and buildings that had become part of the scenery for her. "'Cause it's really empty," she added. "You know, and everyday I look out this window, and I'm like, 'I should be taking pictures myself.'"

"It all happened too fast"

Brodsky's style of stark documentation gave the demolition the tragic tone it deserved. Her photographs did not, however, change the interpretations townspeople had of what happened to them. There were elements in common in these interpretations, just as there were in reminiscences of the good old days. Individuals talked of the "total shock" and of the lack of warning from and betrayal by USX. They also revealed their deep anger at the country for which they had produced tons of steel, enlisted in the army, and marched on the Fourth of July. The loyalty and patriotism of a town "was nothing" in the eyes of a steel company, the federal government, and the Japanese, "who flooded the market with cheap steel."

Residents claimed they were "stunned." The story was that warnings were inadequate, ambiguous, and unclear. Why was that the story in Homestead, when steel plants were closing all over the country?[1] In part it was an ordinary human response: what happened to *them* will not happen to *us*. And in part it was a defensive version of events, a justification for failure to react to the warnings that did come. Together, individuals in the steel town operated with a collective viewpoint that on the one hand allowed life to go on and on the other explained the numbness when the closing appeared to be final. In retrospect, townspeople seemed both to know and not to know what lay in store for them.

Residents' interpretations reflected a reality: USX did *not* reveal management decisions in advance to workers in the Mon Valley. "In particular, 'shutdowns and cutbacks are not negotiated. They are always announced.'"[2] Until the Park Corporation arrived, Homesteaders harbored a hope that USX would reconsider the "death" of the mill. "It's just so unbelievable that I can't believe it," said a thirty-five-year-old woman who had been employed in the mill for nearly ten years. Almost as if feeling the shock again, she several times repeated "how incredible" it was that the Homestead Works had stopped running. Looking back five years, she recalled that nothing had prepared her for the final move, not even her knowledge of "the imports" that, as she put it, were "destroying" the American steel industry. She had observed, she told me in 1991, her fellow workers being sent home week after week, but even this did not seem dire; pink slips were familiar in a steel town that had weathered ups and downs for generations. It was not unusual, either, to regard these periods positively, a time of rest and relaxation after the grueling demands of work in the mill. This woman remembered being happy to spend more hours a day with her children.

"The initial time of unemployment is often viewed as a time of relaxation," concluded an analyst of a mill shutdown in Shenango, forty miles north of Pittsburgh.[3] The initial response filled individuals in Homestead with bitterness when they repeated it to me; they felt foolish on top of their fury at a company that told them so little. Given the history of Homestead, layoffs were not a sufficient warning of a shutdown, and a corporate defense of actions on that basis did not fly in the steel towns of western Pennsylvania. A number of people in Homestead claimed the purchase of Marathon Oil, like the failure of USX to improve equipment in the Homestead Works, served as a smoke screen rather than an indication of disaster to the workers.

In addition, Homesteaders had learned how to cope. Generations of parents and grandparents had managed through crises in the industry, stretching the budget and waiting out the emergency. Taking pride in home-grown strategies of survival, residents of Homestead looked away from international developments in the steel industry and toward their own kitchens and parlors. Every boy had learned to find a job through fathers and uncles, and every girl had learned how to stretch a pot of soup: the upbringing of Homestead children was sorely tested by transformations in a world economy. "Expenditures in many households were cut to the quick, money that had been saved was taken from the bank, and food was purchased on credit."[4] Thus Byington described Homestead's response to crisis in the first years of the twentieth century. The same methods were used eighty years later and with the same sense of pride. Randy, for instance, told me, "Things that we once fixed just lay broken." Concentrating on coping, individuals did not have time to lay blame or to take a stand against a corporation that seemed an abstract enemy.

Moreover, until the mill buildings were demolished, some residents continued to hope industry would start up again. Peter, the carpenter I interviewed on three different occasions, went through several phases, from hoping USX would change its policy to bitterness at the closing down of steel all over the valley. Early in the disaster he had gotten a job at the Clairton Coke Plant eight miles from Homestead. But that soon stopped too. During our first interview in 1987, the heavy Homestead Works was still visible from Peter's front steps. Peter looked at the massive structure and asked me rhetorically: Why would the corporation destroy the plant that represents American industrial triumph? Homestead, he said, "was too big to close," and "big" meant reputation as well as size.

Other residents shared the view: the biggest and most famous steel plant in the world simply could not close. History argued for its reopening—a site too significant to vanish. The wife of a retired steelworker compared the Homestead Works to the telephone company, which would never disappear from the American landscape. "I mean, U.S. Steel being the corporation it was," she said, "I really found it overwhelming. It was overwhelming but downright scary the way—you know, it was like Bell Telephone." Taking steel away from Homestead was like ripping up Bell phone lines across the United States. In the perception of Homestead residents, if Bell was equivalent to phone service, USX was equivalent to steel production. It was impossible to think of such companies closing.

"Shock at the news was commonly accompanied by disbelief. Numerous workers reported that they simply had not accepted the company announcement. Among some displaced workers, such denial persisted for years; there were a few persons who, at the time of the interview, continued to insist that the companies would eventually 'come to their senses' and reopen the plants and rehire their former employees."[5] The situation described for Shenango was repeated in Homestead—and, of course, not only there. "Like the mills, when they closed down, everybody was shocked," a woman in Homestead told me. "They couldn't believe it. Nobody ever thought something like this would happen. They thought they had a job for the rest of their life." She repeated: "It was always here, such a big company, how could they do a thing like that?"

"Yeah, I think there has to be older fellows around here still walk around in disbelief as to what happened," I heard from a businessman on Eighth Avenue in the fall of 1987. "I still don't think they believe it can happen, the idea—," and he lapsed, perhaps recalling his own experience of shock. "Nothing could be big enough to cause that to close, they would think." Men and women said the same thing to labor reporter William Serrin: "Rumors had gone around for years that the mill would close, but few people believed them: that is, few had believed the entire mill the

"To Hell with Spare Parts—I Want Spare Time"
(R. Wurtz collection)

vast Homestead Works, such a storied and famous place—would close. Who would have thought that?"[6] But the corporation *was* big enough to close even the vast Homestead Works. The term *shock* underlined the impact of the event and did not mean that residents had had no foreboding before.

"Then it was layoff and call-back"

In my interviews, it became clear that residents had intimations of disaster well before 1986. When I was shown the new pollution control equipment, for instance, my guide would explain it as something "foisted" on USX by the government, nothing management "wanted to do." In this view, USX had long before stopped modernizing the mills and given up on American steel. "Throughout the last decade [1970s], many of the nation's leading steel companies used the profits from their existing operations—profits enhanced by the savings derived from not investing in new, modern equipment for existing mills—to acquire non-steel businesses."[7] People I interviewed had seen that development and understood its implications, up to a point. One retired steelworker remembered, "We knew something was happening because they weren't buying new parts. They were repairing all of them." Under prodding, George repeated this hindsight: "All they were doing was repairing them [parts] or welding them. We had a welder there welding a line shaft. We knew something was up. They were saving money. How come they weren't buying new parts? They didn't buy new parts unless they had to."

His wife Marie had a different version of the company's allocation of funds: "I always thought that instead of taking all this money, because a lot of people couldn't afford a vacation—," apparently referring to paid vacation time, "they should have modernized the mills." In Marie's view, instead of paying workers for vacations they did not want, the corporation should have paid for equipment the mills needed. It amounted to the same thing: USX was "disinvesting" in the mills by ignoring the degeneration of machinery and by neglecting the real needs of a working community.

Yet men and women continued to apply for jobs in the mills that were still open. George and Marie's son applied for positions in plants along the Mon River, from Homestead to Clairton and back. He, like his parents and grandparents, was used to an intermittent schedule and initially refused to read doom in the layoffs. Marie described the pattern: "He worked there for about four years, but it wasn't steady. I think steady was about two years. Then it was layoff and call-back."

Homesteaders were not unique in this response. As long as some steel production existed, generations of workers continued to walk "down there" for jobs. "Many of the workers interviewed," write two social scientists in their study of the 1980 Youngstown shutdown, "expressed shock and disbelief at the actual shutdown announcement: How could the steel mills, which had provided their livelihood for so many years, simply pack up and leave the area?"[8] Steelworkers went on working temporarily and hoping for permanence until fate hit unmistakably with the arrival of demolition crews. By that time it was too late to prepare another course of action. Stunned, steelworkers in Youngstown, Shenango, Homestead, and other mill towns reeled under the blow.

From his store on the hill, Sam gave his opinion. His neighbors, he said, had experienced slowdowns all their lives; on the other hand, he added, the situation in the 1980s was different from what it had been anytime before: "My neighbors saw the writing on the wall." But, he added in the next breath, "no one would have guessed what was happening." The contradictions came out of the uncertainty that surrounded the event itself and also from doubts about where to place blame. An ex-steelworker in Buffalo, New York, described it poignantly in conversation with Michael Frisch: "Well, it slowed down awful quick, you know. It just seemed like one day there was no more overtime. Then, about two years, there wasn't no more work."[9]

"They want to forget Homestead altogether"

Did steelworkers and townspeople blame the corporation for events of the decade between 1975 and 1985? Not explicitly. Constant references to shock and disbelief replaced cause-and-effect explanations, so that the closing seemed like a natural disaster. Most of the people I interviewed in Homestead stepped gingerly around the issue of blame. Even when they criticized USX for not modernizing the plant or for pacifying workers by granting long vacations, Homesteaders were reluctant to call the company a villain. A habit of putting up with distant decisions made by bosses died hard. And the residents whose history included a famous American labor walkout did not blame the demanding steelworkers union for the downfall of steel in the valley.

The nearest attribution of blame appeared in statements accusing the company of not warning workers of what was coming. "Like I said," a woman who worked at the mill after high school complained, "they just kept giving me the update, as I was home with my daughter—'four people got let go today.' When I came back, there was hardly anyone." But that was it, according to her—nothing more explicit. The company, in other words, mystified its employees and their families. Two, five, and nearly ten years after the closing, individuals in Homestead claimed that had they been better informed, they would have responded better to the disaster. This may or may not be true. There are few test cases in the United States, since most companies do not warn their workers far enough in advance to make retraining a possibility. "People have no chance to prepare for the deindustrialization process or to obtain the training and skills necessary to be reabsorbed successfully into the dynamic sectors of the economy."[10]

The wife of an ex-steelworker explained the situation to me when I interviewed her in 1987: "Several years ago, little by little, men were getting laid off. But they [management] didn't say they were laid off for good, they didn't say . . . , [which left] workers thinking that they're gonna be called back. Where the company had different things on their mind. And the workers, they were sort of like leaving, [thinking] they're gonna be called back. Until they seen what was happening. Little by little, one department after another, slowly they're laying men off." She unfolded a tale of betrayal and deception. "And it kept on going that way until the point where one department was shut down 'cause they didn't have orders. Some of the workers from that department, they would be transferred to other departments, if there's an opening. As it went along, little by little, the departments were dying out. Till it came to the end."

Behind her cautious explanation lay a picture of the pitfalls a worker was bound to encounter when decisions appeared "little by little." At the end she did come out and blame the company for imposing yet another burden on workers who had suffered years of oppression in the mill; insufficiently prepared, these men and women had no options. "Each of the workers," she continued, "men [who had] worked there for years, they see what happened, how they were treated. They [workers] called 'em [managers] a bunch of crooks. Liars." She concluded with one of the frankest accusations of the company I was to hear: "The company was for the company. They didn't treat the workers like human beings. They were nothing, they were just like a piece of machinery."

Few of the ex-steelworkers I met were as forthright as she. Older, more skilled, and white workers were especially careful about what they said. A craneman in his late sixties ready to live on a pension, even if smaller than he had expected, an open hearth worker looking forward to being with his grandchildren, a man in his fifties whose wife had a job—these men were not loud in their condemnation of a corporation that had given them nearly a lifetime's livelihood as well as a sense of dignity and manliness. Such men stepped agilely around who was to blame, at least when they spoke to me in interviews or casual conversation. They tended to portray the mill as if it were a stern parent, correcting the behavior of (occasionally) rebellious children—children who went on strikes, organized unions, protested working conditions.

Occasionally, however, even a committed steelworker admitted his resentment at the actions USX took. The sight of the huge space, once the site of American industrial strength, led to angry remarks. So, for example, Ken used his bitterest tone when he drove me past the skeleton mill on Fourth Avenue. "I can't figure all this equipment they have down there. They just put a new filtering plant at the—, along the river. I heard anywhere from twenty to thirty million dollars it cost them. They only operated it for five years." To make sure I understood, he drove me to where I could see the now-useless improvement myself. "I'll show it to you from up on the hill there."

As we stared down at the concrete yellow filtering plant standing out against the tree-lined riverbank, he continued his complaints: "There's millions and millions of dollars in the mill. I can't see them letting it go to waste like that." Taking up his point, I asked why he thought they had closed the Homestead Works even with all the "millions" in it. He answered without pause: "I think they're trying to forget the strike of 1892. That comes up all the time, and I think they were trying to get Homestead out of the way." He assured me: "That's my theory. I think U.S. Steel wants to forget Homestead altogether because of that 1892 strike and these other strikes." Among "these other strikes" was the strenuous one of 1959 in which he had actively participated. The long months out of work were an important part of his biography: "That was the long strike. That was 116 days. . . . So it was rough then. I know. I just got married—oh, no, I was married, I was married in 1949, but I just bought a home then, that's when it was rough. I had three youngsters, and I tried to support them on a 116-days break with nothing coming in. So that was pretty tough."

The account of his own endurance and difficulties distracted Ken from developing an argument about the downfall of steel. I was uncertain whether he thought strikes were justified and U.S. Steel irrational in its responses or whether he had some ambivalence about the "troubles" caused by workers like himself who could stand to be out on picket lines for months at a time. He did return several times to his "theory" that USX closed the mill because of 1892, suggesting the famed protest was the root cause of the punitive measures that followed throughout the history of steel in Homestead. "In fact, just before I left, it was one turn, we used to be putting out fourteen hundred tons of steel in eight hours—in eight hours! I just can't believe that they shut it. That's my opinion: they want to forget Homestead altogether. That strike of 1892 lingers in their minds, and I think they're trying to wipe it off the map."

Ken was a loyal union man. In referring to 1892, he was not condemning workers for protesting against oppressive work conditions; he had done the same himself. Rather, he was glorifying those workers who had marched out, enduring the pain of no wages and no security. He held 1892 up as an explanation for USX actions a century later, in the process redeeming his neighbors in the eyes of history. Protests against rampant injustice did not form the story in the early 1990s, and the centennial did not send workers to the streets. But the solidarity of a hundred years ago, according to Ken, permanently dented USX relationships with Homestead.

Ken did blame new workers, those who were selfish and interested only in gain. Like other men of his generation, he accused younger workers of taking advantage of the privileges the union had struggled to win. He described "young guys" sitting around, counting the hours until they

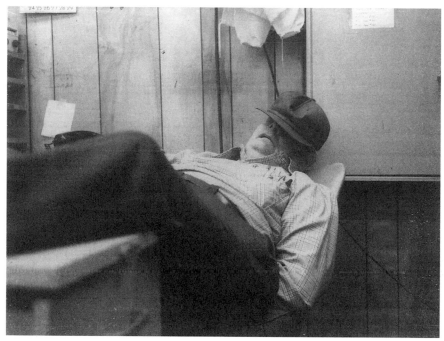

"I Never Had It So Good" (R. Wurtz collection)

could leave and "never doing an extra lick of work." This kind of laziness and greed, he went on, led USX to close the Homestead Works. Whatever its merits, the explanation let USX off the hook.[11]

To say young workers were "spoiled" by promised benefits also let the town off the hook—forgiven for not defending workers who might just have asked for their fate. Dividing the work force, like dividing a community by standards of behavior, was not conducive to collective action. Even workers who had enjoyed the generosity of the company wondered later whether excessive benefits had caused the crisis. George, a steelworker in his sixties, considered this possibility in his interview. He began by attributing the explanation to his wife: "She always thought the thirteen weeks—," and his wife finished: "I always thought the thirteen weeks was the pits. You know why? Like they used to ride [tease] each other a lot. If he wasn't going anywhere on vacation, they would put up signs and everything saying, 'George is going to Porchville. He's staying at home.'" George revealed his own puritanical response to the luxury he had been granted: "We never took our thirteen weeks. Some fellas did. We'd take ten. Then you were allowed to work three. Then you'd get paid double." The union had won the possibility of thirteen weeks off, but workers like George, and his wife Marie, argued that a sure pension would have been a better reward for hours spent in the mill.

Men and women in a younger generation were more forthright in their complaints about USX. Unlike older workers, they had been laid off before their pension plans matured, and they got little beyond unemployment compensation from the company. Vigorous and usually with children to support, these men and women did not appreciate early retirement or a chance to relax all week long. In conversations with me, they treated USX like a villain: the company had milked them dry and then abruptly pulled the plug on the whole operation. "You have people down there dedicated. Like I say, you had [workers with] anywhere from thirty- to forty-five-year . . . service. How many industries are you going to have people with that kind of service?"—only, this man implied, to be kicked out.

On the other hand, individuals in the younger generation tended to leave union gains out of the interview. They did not, as some older workers did, blame the union for "conspiring" with the company, or demanding more benefits than the company could afford, or allowing work hours to go down. They reaped the benefit of such demands, and if they had learned (as they almost certainly had) the stories of one hot turn after another, they appreciated the fact that that had not been their experience in the mill. Nor were these individuals as emotionally bound up with the union as their fathers and, in several instances, grandfathers had been. The United Steel Workers of America (USW) was in place when they entered the mill gates, and it was a strong and well-organized association. Gains had been made, and protests against the company did not have the drama that once surrounded strikes and walkouts. The influence of 1892 on a steelworker's self-image was fading.

"All steel workers—we're wrote off"

Townspeople blamed the "government," a word that blurred all administrative units. Bureaucrats and politicians were evil. One young ex-steelworker was especially outspoken on the issue. He began mildly: "I hope that towns that start up out in the Midwest and Colorado . . . , they should get two, three major businesses. If one fails, you still have two," he said, with practical economics in mind. But as he continued, the story changed its tune: "That way you have a chance of making it. This way you got nothing. There's a lot of people hurting. And Reagan, there's another story. I refer to him and his wife as Mr. and Mrs. Asshole of America. I don't like the guy. I don't like his policies. He surrounds himself by millionaires. He's a millionaire." Providing as close to a class analysis as anything I had heard, Dan went on: "And so you think like a millionaire. He wrote us off. All steelworkers, the farmers, we're all wrote off."

Bitterness like his burst out in others in the years that followed the Mon Valley closings. Townspeople who prided themselves on loyalty to a country, who knew their steel had won wars, and who constructed monuments to American history, resented the fact that they had been "X'ed" out. But loyalty died hard, and one president's policies did not spur rebellion in towns that had gloried in the recognition accorded by earlier presidents. Unlike auto workers, steelworkers refrained from hanging politicians and bosses in effigy.

"Government officials have cast their lot, workers believe, not with the people who elected them, but with the big business leaders who pay them off," Kathryn Dudley writes about the auto workers. "And if the interests of multinational firms and the American government have become inseparable, then who is representing the will of the people?"[12] That is what Dan said to me, but neither he nor anyone else succeeded in organizing townspeople beyond sporadic protests against bank foreclosures or at a Reagan appearance. Nor, apparently, did Dan convince many of his neighbors to attend city council meetings with him.

When I interviewed the mayor of Munhall, he clearly was aware of the perceptions of some of his constituency that the borough was "doing nothing."[13] At the same time, he told me his hands were tied. Like his neighbors, he blamed people in power—in his case, a state and a federal government that failed to give support to distressed industrial communities. He also returned to the theme I had heard often: if only USX had warned the towns in advance, the closing would not have been so devastating. "But as far as the steel mills closing themselves, it's very unfortunate," he told me. "I'm kind of disappointed that it had to occur in the way it occurred. Obviously, they had a cost factor which they brought in consideration . . . , but personally I felt maybe it could have been done in different stages rather than just one big shutdown." Like virtually everyone else I interviewed, he did not regard the pink slips and department cutbacks as sufficient warning of a permanent closing. Given all this, the lack of protest was understandable; shock, he intimated, threw people into passivity and inaction.[14] "As far as people, no doubt it was a crushing blow to the community and also to the borough, the Munhall borough and the other surrounding boroughs. Very much so."

Not only had there been no warning of the final event, he continued, but there had been no effort on the part of the corporation or the federal government to lay the groundwork for new economic institutions in Mon River mill towns. That this experience was not unique to steel towns did not make it less painful; industry pull-outs of the 1970s and 1980s occurred without consideration for the communities left behind, leaving depressed populations in all regions of the country.[15] A team of labor economists stated the case forcefully a decade earlier in a study of displaced miners: "There are very few 'good corporate citizens' willing to voluntarily go the extra mile on behalf of their displaced workers and the impacted community once the decision to shut down has been made."[16] In the years following a closing, as the mayor of Munhall noted, unprepared workers had an increasingly difficult struggle to regain anything like their former circumstances. "But now the time's come—it's a period of time where everybody's benefits are down the tubes, more or less, and people are really desperate," he said. "And, you know, they can't live on a job making $3.50 an hour. It's just impossible now. There's too many people with families, and they have to work a couple of jobs in order to survive." He concluded tersely: "It's just the mill itself closing must have played hell with a lot of people."

Sympathetic as he was as a neighbor, the mayor was voicing the politician's view: the impossible task he faced of having to revive a town where there was no tax base and precious little help from the outside. "We need the income that the mills produced, and we need, naturally, the wage taxes and everything else." For ex-steelworkers, however, beyond the difficulty of living on $3.50 an hour, there was the symbolism attached to taking a minimum wage job. The personal meaning of being in hell belonged to the laid-off steelworkers and their families.

"Without the mill, I have no life"

Peter gave vivid expression to the "hell" an unemployed worker faced. For him, the days stretched ahead, empty hours despite his involvement with two young children. In the mill, he recalled, "I always did the same thing. Was regimated. I get up, I work Monday through Friday daylight, with weekends and holidays off. That's what I did." This was not a bad life, especially when a man looked back on it from empty hours. "And then all of a sudden, bingo, I didn't do this anymore, and now what do you do? Well, you know every day can't be Saturday. A lot of times I sit here, and I try to figure out what the heck I should be doing. I should be doing something here but I'm not. 'Cause I'm an achiever." A man, he said, felt better simply being *at work*. "And I don't want to be the president, but I wouldn't mind cleaning his office, you know what I mean? Long as they'd pay me, I'd go do it."

Work at home and without a paycheck did not count in this equation. Work at home also did not provide the companions and stimulation Peter had known in his years in the mill. He grew up on heady stories of risk, danger, "hardness," and a certain definition of maleness. Like others, he lost more than a job when the mill shut down. As if to ward off the devils that come with a collapsed self-image, he kept himself busy. He refused to let himself follow the route downhill reported in social scientific studies of unemployment.

Peter told me about men in Homestead who sat around all day, a visible reminder of what he did not want to become. He described fellows he knew who were lazy, fat, soft, and solitary and, just as Homestead refused the horrible image of Braddock, so Peter refused this image for himself. He offered worse scenarios: "There's been a few people that have committed suicide over it, that have taken the bridge. Or if you call hitting the bottle, where you actually, you die of cirrhosis of the liver, but it's suicide, it's a form of suicide." Bluestone and Harrison report, "It is likely that permanent layoffs cause even more 'social trauma' than unemployment arising from other causes. For example, in the aftermath of the Federal Mogul Corporation closing of its roller-bearing plant in Detroit, eight of the nearly 2,000 affected workers took their own lives."[17] Peter had a prescription against that, at least for the time being: "If you sit here long enough and you don't have nothing to do, you'll get into something. Whether you chase it away at a beer garden or if you volunteer to help Boy Scouts, you have got to do something." He paused, then added: "Yeah, I have an application in just about everywhere." He also insisted he was "never gonna" take a job at minimum wage. Stubborn and proud, child of a mill family, Peter did not want to relinquish everything he knew—not until the only other choice was "hitting the bottle."

"Without the mill, I have no life." It is not surprising that observers and social analysts translate the statements men like Peter make—men in their thirties, too young to retire and too old to retool—into the language of despair. "Persons still unemployed several months after their job loss may experience insecurity and self-doubt, depression, feelings of inadequacy, mood swings, and marital or interpersonal problems," Zippay writes about the Shenango shutdown. "This may be followed by the onset of malaise and an increase in listlessness and resignation."[18] As he talked, Peter emphasized his efforts to be the exception to the rule Zippay and others found in one deindustrializing area after another: "I'm one of the lucky guys, my wife sticks with me. Money didn't make a big difference in our relationship. Whether we have it or not, we love each other. But a lot of my friends, they—whoosh. They broke, it broke—."

Around him, in his town, families were breaking up, men and women turning to drink and drugs, and a few "taking the bridge." In this respect, Homestead was no different from hundreds of towns in the United States. "The costs of disinvestment go well beyond lost wages and foregone productivity," Bluestone and Harrison write. "Workers and their families suffer serious physical and emotional health problems when their employers suddenly shut down operations."[19] I met individuals who had not survived as well as Peter had, and they talked about that to me.

In the car wash where they worked, Randy and Bobby compared the havoc wreaked in their lives by the closing of the Homestead Works. Each had gone "way downhill" for a while. Bobby, who had been in the prestigious position of craneman, admitted that when the gates closed he took to the bars. "My wife ran out on me," he said, "because I was spending more time on bar stools than at home." The black man, Randy, also had a tale of personal collapse. "My marriage collapsed because of finances," he told me, clarifying, "*lack* of finances." Equally knocked off their feet, the two men were now equals in a way they had not been in the mill; grabbing the hoses and cloths to clean yet another car, the difference in race seemed to make no difference at all. And there were no bosses or foremen to impose crew distinctions. Bobby and Randy experienced the humiliation equally, as well as the loss of income that the move from a steel mill to a car wash brought to their lives. Yet they were better off than many—especially many blacks—who had no jobs at all.

Over sixty years ago, three sociologists described the psychological malaise that spreads through a town with the disappearance of jobs. Written during the Great Depression, *Marienthal: The Sociography of an Unemployed Community* stands out in its evocation of the hopelessness and despair that shadow every life in such a community. "But the future, even in the shape of plans, has no longer any place in the thought or even dreams of these families."[20] Sam, who had never worked in the mill, told me sadly one afternoon: "Everything I've got is going down." Mon Valley communities, too, received scholarly eulogies as their mills went down and rates of divorce, bankruptcy, alcoholism, and suicide went up. John Hoerr's *And the Wolf Finally Came*, a detailed description of the downfall along the Monongahela, conveys a bleak and deathlike region. Mill towns, Hoerr writes, "are condemned to wither and fade," adding, "one cannot help but wonder about a social and economic system that sentences the thousands of people who are left—who cannot move—to lives of despair."[21] The devastation was terrible, in ways that statistics and graphs cannot capture. In deindustrializing communities, "suicide rates are double the national average, while crime rates, divorce, wife and child abuse, and the use of drugs and alcohol all mount,"[22] and these numbers reflect the experience of particular individuals. None of this was missing from Homestead, and residents saw proof of the statistics on Eighth Avenue, in local parks, and on a next-door neighbor's porch.

William Serrin links the present malaise in Homestead to a past pattern of resignation. "Even today, the Homestead workers—ex-workers now—and the townspeople have about them the atmosphere of defeat; time after time they are put upon, but they never seem surprised."[23] For the residents I interviewed, apathy and despair did not represent Homestead's history but were a brand-new development. "If this would have happened a hundred years ago," Peter commented, referring to the 1892 strike, "we would have had our guns out. They wouldn't have gotten away with it." Referring to his own generation, he noted, "Most of the guys in the steel mill, they are deer hunters. They have two or three rifles. A lot of them are national guard." A century ago, he concluded, "there would have been a revolution if they had tried to pull the mills from this valley."

His remarks were at once a reminder to himself about why he ought not to despair and a reminder to me that Homestead had once been a different town from the one I now saw. Peter's comments also took him back to the earlier years of shutdowns, when some men and women did take to the streets, if not with rifles at least with anger, aggression, and assertions of their claims against the corporation.

"The soup kitchen just keeps going"

On the corner of Eighth and Amity, the Rainbow Kitchen underwent a noticeable transformation in the years I spent in Homestead. Initially a banner of hope, its bright rainbow painted boldly across an outside wall evoked the proverbial pot of gold, the light after a storm, and the political party created by Jesse Jackson. Inside walls contained further signs of the original purposes: snapshots on bulletin boards documented the protest marches, sit-downs, and oppositional strategies that were part of its founding. Over time the snapshots faded and were pulled down. The job ads that once peppered the front windows disappeared; instead, small signs appeared advertising clinic hours, family planning services, and drug counseling. At the beginning, food banks throughout the Mon Valley were centers of political action.

> As it became clear that more mills would close, the resistance among activists in the Monongahela Valley grew, and new groups were formed. The Mon Valley Unemployed Committee was founded in December 1981. The Homestead Food Bank, which operated out of Local 1397 and provided bags of food to unemployed workers, was organized by Michael Stout and others in May 1982.[24]

Stout was the president of the local branch of the USW and a militant labor unionist. With several colleagues, he spent a good part of the 1980s trying to organize workers and their neighbors.

Bob Anderson was one of Stout's colleagues, and I spent several hours with him one afternoon. The interview was constantly interrupted by phone calls and by individuals who asked Bob advice on one issue or another. Interruptions, however, did not slow his narrative of failed efforts to organize the valley. He began by telling me he lost his job as a steelworker because he had been outspoken in his criticism of mill conditions. Bob had worked in the Edgar Thomson Works in Braddock, and he insisted "they fired me because I had ran for the union presidency." Of course, it was his platform and not the simple fact of running that did him in. In the balmy days of union success, he was fighting against arbitrary management decisions, persistent discrimination in promotion policies, and, eventually, the flood of unexplained pink slips. He was as annoying to the foremen and managers as Thomas Bell's hero Dobie had been in the 1930s: "Then resentment stirred within him. 'No, by God, I've been getting pushed around till I'm God-damn good and sick of it. We'll get this straightened out right now.'"[25] Then it was getting a union accepted. For Bob and his generation, it was getting a union to act.

The first act consisted of providing a place of refuge, resources, and referrals. The food banks were not just "kitchens" in those days; they were at the core of grassroot protest movements. Bob made it clear that his motive was primarily political and secondarily food distribution. "In the other locals, there were a lot of other people who had tried to do things, so we all had food banks. So we joined them together into what was called the—what did we call it? Mon Valley Employment Organization." His talk of the early unity broke up against the eventual dissolution of coordinated activity in the area. Bob referred to these splits indirectly: "A few of us lived here in Homestead, and we started to organize right up here in Homestead. We shared an office with Tri-State Conference on Steel right up the street here. They had rented a storefront. We had a desk and a phone there and we sat there." After awhile, the agendas diverged and they stopped sharing the space.

Bob's group intended to battle the structures of economic inequality in the Mon Valley by not only providing jobs but also convincing workers they had interests in common. Though Bob did not use the words *class consciousness* or *class struggle*, such concepts lay behind his practices. His motivation, clearly, was to get men and women to see mill closings as life-and-death struggles in which the strategy was confrontation, not conciliation.

By the time I interviewed him in 1989, he was depressed and discouraged. The Rainbow Kitchen itself remained, but Bob's neighbors had given up even the scant protests characteristic of the early 1980s. "The soup kitchen just keeps going," Bob said, while other activities lost their momentum. A year after its founding, Serrin writes, the Rainbow Kitchen was "feeding five hundred people a day."[26] That, however, was not Bob's goal. Perhaps he, like Elaine, looked across the street to see the signs of his defeat: the Army Recruiting Center on the next corner absorbed the restless energy of young adults who wanted to keep on a "straight" path; the stately Mellon Bank on the other corner loomed darkly and quietly, no longer the site of marches and signboards.

The Kitchen kept going, but efforts to organize mill town residents had definitely failed. Bob had started with optimism, he remembered, and a conviction: "Organized workers and the industrial workers were going to work on social change." In 1982, the Rainbow Kitchen helped host a large event at which the popular singer Bruce Springsteen, drawing on his own working-class origins, gave a concert to raise money for food banks throughout the steel valley; the result was ten thousand dollars for those towns. In 1984 the Kitchen invited Jesse Jackson, founder of the national Rainbow Coalition Party, to speak; a snapshot shows Jackson looking ebullient, his arms around the shoulders of two Kitchen workers. The celebrations brought support to the Kitchen, but they did not accomplish the purposes Bob had in mind. The morning after—and the years after—Homesteaders returned to their private efforts to make a go of it.

Bob recalled: "In the election of '84, we got Jackson to come in here. So that was a part of our strategy. The other strategy was to empower people by getting people involved in organizations like the Rainbow Kitchen." With a wry cynicism, he admitted he had been naive about what it took to bring a working-class community into the streets in the late twentieth century, persuade them to confront the elite, and convince them to support an African American in his bid for the presidency. The "cultures of solidarity" in America's steel towns competed with racial, ethnic, and religious enclaves.[27] Work held working people together but, except for the high point of CIO activism in the 1930s, other interests spread them apart. Bob analyzed this, with regret in his voice. He could not, he admitted, break down the cautious conservatism of his neighbors. Homesteaders were not likely to string up effigies of the figures who oppressed them for years and now did nothing to help them out of a tragedy.

Coping had taught people in all three generations to rely on kin, neighbors, ethnic clubs, and churches. These familiar strategies did not encourage class solidarity, as Margaret Byington had observed at the beginning of the century: "In isolated groups they are trying to solve the problem set by the economic and social conditions which confront them in this town."[28] But "isolated groups" did carry Homesteaders through the crises a steel industry brought to the town decade after decade. Whatever a Progressive like Byington, a labor historian like John Bodnar, or an activist like Bob might wish, tradition won the case against radical political action in towns like Homestead. The nickname for the Rainbow Kitchen— the "Kitchen"—aptly conveys the domesticity of forms of help in an American industrial town. During the period of my research, individuals increasingly spoke of the role of the Kitchen in providing food and clothing and minimized its role in stirring up collective action. Men and women in Homestead supported the Kitchen while rejecting its origins.

The wife of one steelworker, for instance, revealed her feelings about the behaviors encouraged by leaders of Local 1397. "In fact, they got into—." she began, without filling in the word that seemed to be *trouble*. She continued: "Ronnie Wiesen was the head of the union. Well, we invited him—he knows Luther [her husband]. Luther knows him personally, and the secretary of the union, Joe Stanton. They both came to our house for dinner. And my dad came over, and I mean they got into this real heated-up discussion because Ronnie Wiesen, he had his strong views and everything. And now even like my husband says, 'I like Ronnie a lot . . . but some of the things that he did, with the protesting and that, with the churches, you know, involving Mellon Bank and all that,' he said, 'I just didn't quite go for that.'" Apparently accepting her husband's perspective, this woman concluded: "And then with the union itself, there was so much on the news and everything."

From such a point of view, the union represented neither the real working man nor the spirit of a genuine working-class community. Instead, the union—and specifically Local 1397—represented outsiders, individuals with different ideas about getting through hard times. Yet this was the union the majority of working men, and some women, in Homestead belonged to; perhaps only a nonmember could speak critically of its leaders. I usually encountered a pause when it came to the Rainbow Kitchen's founding or a pause followed by praise of the "good things" the Kitchen did.

As long as the Kitchen was primarily a food bank, it was acceptable. The place could be "homey," as several individuals said about Homestead, and it could be looked upon as an extension of the coping strategies families had always utilized in bad times. The inclination to depoliticize soup kitchens was not unique to Homestead. In their study of a dying steel community in South Chicago, Roberta Bensman and David Lynch observed a similar tendency; the more homelike a soup kitchen was, the less it stood out in neighborhoods reeling under a wounded economy. South Chicago's soup kitchen was not downtown but alternated between a parish hall and the front porch of a volunteer's home. "Bob and Lolly run a food pantry out of the parish hall on a periodic basis and out of their home on a daily basis."[29] In Homestead, as in South Chicago, the emphasis on food and clothing overwhelmed any association with worker activism. Over time, patrons of a pantry were less likely to be the population that participated at a rally.

"The Rainbow Kitchen, they feed everybody, every single day, breakfast, lunch, and dinner," remarked a white woman in her thirties who five years earlier had moved to Homestead because it was "a comfortable place to live." She admitted with some self-mockery: "I always seem to come back here. You know, it just feels the most comfortable for me." Out of work because of an injury, she was raising her young grandson and needed all the help she could get. Still, for a while she spoke of the Kitchen as if it were a resource only for *others*. "There's clothing down there. If you would take clothing down there, they just put it all on the table, and you just come in and take whatever, you know, size you need. I think they've really done a wonderful job with that." Only as she came to the end of her story did I realize she was talking about herself. "Like if you don't have no food or anything, you can go down there and they have a, like a pantry, and you just take a bag in there, and you just get whatever you need." While domesticating the place through its nickname, individuals insisted they only went to the Kitchen in times of dire need. The young grandmother concluded: "When you're hungry and you have no food and no money and no job, you're going to go down there and get something to eat."

Another strategy for minimizing the difficulties of going to a soup kitchen was to make fun of it and oneself. Laughter disguised the sad fact that going to a soup kitchen meant not only that an individual was in need but also that she had no one else to turn to. The main staple of beans and corn, for instance, prompted remarks about iron stomachs and tough digestive systems. Gregory Pappas reports a similar approach to charity in Barberton: "That the proud people of Barberton would line up for a handout demonstrated that a need existed. Some citizens expressed fear that the food would be wasted, others were concerned about its quality. A joke circulated, especially among the older residents, about the effect of large quantities of cheese on the bowels."[30]

Women also joked about "shopping" at the Kitchen and choosing particular items from the pile lying on a table as if this were a fancy boutique.[31] One afternoon, I became part of the clothing exchange that often followed such a shopping trip. In the middle of a three-way conversation, a woman abruptly ran off to her house across the street from where we were standing. She returned with a pair of well-pressed blue jeans and handed them to me. "I picked them up at the Kitchen," she said, "and they're too small for me. They would only fit someone like you!"

Jokes about free food and a soup kitchen boutique are survival techniques. They are effective in their way—and better than bringing out rifles, if less likely to draw the attention of newspapers and politicians. By the early 1990s, use of survival tactics was tinged with alarm that the town was going the way of Braddock. The soup kitchen, there for over a decade, looked like a permanent feature of the landscape and a sad replacement for the awesome mill buildings. To notice that you were not alone in the soup kitchen, and that everyone needed help sometime or other, was a small and increasingly bitter comfort. "The person that you was afraid of seeing is also going to be standing right there next to you," said one woman.

"And that's the way I look at it. That's the way it is." But "that's the way it is" did not cover up the humiliation of having a soup kitchen "just keep going" on the main street of town. "They'd rather that we go away," Bob, the director, said to me in 1989, "so the problem would appear to go away."

The problem was not going away, but spreading. Over a decade, the Rainbow Kitchen expanded its health services and cut down on its job-related services. In the mid 1980s, at a desk in one corner a volunteer counseled individuals about job opportunities, handing out names of possible employers. By the early 1990s, the desk had disappeared; a few signs hung on the windows, advertising temporary positions. By contrast, the Rainbow Clinic had grown so much that it moved into a separate building next door. But only a few people I interviewed mentioned the clinic.

"Patients were encouraged to become volunteers at the clinic," wrote Pappas about the clinic in Barberton. Homesteaders could look in the plate glass windows of their clinic and see patients taking on the role of helpers. Such compromises were necessary in a depressed town, and Homesteaders were not spared this view of what their town had come to. Pappas continues: "Most important, the clinic had no strict eligibility criteria and was open to anyone who could not afford a doctor."[32] His sentence evokes a view I heard expressed the rare times the Rainbow Clinic was mentioned: its doors were "wide open." Street-front health services contrasted with the large hospital up the hill, a symbol of the health care a prosperous steel town had provided.

"At least they're trying"

The Rainbow Kitchen filled in for overstretched church charity and the inadequate resources of neighbors and kin. Yet for residents who did not actually go to the Kitchen, its agenda remained a mystery and its goals not altogether clear. Away from Eighth Avenue, in Homestead, West Homestead, and Munhall, an individual might know the Kitchen through the representatives who came around asking for donations. That was true for Corinne, who told me of a personally uncomfortable experience with the Kitchen. "A couple of people," she recalled, came to her door selling pot holders. "They were around, you know. And I said to her [sic], 'I'm sorry,' I said, 'I could give you some things to sell.'" With pride in her own craftsmanship, she refused to buy other people's crafts. Corinne went on with the story: "And I went upstairs, in my suitcase, I brought it down. And I gave her seven different articles." She admitted: "Anyway, she was tickled pink. So yesterday . . . , I got a letter. They're having a meeting this Saturday, at eleven o'clock, and they want me to attend. So I went down there to find out what it was all about, and I told her, I said, 'Gee, I'd like to make some things for Christmas for you folks, you know.' 'Oh,' she said, 'that would be wonderful.' I said, 'Well, what did you do with the things that I sent down the last time she was here?' And she said, 'We gave each one of them [away] for nothing.' I thought, 'I'll be doggoned.'"

Corinne was visibly distressed as she told this. She apparently had no idea that the Kitchen was going to give away her work for *free*. "There was two things in there that I said they could have sold for ten dollars." Her disapproval of Rainbow Kitchen policy was unmistakable: "I'll be doggoned if I'm gonna sit here and knit and knit and knit or crochet and then you give 'em out for nothing. The heck with it. I'm not gonna do anything." Lydia, who was sitting with us, explained that the Kitchen always gave things free to people in need: "So that they would have food and things around the holidays to give the other people that really couldn't afford a dinner as they are, you know, so much out of work."

Lydia was reminding us that even in a depressed town, needs differed. With her own house and Social Security, Corinne managed better than many others in town. The Kitchen anecdote led to a general discussion of conditions in the Mon Valley and the ways in which Homestead was coming to resemble neighboring dying towns. When USX left, Lydia continued, "that took away all that bundle of tax money that the borough was collecting every year. They don't get that anymore, so subsequently it comes back on the individuals and no jobs." There was little leverage and lots of poverty. On the other hand, the friends agreed, Homestead was not exactly like every other declining community. On Eighth Avenue, after all, there were social service agencies and an occasional new shop. "And thank god for Heritage House and Rainbow Kitchen," Thomas added. Heritage House was a senior citizen center that provided lunch, activities, and referrals to older residents of the community.

In an attempt to persuade me, and perhaps himself, that the presence of charity institutions on the main business street did not spoil the town, Thomas remarked, "Now, if you notice down on Eighth Avenue, sure there's a lot of stores that closed. Every time you go down there, you see a storefront boarded up. But inside of a month or so, there's something else opening up down there, trying to make it. We got brand-new pizza shops, we got any number of a variety of small stores opened up. At least they're trying—." His wife chimed in, remarking on the good spirit of Homestead residents: "People are glad to give to help somebody out. Even if they only have a little bit. They're gonna share, you know."

Her husband described the array of helpful institutions: "Well, mainly the Meals on Wheels down there. They have to feed those people every day, six days a week, from twelve to one," he said. Then, as if he really started seeing the situation he had been describing, negative images floated to the front of his account. Apparently referring to the Rainbow Kitchen, he said, "Some of the people that come in there, it's just a handout for them. But they can't refuse 'em." His words—"some of the people" and a vague reference to "them"—were accompanied by a wince of distaste. He went on: "'Cause, probably, many of them not working, they slide across the street from one of them bars at twelve o'clock and come over and get a free meal." In the end, he was more critical of the Kitchen than Corinne was. For him, as for others I interviewed, the Kitchen was full of drifters, disreputable members of the community, and individuals who did not live in the community at all.

In 1991, when I interviewed a shopkeeper whose store was just up the street from the Rainbow Kitchen, he told me to "watch out" and "not hang around here." Outside his window, I could see people "drifting" in and out of a nearby bar. That afternoon, Bob dropped in—taking a break from his duties at the Kitchen—and, in different words, also cautioned me about hanging around in the early evening. Neither man said anything explicit, but each was translating an observation into a warning. Bob faced a dilemma, the one various residents mentioned but could avoid by simply not traveling down to Eighth Avenue. Bob's obligations were to the Kitchen, and he knew the doors should be "open to everyone."

The Rainbow Kitchen was eventually taken over by individuals who expanded its efforts to feed and clothe anyone in need. Bob had talked about the inability of local churches to do their part: "Most of the churches have lost so much membership that they don't have the wealth and stability that they used to," he said. "The Catholic Church is in the process of closing down a large number of its parishes all through the area, in the process of retrenchment." He was also disappointed in the conservatism of Homestead churches. "The membership is an older base. They lack youth and young members." He finished his thought somewhat pessimistically: "[People] do not look to the local community-based groups like us to make change or the churches."

The fact was the Rainbow Kitchen served one clientele, Heritage House and the churches another. The town was dividing on new lines, religion and ethnicity less significant than race and "stability," a code word for those who were acceptable in the changed environment of the steel town. Stability, sobriety, and security combined with race when residents redrew the social boundaries of Homestead.

"A shell of its former self"

Cultural changes are not documented in snapshots or in family photo albums. They are evident in verbal images, in metaphors that contrast present with past. When photographs appeared, people noted the contrasts between then and now; at those moments, the "lost" town was visible. Coming across a photo of a day at Kennywood or a formal portrait of a confirmation ceremony, an individual recalled the "good feelings" and solidarity of the community *then*. In the eyes of the observer, snapshots showed a cooperative, self-sustaining, and vigorous community apart from the mill. If nostalgic, these interpretations also offered a ray of hope.

Hope existed in a community outside the mill, the community of churches, schools, playgrounds, and bars. But little of this was left in the contemporary physical landscape.[33] Baseball diamonds had disappeared, and snapshots of kids playing ball were individualized, a pose in uniform on a front porch. Playgrounds had been appropriated by adolescents and Eighth Avenue emptied of holiday parades. The emphasis on recreation in photos of the past contrasted with the situation now. I had seen pictures of lavish Fourth of July parades, in personal collections and in the *Homestead Messenger*. On July 4, 1990, I went to Homestead; there was no parade that day and virtually no one on the streets. I stopped at Isaly's for ice cream and chatted with a few townspeople celebrating their holiday there. There were flags on front porches and public buildings, and there may have been barbecues in backyards. On Eighth Avenue, however, it was quiet, and Homestead seemed, as a woman said, "just a shell of its former self."

Two years later, in July 1992, scholars arranged a celebration of the centennial of the Great Homestead Strike. Few residents attended. The food stands and crafts tables looked forlorn in the dripping rain of a Pittsburgh summer day; the audience for the speeches given at the Carnegie Library included more visitors than townspeople. Charlee's photograph of a motorcycle parked in front of the deserted mill, a tiny American flag waving from the back of its seat, offers another angle of vision on the former steel town. None of these views, however, tell us or Homesteaders exactly how the town is going to move into the future.

THE MILL

The "hole in the wall," where wages were distributed.

BEYOND THE CLOSING

10

Changes in Homestead

> Mutual understanding would be achieved the sooner were the American fraternal organizations to adopt the policy of welcoming these aliens; or were the Catholic church to exert a more definite influence to bring men of all races together as well as to hold each race firmly intact, to interpret America to them no less than to preserve the religious heritages they bring from the churches of mid-Europe. In politics, social bonds are less personal and an aggressive, thoroughly democratic civic movement in Homestead . . . , might serve to bring men of all races to touching elbows.

—Margaret Byington, *Homestead: The Households of a Mill Town*

In *Homestead: The Glory and Tragedy of an American Steel Town*, William Serrin remarks that, after awhile, most of the clientele at the Rainbow Kitchen "were from the poor population that had begun to drift into the area and were not laid-off steelworkers."[1] Though he does not specify their negative attributes, his word *drift* suggests a contrast between this population and the people who had lived in Homestead all their lives—steelworkers, members of steelworking families, their neighbors, and their friends.

As Serrin observed, in the decade after its founding in 1982 the Rainbow Kitchen accumulated an increasingly disparate clientele. Not only did the Kitchen have a reputation throughout the steel valley that drew people in, it was also located in a business district that was the transfer point for buses going to and from downtown Pittsburgh. People waiting to go somewhere else would catch a glimpse of the rainbow on the wall, or notice a sign advertising lunch, or just wander in aimlessly. Serrin also remarks that the clientele were recent arrivals in Homestead, individuals without family networks to depend on. His characterization of these new residents as "drifters" echoes descriptions I heard in interviews, especially as conditions worsened in the steel valley.

Newcomers were not a new phenomenon. The question now, however, is what the difference is between 1990s newcomers and those of the past. What will the impact of their arrival be on an ex-steel town, and how will their lives influence the route the town takes in the future? Such questions were not raised explicitly in my interviews, but they constitute the explicit theme of this chapter. The faces staring out of Brodsky's portraits show the changes in Homestead's population. During the summers of 1992 and 1993, she took pictures of kids bored on their bicycles, men sitting on the backs of pick-up trucks, and couples lounging on a downtown bench. Like the people of Homestead, Charlee tended not to record the "drifters" in the Rainbow Kitchen or the empty pews of a church. *That* Homestead was not picturesque or dignified. Yet it is the Homestead residents conjured up when they talked about what might happen next.

Residents of dying industrial towns do not take snapshots of the disaster. At the same time, visual evidence of decay is present for every Homesteader who crosses the High-Level Bridge or shops on Eighth Avenue. Perhaps, too, reluctance to preserve images of the town in its current state represented a hope that this was a passing phase in town history—the future would look different again. And so residents looked eagerly at pictures of Homestead *then*, a time when community seemed good despite the oppression of work in steel, and when harmony seemed to reign despite discrimination in jobs, schools, and housing. Ironically, the "good old days" are especially significant in describing the end of an era in Homestead; the best way residents can save their town is to consider their stories a map for the future. With an echo of Byington, their histories push the households of a mill town into prominence over its mill.

Residents feared that these family structures, too, were falling before the wrecking ball of corporate decisions. Talk of crime, drug use, and wandering gangs suggests the precarious nature of hopes for the town. Little seems to be left of the households individuals remembered when they thought back to childhoods in the 1930s, 1940s, 1950s, or, my youngest interviewees, the 1960s. In their accounts, blame fell on the newcomers, people who came to a town that had no jobs, declining schools, and collapsing religious organizations. There was no "pot of gold" in this town, despite the rainbow on Eighth and Amity.

"Homestead is horrible now"

When I drove over the Homestead High-Level Bridge in 1992, I saw a different town from the one I first encountered in 1986. For me, as for residents, Eighth Avenue was less welcoming than it once had been; the mood inside the popular Isaly's was gloomy and somber. Inside the ice cream parlor, clients were white, in contrast to the people on the street, a majority of whom were black. Old boundaries were being reasserted, and lines once drawn implicitly were now visible and explicit.

"Bad place here," concluded an Italian tailor whose shop was up the street from the Rainbow Kitchen. He nodded at the bar across the street, where an odd assortment of teenagers and older men stood around on the sidewalk. On a subsequent trip to town, Brodsky set up her camera near that bar and asked several of the teenagers if they minded having their pictures taken. One African-American girl of about fourteen, her hair in a tight roll on the top of her head, cheerfully posed for a sequence of portraits. Throughout, she kept up a running set of complaints about "how *boring* Homestead was in the summer." Shortly afterwards, two white policemen in a slow-moving squad car beeped at Charlee and me. The round-faced, middle-aged driver rolled down his window and shouted: "Well, did your film burn up?" I had no idea what he was talking about, until he explained that the young girl we had just been photographing was a "hot prostitute." He went on to say, still half-laughing, that she supported her coke habit by doing anything anyone wanted.

These were street signs of decline. The decline going on behind the shaded windows and closed doors of Homestead houses was a parallel. For many residents, the tragedy of the closing was in the breakup of families, the spread of hard drugs, and the high rate of suicide. A white ex-steel-worker in his thirties, Dan had lived in Homestead all his life. When the mill closed, he told me, his life collapsed. His wife left him and he moved into the basement of his mother's house, with his dog as company. He had initially reacted to the closing with vigor, supporting the Rainbow Kitchen in its protest marches, actions against the banks, and pleas to the borough council to "do something." Now his anger turned inward, expressed in bitterness at himself and his "lazy" neighbors. No one, according to Dan, was doing anything to help the town. Crime, he told me, was rampant, and the police just sat back and let it happen. More charitably, he added that perhaps the "cops" simply did not have the resources to make any changes in street life. "I think we need beat policemen," he asserted, but the politicians "don't like that. I think you need it for more business hours or maybe at night. 'Cause I been down when the stores are open, and they [other residents] won't come down because of the blacks. Because at night *they* take over down here."

Blacks did form a large proportion of recent arrivals in Homestead, and they tended to be poor, unemployed, and members of single-headed households. They did not look like the blacks Dan had grown up with and, for a while, worked next to in the mill. He described junkies, dope dealers, and muggers on the streets of Homestead, and in his remarks on police reactions, he used the word *doper* interchangeably with *black*. Local newspapers encouraged the association by noting the growth of crime in Homestead in paragraphs that also reported on the "population change."

At the same time, throughout his interview Dan stood up for the underdog, those who were victims and vulnerable. When he talked about the rich and powerful—the corporation and the federal government—his became a class rather than a race analysis. From that point of view, the less well off were equally oppressed by the elite. By "elite," Dan did not only mean the businessmen, bankers, and congressmen who regulated life in a steel town; he also meant local politicians.

"Got a couple of assholes up here who won't do nothing, on council. They just grease their pockets," he proclaimed, and went on to describe what they *did* do: "But just a few of them up there who don't do nothing, just fight [with each other]." The president of the Homestead Borough Council particularly infuriated Don, and he gave me an extended, sarcastic imitation. "Your opinion is well taken, Mr. Murkle," were the stilted words Dan quoted—words that led to nothing: "And that's it. And I swear the next time he gets up, I'm going to go up and punch him. I say, 'You keep telling me that and you don't do nothing. You just sit up there, pounding your gavel, go home, and that's it.' Nothing is ever done."

However pompous a council meeting was, lack of funds, the collapse of an infrastructure, and the visible demoralization of a population set up obstacles to urban planning. Yet this was a town with a history of uniting against the "enemy." Where was that history now? Like Dan, a white woman in her early thirties wondered at the apathy of her neighbors. Like Dan, too, she expressed sympathy for those who had been thoroughly victimized by the closing and saved her most bitter criticism for politicians. "Homestead is *horrible* now," she claimed, recalling the feelings she had upon moving back after ten years away. "Before I left, there were stores, places to play pinball. Now the only thing on the corners is junkies—junkies and drunkards." Junkies, she went on to note, had the run of the streets because the cops did nothing. But she was also sympathetic, adding that Homestead cops did not get paid enough to do anything. "Cops get paid $4.25 an hour to sit in their cars and eat donuts. They don't get paid enough to do anything else." Forgiving the cops, and their donuts, Jackie blamed city council for letting the situation remain horrible. "The trouble is people running for city council don't have the brains to get the grants [for services and improvements]. There are grants out there; people could get them." This led her to attack other institutions she felt were just "sitting on their asses" when they could be helping the people of Homestead. "Like the Rainbow Kitchen, Y [the director who replaced Bob] doesn't have sense enough to get them [grants]. Now the Kitchen will close because Y doesn't know how to get grants."[2]

Practicing what she preached, Jackie had herself several times marched down to Homestead City Hall to demand action. The issue she fought for involved parks and playgrounds. In her neighborhood, as in others, the park was being "overrun" by teenagers; it was unsafe for young children who regularly discovered needles, condoms, and empty beer bottles. Jackie wanted the borough council to put money into the parks, to provide protection, and generally to revive a part of Homestead life that had always been important. But a poor town could not fix up its parks, and Jackie's petition was denied.

Exacerbating the anger Dan, Jackie, and others expressed was a sense that they were acting alone. The solidarity of remembered strikes was gone; communal action looked like a thing of the past. And in many ways it *was*, not just in Homestead but in towns suffering from the pull-out of industry throughout the United States. The 1980s and 1990s were not periods of protest in ex-steel towns but of withdrawal into a private domain whose stability itself seemed at risk. In many ways, protest had always been the choice of a few: the early labor activists and union organizers, the later outsiders who came in to organize grassroots coalitions. Patterns in Homestead in the 1990s were a version of what Byington described: households coped, drawing on familiar familial strategies.

Residents who were older than Jackie and Dan did not express bitterness so much as regret at the failure of neighborliness. Members of the first and second generations referred to the Depression, to sharing resources rather than taking to the barricades. In a typical interpretation, an African-American man characterized the present as "every person for himself" and bemoaned the selfishness that followed the departure of USX. Behind his statement lingers the possibility that an industrial town needs a corporate enemy in order to unify.

A visible sign of the withdrawal of Homestead residents from collective action was the transformation of the Rainbow Kitchen. Once a center of discussion and of organization, the Kitchen had become a place to go for a meal, a box of diapers, or a pair of secondhand blue jeans. The founders had left and the new staff struggled to keep food on the pantry shelves. By 1993, the Kitchen's early history of jockeying for place in the hierarchy of steel valley protest groups had become an event of the past.

"It burnt out a lot of people real fast"

In my interview with him in 1989, Bob gave me his history of protest movements in the tri-state area. "Another thing that fits in was the rise of the DMS, which I think really destroyed the—," and he paused. The Denominational Ministry Strategy, or DMS, was a group of ministers and citizens who organized in 1982, using church services to marshal protest. Sunday mornings in the Mon Valley saw ministers preaching against banks, bosses, and mortgage brokers. Parishioners were upset, congregations split, and police barred so-called "radical priests" from their own churches. According to Bob, this was not surprising. In the conservative towns of the Mon Valley, radicalizing religion was not a good idea. The DMS movement posed a challenge in communities where church had historically been a refuge from—not a forum for—debating the decisions imposed by "big" companies and "big" government.

Bob never said exactly what the rise of the DMS destroyed, but I took him to mean that the DMS had nipped activism in the bud by locating it in the wrong place. He summarized the attitude of steel town residents: priests and ministers could support a labor strike or a protest march, but not at the altar. Pictures of cops running up church stairs to arrest a minister or of a clergyman riding in the back of a squad car were distressing, not an inspiration to act. The DMS, Bob implied, drove residents of steel towns away from all forms of collective action.

Referring to his own group, the Mon Valley Unemployment Committee, he said, "We had a big movement of unemployed people and a lot of resentment and anger." There was something to build on. "Because it was a sort of anarchist-socialist concept they were operating under, it got a lot of people fired up and involved in some actions and demonstrations around the banks and things." But, he added, "there was this movement which resulted from the churches, among the middle-class white churches in the Mon Valley, that was very reactionary." The problem was too much competition, too many groups trying to win the loyalties of laid-off workers.

To pinpoint the differences between the DMS and the Mon Valley Unemployment Committee, Bob described the strategies his group used. "*We* were directing them [people] into the political arena and [trying to] get people to run for office and social change in the government and legislation. And *they* were trying to direct it into church. The combination of things wasn't very clear, and it burnt out a lot of people real fast." In the end, he concluded, factions and feuding dissipated the resentment and anger that could have produced effective action in the Mon Valley. "Most of us that were steelworkers just got out of it. It just destroyed a lot of hope that people had of organizing and fighting back because here were these people in the clergy and symbols of legitimacy—but all that was coming out of it was division. It just destroyed a lot of hope that people had of organizing and fighting back."

Established in 1982, the DMS had died by the late 1980s, defeated by disputes within its own ranks and by the hostility it prompted in steel town residents. But the biggest obstacle for the DMS may well have been what it was for the Mon Valley Unemployment Committee and for every other organized group: the desperation and despair of the people these groups intended to mobilize. In Homestead, residents concentrated on surviving a trauma that was social and cultural as well as psychological.

The story is the same throughout America's rust-belt communities. In such communities protest historically came attached to work, a reaction to jobs that denied workers dignity, time with families, and health benefits.[3] The presence of industry established the terms of protest. The loss of jobs pushed workers into time-consuming efforts to find new positions or, alternatively, into lassitude.[4] By 1990, steel towns of the tri-state region witnessed apathy on the part of women and men who had once endured 180-day strikes in order to gain their rights. By 1990, residents of Homestead lost the will to revive that past script. Yet throughout the early years of the decade, "below the tracks" continued to appear in interviews, a banner for what the town might become: a community of shared values and understandings that existed way beyond the shadow of the mill.

Retired steelworkers (R. Wurtz collection)

"An investment in paradise"

The phrase "below the tracks" evoked a life independent of the mill and the oppressive work in steel. "Below" referred to strategies of survival and of solidarity that were domestically based, informal mechanisms of sharing and taking responsibility. "Below" hid the steelworker behind the *worker* who managed his livelihood in all possible ways. As representative of a golden age of working-class community, "below" was perhaps the best plan contemporary Homesteaders had.

Evocations of "below the tracks" did not stop individuals from citing pragmatic solutions to problems currently visible on the streets of Homestead. Force the politicians to act, some said. Clean up the drug problem and all would be well, others argued. Ideas for change were voiced by business people and merchants on Eighth Avenue, by residents on the hillside blocks of Homestead, and by newcomers who settled on Ninth, Tenth, and Eleventh Avenues. The ideas were not always the same, and public statements revealed rifts in the three boroughs that had not historically been there.

A prosperous businessman genuinely devoted to the welfare of his town, Frank Morrison began implementing his plans for improvement before the mill actually closed. In the early 1970s he supported the beautification of Eighth Avenue, in the hopes of bringing new business into Homestead. After the USX pullout, he urged his fellow businessmen to support the establishment of "high tech" and service industries in downtown Homestead. Sitting with us, his mother added a note of caution: "But they're going to have to employ enough persons to create business in Homestead. Because of our malls and everything." No matter how bustling and how well-appointed Eighth Avenue was, "down street" still had to compete with thriving suburban malls.

A bit defensively, Frank insisted that shopkeeping was not what he had in mind. "So I disagree with my mother, to the extent that I see the future of Homestead being different. I don't see it depending that much on shops and stores, as much as it used to." But he also admitted that new shops and shoppers were crucial to carrying mill towns into the future. With its wide, pleasant boulevard, Homestead, he said, was particularly well suited to competing with the nearby Century III Mall. "So I would submit," he concluded: "number one, just the visual appearance of that main street is number one. Number two, the fact that Homestead being at the end of that bridge, which was, let's say, the gateway to the South Hills." Given these features, "People would see Homestead and they would say, this is a place where I can do business, this would be a place to live."

Frank may not have known that some of his neighbors found the geranium pots and trees on Eighth Avenue more a bother than a benefit. Downtown gentrification substituted one physical commemoration for another, emphasizing the commercial establishments rather than the industrial foundation upon which Homesteaders had built their lives for generations. Beautification violated the sense Homesteaders had of the heart of their town, which involved hard work and struggle. From that point of view, the steel gazebo near the Carnegie Library in Munhall and the stone memorial to steelworkers near the High-Level Bridge better represented Homestead.

Most residents I interviewed, however, noticed what was missing from Eighth Avenue, not what Morrison and his fellow entrepreneurs had put there. Where there had once been five five-and-tens, there was now one. Homestead's proud Leona Theatre had been replaced by a Quik-Shop. Isaly's, still open, looked decrepit and deserted on a sunny afternoon.

And no one really knew who would take charge of Homestead's future, workers or businessmen. Could Homestead move forward without completely relinquishing a past built on steel, on pride in manual labor, and on a sense of solidarity under the shadow of a mill? Disagreements over what the town should *look like* were the tip of the iceberg of a profound conflict of values. Reconciling various perspectives on the town's historical identity, not simply rearranging its economic structures, must be part of envisioning the future.

In his interview, Bob expressed the resulting inconsistency. After voicing regret at his failure to politicize the unemployed, he wondered about the possibilities for Homestead. A partisan of the working man and of "victims of capitalism," Bob constructed an agenda that at first resembled Morrison's. "Cut the red tape," he said. "Build housing, put money in here for a lot of these old structures. Upgrade them." He went on to suggest alternatives that more closely captured the viewpoint of most Homestead residents. "Education alone [would help], grants for students of former steelworkers and industrial workers in this area. Put them to school as far as they want to go so they don't have to join the military, they don't have to leave the area. They can stay here and get well educated." He concluded with a heartfelt plea: "Build programs whereby people feel they have control over their lives."

Here Bob really hit the nail on the head. Having control was a persistent theme in my interviews—pride in controlling the domestic arena if not the work place; pride in controlling the moral community if not the material basis of that community; pride in controlling social interactions so that diversity did not erupt into dispute. Bob's idea of restoring a sense of control did not necessarily require *formal* education, but rather some kind of program that gave individuals leverage over their circumstances. Later in the interview Bob offered a concrete plan.

He talked about the summer of 1988 when Pittsburgh sponsored a visiting team of architects to look over the old steel towns and propose changes. The team got a lot of attention, partly because Prince Charles of Britain was among the visitors. In his interview, Bob expressed a certain amount of sarcastic amusement at the proposed renovations. One aspect of the plan involved converting mill structures into greenhouses. This was not entirely ridiculous. Mill buildings had open roofs that could be glassed in and, on the riverbanks, had access to a water supply. Yet, more than geraniums dotting the sidewalks of a commercial street, growing flowers in a steel mill offended Homestead history. Bob tried to find a virtue in the plan: "Put greenhouses in these old mills, ludicrous as it sounds, if somebody had the money to do it, it would go."[5]

Then he proposed a use of the mills that sounded less ludicrous and more practical to a former steelworker like himself. "Open the steel mills," he ventured, "and put the bedrooms out here, put the condominiums out there. If you have the money to bankroll it and do something that architects think—." He trailed off, stymied by the daunting task of converting a huge mill into bedroom apartments. Still, he ended optimistically, "it's an investment in paradise."

If somewhat tongue-in-cheek, his word *paradise* was not a mockery. He believed in Homestead, as did many of the residents I met. And like them, Bob stayed in the community until he lost all hope of being able to do anything there. Instead of greenhouses or apartments, the borough of West Homestead saw a water park on abandoned land belonging to the Mesta Machine Company. For residents of the area, the contrast between the tinkly sounds of an amusement park and the noise of an enormous machine shop was painful—the more so, since the admission fee Sandcastle charged discouraged attendance by residents. And the only residents who would be employed there were teenagers in need of summer jobs. No "man of steel" would take a job running a slide, and no woman would leave her children to work for a minimum wage, and for only three months of the year. The park existed for *others*, whether well-off Homesteaders or the tourists who came to consume.

"I seen license plates from Maryland, Ohio, Virginia," one Homestead woman reported to me. "They're probably coming up here and staying up here just like they would in Atlantic City or New Jersey." Sandcastle visitors, she said, were not from the steel valley. As she continued assessing the brand-new amusement park, she came down harder on the strangers who seemed to be running her town and benefiting from its downfall. "They're going to rebuild everything there. There's supposed to be a lot of apartments for the elderly and for people that come in from out of town, like another Sheraton and stuff like that, like four hundred rooms." What good would four hundred fancy hotel rooms do her?

For Homestead residents, the gates of Sandcastle were effectively slammed shut by the entry fee. "Who can possibly pay $13.50 just to get in for a day," one mother asked me rhetorically, possibly seeing the groceries the same amount would buy. Furthermore, fond memories of Kennywood secured the condemnation of the new park. Sandcastle did not carry the

traditions that Kennywood did—the ethnic day parties, the picnics mark-
ing Labor Day, or simply the Sunday afternoons of wandering from roller
coaster to fun house. Clean and white on the banks of the Mon, Sandcastle
makes no more of a dent on Homestead life than the imagined greenhouses.

An African-American woman in her mid-thirties told me that what
Homestead "really" needed were not recreational spaces but drug treatment centers. She dismissed amusement parks, greenhouses, and bedroom
apartments, and said the town should build "one big rehab." Flora continued: "Then you could go around town and snatch 'em all up. Snatch 'em
all up and just throw 'em in—not on their own will, because they're not
going to go on their own will." She did not make any distinctions then,
but in other parts of the interview she implied that newcomers were "worse"
than old-timers; it was the newcomers, black and white, who brought drugs
and crime. It was the old-timers, black and white, who knew what Homestead ought to be like. From her perspective and that of others I interviewed, Homestead was losing its "homey" character and falling prey to
the blight of any urban center. When Homestead lost its industrial base, it
seemed also to lose the neighborliness that once allowed residents to forget the steel that supported the town.

"Rough language and violent ways"

> A new immigration was occurring in Homestead. As Slavs had
> replaced English, Welsh, and Germans, and black people had replaced
> Slavs, now poorer people, black and white, some from Appalachia,
> were replacing the families who were moving away. But whereas
> immigrants had once come with the hope of getting ahead, the
> newcomers had no hope. They brought with them the problems of the
> poor everywhere. Many were unkempt and did not take care of their
> homes. They used rough language and had brought with them violent
> ways.

So William Serrin described the changes in Homestead after the mill shut
down in 1986.[6] His characterization of newcomers rings true to some of
the comments I heard. In the eyes of residents, arrivals in the 1990s looked
unkempt, unhappy, and unhopeful. The characterization, too, reiterated
the contrast between past and present: in the old days, immigrants had
been hardworking, hopeful, and upwardly mobile.

In his house in the middle-class neighborhood of Homestead Park, Luther talked about the disorder now "coming into" the area. He told me he rarely drove down to Eighth Avenue, and when his wife had to go there to do an errand, he gave her a special route to drive. She was to avoid West Street, the main route into town, and circle around through the predominantly white neighborhoods of West Homestead. The corner of West and Fifteenth, he told me, was "really bad." In fact, he asserted, they changed the traffic light from red to blinking yellow after dark "so no one would have to stop."[7]

I often drove down West Street on my way to the Homestead High-Level Bridge and back to Squirrel Hill. After the interview with Luther, I took a special look at the corner of Fifteenth and West. I saw several storefront churches, their evangelical signs suggesting an African-American population. Further down Fifteenth, I knew from interviews, newly arrived black families had moved in, checkerboarding the blocks more than in the past. Was Luther, then, being racist in his perception of the source of danger in Homestead?

The question is not easy to answer, either for Luther or for any other white resident of Homestead who observed radical transformations in a town that had once been as familiar as the back of one's hand. The individuals who drifted into the Rainbow Kitchen or sat outside on the front steps of houses along Fifteenth or Ninth or Eleventh Streets were more often black than white: the population of Homestead shifted so that in 1990 whites made up slightly less than half the total. The association of disorder, despair, crime, and drugs with blacks was not surprising; there was, as discussed in previous chapters, a legacy of racism upon which older white residents could draw in greeting the new blacks.

One young woman who came to Homestead for the traditional reasons confronted this racism and talked about it. A white woman, she came in 1990 with her black boyfriend because, she said, Homestead was "homey, comfortable, and safe." She told me, "Then I moved out here with him in probably the end of August, the beginning of September. He would bring me out to meet his mom and his family and stuff. I just liked it so much." They moved in with his mom. "OK, you know where the projects are in Whitaker? OK, that's where we live. I like it there because you can go for walks and be in trees." Like old-timers, Joy ignored administrative boundaries, blurring the steel town boroughs under the adjective *homey*. Whitaker was not politically in Homestead; in terms of social geography and community feeling, it was. "Yeah, we sit outside a lot in the yard. We put a blanket out and set a TV on the porch and just sit in the yard."

Like old-timers, too, Joy separated households from mill. She came to *live* in Homestead, a decision she claimed was independent of the fortunes of steel. Her view of the town as a good place had nothing to do with the lower costs resulting from the USX withdrawal. But Homestead was not "paradise" for Joy. Her visits to the local ice cream parlor, she told me, were terrible, embarrassing, and humiliating. The waitresses and clerks refused to wait on her when she tried to use food stamps to buy a snack. "They're getting really rude to their customers," she said. "I think they don't like for welfare recipients to go in because if you have food stamps, they don't want you to eat what you buy in there." She implied that people with food stamps were scorned and condemned on Eighth Avenue. "But just lately I get food stamps, and I went in there and I had bought some pop and I sat down to drink it and she said, 'You're going to have to leave because you bought it with food stamps.'"

Joy also experienced the racism that surged up in the 1990s. She told me this at first rather casually: "Sometimes when we're [she and her boyfriend] sitting together, some of the older people will look at us and wrinkle up their face. A lot of old people are like that." Later she reported an incident that seemed more painful to her: "I know one day I was sitting on the bench down there near Sheetz waiting to catch the bus, and this man sat down and started telling me this joke about a black man. It was an old man, and when he was done he started laughing and I didn't really laugh, you know. And he said, 'You know what, you remind me of this girl in Squirrel Hill because I told her the same joke and she didn't laugh. She told me it wasn't funny because she's married to a black man.' I said, 'Well, my boyfriend's black.' He said, 'Oh.'" The anecdote conveys the casualness of racism and its ordinariness in a depressed area. Joy also recognized that racism had practical implications. Mac, she reported, could not get a job because "no one" wanted to hire a black man. "He's having trouble," she said, "he hasn't been able to get anything."

The inconsistencies in her account were echoed in other interviews after 1990. Those who had chosen to stay or had recently moved into a visibly impoverished town expressed their loyalty in terms of neighborliness and "hometown" spirit. Yet almost everyone said something that revealed a racism no longer smoothed over by prosperity. Joy herself expressed ambivalent feelings. She wanted to leave town, she told me, right after the baby was born. "We've been trying to find a house because we don't want to raise our baby in the projects where all the other kids are. There are just too many problems." The problems, it turned out, stemmed from hostile attitudes toward mixed couples and, in her words, "half-breed babies." This was a kind of mixing few townspeople tolerated: a striking sign of the breakdown of parameters.

Behind the barred windows of her shop, Mrs. Wozeck brought her account of Homestead into the 1990s. In the "old days," she explained, "you could be generous to customers who needed help" during a crisis. "Years ago," the store extended credit to families caught in a slowdown, a strike, or simply without ready cash. By 1990, that was no longer the policy. As Mrs. Wozeck put it, "Yeah, well, if we got someone who really needed it, you know, we would just give them food. There were times when there were people that would come up from—your tape's running, I don't want to say it." She paused, then continued: "Different people would come in. And they would say, hard luck story or something like that, and Sam would just say, 'Well, here, you take the bread, lunch meat. Here is some fruit, you know, you just take it.'" She explained: "Because we knew if we were to give them credit that we weren't going to see the money anyway. So this way they didn't have to feel that they had to pay back anything." Going on with her narrative, Mrs. Wozeck revealed the fine line she walked in trying to help while not losing her own livelihood. "So if we really felt someone needed it, yeah, we would give it to them. But a lot of people that ask for credit, they would ask for credit and then they would go out and buy a new car the next day."

She did not name the "troublemakers." But the local newspapers did, attributing a rise in crime and in disorder to the new population of blacks who came to Homestead in the postclosing years. The media addressed an audience with similar values, residents who had long before spoken of a "darkening" town and who knew the story of blacks arriving as strikebreakers in the first half of the century. As a way of life and a century came to an end, white residents of the steel town voiced their fears openly. With my tape recorder on or off, an increasing number of Homesteaders blamed blacks for the trouble in town. So, to my initial surprise, did longtime black residents.

Identification of oneself as a longtime resident had as much to do with commitment as with years spent in the town. An African-American woman who had moved to Homestead after the mill closed in 1986 had harsh words for "recent blacks." She blamed "them" for the spread of drugs and violence, and for making Eighth Avenue unsafe. We sat on her front porch where, she said, she had a view of "cop cars day and night." To further differentiate herself from the "druggies" and criminals, she took on the language of older residents, talking of the town's legacy of "homeyness" and generosity. Flora did not come from a "below the tracks" family, but she had acquired the myths that attached a person to the town. "Homestead," she assured me, "is a good place to raise children."

She underlined the good qualities of Homestead by deurbanizing the town. "Here in Homestead, it's real peaceful and quiet." A few minutes later, in a similar tone, she recalled her reasons for moving there in the first place: "The people were nice. You didn't have problems, you know, the neighbors were always nice. Everybody was like one big, happy family. That's what brought me to Homestead. And that's what's keeping me in Homestead now, because it's still like one big, happy family. I mean, almost the whole street, everybody gets along with everybody."

She also did not minimize the changes the last few years had brought. "You know, it's been a little more lively than it's ever been, 'cause this has always been a real quiet town." Lively, it turned out, was a euphemism for noise and fighting on the nearby streets. Such liveliness could be deadly. Flora described a murder that had occurred not long before our talk, a brutal stabbing in a house just up the street from her own. That very afternoon a police car drove up to the door and two policemen rushed inside. Watching, Flora commented, "*those people* are always in trouble."

The categories of "us" and "them," insider and outsider, responsible and lazy were shifting along with everything else in Homestead. Talking about the present, white and black residents increasingly used "black" to stand for the negative elements in Homestead. Thomas, who had recalled the racism directed toward him, pulled his narrative forward to describe current developments. "People are moving in, now a lot of people are moving out, and I notice most of the families are black." Some, he acknowledged, "have a willingness to work, to bring their house up [that is, take care of the house]." But when he concluded that "most" were careless about the upkeep of houses, refused to work, and turned to drugs, he sounded just like his white neighbors. By the 1990s, attributing crime and disorder to blacks was part of Homestead culture.

Blaming "new blacks" reflected the increasing presence of blacks on the streets of Homestead and the fact that blacks were frequently picked up by town cops. Homestead history justified the attitude; blacks had never had a warm welcome in steel towns of the Mon Valley.[8] When there were no jobs and no visible opportunities for a new resident, the reasons for coming were even more suspect. The older African-American man finished his assessment: "Because they can actually get more money out of welfare than they can making the minimum wage. So they say, 'why go to work?' And they get that defeatist attitude, and the next thing you know they're on dope."

"Kids, like fourteen, fifteen years old, are carrying these drugs"

Homesteaders fell into blaming individuals rather than the system. In this respect, they were typical of conservative industrial workers throughout the United States.[9] Joy, for instance, avoided attributing her boyfriend's failure to get a job to racism. "He had put applications in at Shop 'N Save," she told me, and "at the Kennywood Plaza, at all the places in the Kennywood Plaza, and down here at this Shop 'N Save, I think. And I'm not sure where else. He hasn't been able to get anything." She explained that Mac got sick in air-conditioned spaces, which made it hard for him to hold a job. "He's worked at the Giant Eagle in Greenfield, as soon as you go across the bridge. And the air conditioning, he can't be in the air conditioning for any length of time because his asthma is so bad. He only worked a couple of days, and he had to call off because he couldn't breathe."

Mac tried to stay out of trouble, she said, but he was "always getting into fights." In the photograph Charlee took of Mac and Joy, Mac has an arm flung proudly over Joy's shoulder. The arm is bandaged, a result of his having thrown a cousin against a wall after a quarrel. Joy forgave Mac his temper, she said, just as he forgave her for eating too much. The two faced bigger problems.

Beyond issues of race and racism, the world of Homestead had shut down for a majority of residents. White or black, young adults were at loose ends, and kids in school had no idea what their futures would be. The traditional patterns had collapsed, for girls as well as for boys; the departure of the mill took away familiar routes to labor and to life. A snapshot view of Homestead in the 1990s showed women waiting for buses or clerking in a local store; it showed men going to church meetings or sitting on a bar stool. Throughout the community, male and female householders coped by visiting the Rainbow Kitchen from time to time, by using food stamps despite the scorn of a waitress, and by trading around secondhand clothes with as much humor as they could muster.

Under such circumstances, the distinction hardened between those who received help legitimately and those who turned to crime or to drugs. In interview after interview, I heard bitter complaints about illegal businesses in Homestead. Yet often the same people joked about bootlegging, speakeasies, and a "world renowned" red-light district. With the nostalgic aura "below the tracks" evoked, vice in the old days was described as harmless, amusing, and controllable. In the present, illegal activities threatened the moral order of the community.

When residents talked about the red-light district *then*, they claimed it was limited to one neighborhood and did not impinge upon the rest of Homestead life. To an extent that was true. In the years of steel's supremacy, the corporation and the police cooperated to keep things in hand for residents and patrons of illegal businesses. The pull-out of industry in the late twentieth century created a gap in the informal monitoring of such activities, and in the eyes of residents, vice became violent crime and drugs "lured" youngsters in the way a mill once had. "Between the dealers and the people using drugs, it's been, like, really hard in certain areas of Homestead, you know, as far as raising kids and whatnot," Flora told me. "Because you have all this drug traffic." She had moved to get away from the druggies and criminals in inner-city neighborhoods. But she quickly discovered that Homestead shared these problems and that drug dealers intruded on the spaces children should have to themselves.

"Most of 'em linger in the parks late at night, on the corners, mainly up on the hill." It is a terrible problem, she continued, "because kids like fourteen, fifteen years old are carrying these drugs. And it's really terrible." Warming to the theme, she offered a strong version of the fear others expressed, that drugs and drug paraphernalia lay around *all over the place*: "At night, the kids, going down to the store and they come through the back alley and there's needles and stuff laying there. I mean, totally ridiculous. And then they'll bring them up and they'll say, 'We found these here.' Or they'll give them to the policemen and whatnot. But what if one of these kids gets stuck with them, and who knows what the person had when they were using them?"

There was another, sadder scene in Flora's story that she did not tell us herself. One afternoon, several months after I did the interview, Charlee went back to take some pictures. Flora was not there, but her neighbor Henry was, in his usual seat surveying the neighborhood. He explained that Flora was "gone for a while." She had had problems, he said, and was in jail. He did not go into detail, but it became apparent from what he did say that Flora had been busted for drug use.

Flora's condemnation of the town for failing to handle its growing drug problem remains persuasive despite her own behavior. So, too, does her analysis of the ruin in store for the younger generation if nothing changes. A black woman in a depressed economy, she did not see many avenues of escape from drudgery and despair. Neither did a lot of other people. A big rehab center would have been one answer, but only one. In a town without jobs, and with fewer and fewer activities to fill nonwork hours, drugs and alcohol became an increasing danger. As another woman said bitterly, "Homestead is full of crackheads. You never know what will happen when you walk through town." Despite all the proclamations of its "homeyness" and countrylike feeling, Homestead seemed to some of its residents to be turning into another blighted urban environment.

The only way to manage, people said, was to avoid "down street" altogether or learn how to battle the "junkies" who hung around the corners. A young white woman prided herself on her toughness and the defensive behavior she used to make her way through bad blocks in Homestead. Eighth Avenue, she told me, "is like a ghetto—only junkies and drunkards and thugs. I wouldn't drive to get milk at night. I wouldn't take my children into that environment." At the same time, she said she would not give up on her town. "I can fight anyone."

Fighting one's way through a hometown was a paradoxical notion. But it spoke of faith in the community as well—a choice to stay and not abandon the place to "undesirable" elements, drifters, and newcomers. Here differences between generations arose. For those who had lived "below the tracks" and for whom that kind of community was a personal (if romanticized) memory, the change in Homestead was striking. For a younger generation, who knew "below" as their parents' and grandparents' story, facing the town now had a different dimension. Older women and men talked of being victimized by newcomers not, like the woman quoted above, of being prepared to "defend" the streets and neighborhoods of the town.

Louise, who had described her hard-working father unifying the neighborhood with his accordion after a full turn in the mill, told me an anecdote about her ninety-year-old mother. One Sunday afternoon, her mother was walking home from church along Eighth Avenue. Suddenly a man leapt out of an alley and grabbed her mother's pocketbook. Even worse, "They took her old, old prayer book from Europe, thinking there might be money in it."

For Louise, the incident conveyed the totality of Homestead's decline: a lack of respect for age, for religion, and for the sunny peacefulness of a Sunday afternoon. Another woman provided what could have been the conclusion of Louise's story. Once, she said, "we would walk and it was safe for us to walk." Things had changed. "Now, there's too many nuts out there." Later in the interview, this woman revealed that "nuts" were not the issue. In the past, she said, "even with the—, with the blacks, we got along. It's only now. Now I don't know, I don't like to walk now. I don't."

Shopkeepers were even less likely to mince words as time passed and Eighth Avenue declined further. Julio was typical in the sense he gave of being inside a fortress, closed to the street that once would have been his main source of customers. Julio's frequent glances at the black bar down the street revealed the specific source of his concerns. Up the hill, in the Wozeck shop, the sense of a fortress was repeated in the iron bars across the plate glass windows, a new development since I had been going to Homestead. Inside, at her cash register, Mrs. Wozeck kept her eyes on the door and even while chatting about her children and grandchildren did not let her attention wander. Business that afternoon was slow, as it had been since USX pulled out. As I watched, customers came in with small demands and made limited purchases: a quart of milk, a carton of cigarettes, a package of lunch meat. Months earlier, Rosie Wozeck had differentiated the customers her mother now served from those Rosie had known in her childhood: "Once people were buying T-bone steaks, and now they're buying jumbo [bologna]."

Yet Rosie also represents an important contrast to the view Julio and members of his generation presented. Rosie insisted that Homestead was not as bad as it looked and that the town would turn out OK. She remained in the neighborhood where she had grown up, living next door to her mother and to the store. It was safe there, she said, "everyone has known us for years." Carrying forward the vision she inherited from her father, Rosie consistently offered me the good face of Homestead. "I have no thoughts of moving," she assured me, insisting that her siblings "felt the same thing." "I love it," she added, "I feel so safe here."

"Why waste the manpower?"

The picture of Homestead as peaceful and quiet accompanied pride in its industrial might and famous labor struggles. What I was hearing was a version of the households/mill dichotomy Byington had established in the early twentieth century. An emphasis on the domestic and familial affirmed a part of Homestead that did not have to disappear with the disappearance of steel. Pictures of children on a front porch, three sisters hanging out in a park, a man at the side of his backyard swimming pool, brought the alleyways Hine once photographed into the present. Such pictures might even be full enough to distract a viewer from the empty space on the river. Yet residents of Homestead did not relinquish the other part of their history, the steel that had won World War II, girded the Empire State Building, and placed Homestead on a world map. In interviews, that history became a foundation for the resilience of the current population.

Rosie stayed in town because she felt at home and safe. That was why Joy said she moved to Homestead in the first place. "But I like Homestead. It's country," Joy explained. "They treat you like family. And when I lived in the city, that's something you couldn't—go out in your yard and sit and play with your kids. You never knew what was going to happen." The two young women had turned the prism of history to another side, revealing a town that did not hover in the dark shadow of a mill or depend on the hardened open hearth worker for a portrait of work. And through this side of the prism exists the possibility for renewal and reinvigoration of the ex-steel town. A step has already been taken in that direction in the restoration of the Carnegie Library of Homestead with its swimming pool, bowling alley, and auditorium. But these and similar improvements remain cosmetic as long as there are no jobs, police force, or source of tax revenue.

In order to maintain "homeyness," residents recognized, the police had to get out of their squad cars and walk the streets; children's parks had to be cleaned up so that condoms and needles did not decorate the slides and swings; high-tech industries had to recruit former manual workers and train them on the job. In Dan's words, "It's nice here," except "it *is* bad [on Eighth Avenue]. My buddy's a businessman down there. And I keep telling him to go to council and start bitching about it. We have dopers that are down on Seventh Avenue, down on the lower end." In his typical shift between loyalty and bitter impatience, he described the role of the local cops: "They've kind of cleaned them [dopers] up. They usually chase them. Some of the cops will chase them. But they get out. They arrest them, but they get out again. The cops can take them down [to court] and be back in Homestead, and they're free already." In the end the police had no more resources or leverage than anyone else. "Then the cops say, 'why waste the manpower, why waste the gas for the cars, waste paper and everything, if you can't get them in jail and off the streets?'" In the end, Dan concluded, it was not the fault of the police or of newspaper reporters or of his neighbors. Blame belonged to the borough, state, and federal governments.

He was not wrong. And he was not alone in the opinion that without an influx of funds, the town would remain plagued with crime, "dopers," and random violence. Nor was he wrong in arguing that renovation ought to start with the commercial area; inasmuch as this accorded with the view of business people and merchants, it bridged the gap between classes. But renovation had to involve more than geraniums and new storefronts. It had to also involve lighting the streets, expanding the police force, and enforcing laws against drug dealing.

Much of this came up explicitly, and heatedly, at a town meeting I attended in December 1993 in the old Bishop Boyle High School on Ninth Avenue. A small group of people attended, many of them familiar faces: an African-American woman I had interviewed at the Rainbow Kitchen, the owner of the appliance store on Eighth Avenue, the local state legislators, a scattering of citizens—black and white, old and young. The meeting had been called so townspeople could respond to a report prepared for the Pennsylvania Department of Community Affairs. "This plan sets forth a number of recommendations to correct both short and long term fiscal problems of the borough which are intended to restore the fiscal integrity of Homestead."[10] A summary was presented by three men from the state-sponsored Resource Development and Management Company. Recommendations included consolidating municipal services with neighboring towns, a proposal that was roundly condemned by anyone who said anything. (Someone behind me whispered loudly, "It will never happen.") The idea of sharing a police force elicited the most passionate protest.[11] Though some responses sounded simply chauvinistic and resistant to having "someone else" solve Homestead's problems, many were based on a careful assessment of the factors that would allow Homestead to thrive again, as a community and not just as part of a larger metropolitan area.

A good deal of the talk focused on increasing the town's revenue. Along these lines, one Recovery Plan proposal was to dim the streetlights as a way of saving money. The proposal brought vociferous, angry reactions. Without lights, the audience told the men sitting on stage, no one would venture out. In a dim town, residents would not go to the shops on Eighth Avenue or to local restaurants or even down the street to visit a neighbor's house. Making the streets darker by reducing lamp voltage underlined a darkness residents already saw in their town. They knew better than the planners how radically a dark town violated the image of Homestead and how darkness destroyed its best hopes for survival.

Not much got settled that evening. In the end, the Homestead City Council would negotiate with the Resource Development and Management Company and the state about implementing the proposals. There had been much heat and energy expressed by those who attended the meeting but, as one man pointed out, not many residents were there at all. "Look at how few people are here," he said. "No wonder nothing ever gets done."

"Nobody disturbed the goldfish"

By 1993, residents had stopped blaming USX for abandoning the town and started to search for relief from the disaster that had struck. It was not germane to characterize the town as a "deindustrialized" or "rust-belt" community. Rather, it was a "hometown" that was rapidly losing its economic, social, and cultural institutions. It was a hometown, too, that was depressed and dangerous—and to those conditions the small audience at Bishop Boyle demanded a response. Listening to the audience that night in December confirmed the impression I received from my last interviews: residents envisioned chaos and pollution unless something were done soon.

A portrait based on darkness, despair, and disorder did not immediately point the way to specific remedies, though it did reveal the pain residents experienced at the disappearance of a familiar way of life. Certainly, as the Recovery Plan argued, revenue was needed, a source of financial support for improvements and renewal. With the departure of USX, the town had lost the tax base it had come to depend upon. Given the poverty of Homestead, too, the idea of consolidating services across several boroughs made sense; the objections the audience made to that part of the plan indicated that those who stayed did so because they valued the distinctiveness and autonomy of their town. The individuals at the town meeting, like the residents I interviewed, had their own proposals for remedying the situation: clean up the town, get rid of "debris," and round up "druggies." By 1993, those were the crying needs, and they had to be dealt with before job training programs, a reopened supermarket, or a renovated public library could make a difference.

By 1993, a number of Homesteaders acknowledged that the mess could not be blamed on one part of the population—not newcomers, or blacks, or "wild kids." As the metaphor of pollution suggests, the blight had spread, sparing no group in the town. A woman I talked to offered the further perspective that succumbing to violence, alcoholism, and despair had long been a feature of steel town life; the difference was that, in the present, residents had little reason to keep these impulses in check.

She remembered growing up in a steel town where the after-work drink was not necessarily the only drink, and where some men regularly beat up their wives after a hard day. Life in a Mon River mill town, Jackie remarked, was pretty tough, in times of prosperity as well as in times of downturn. But even she suggested that "stuff" *then* was within limits, while *now*, "Did you notice all the locks on my doors?" I barely had time to answer before she went on: "My house is secured tight as Fort Knox." Because, she explained, one sister was a "crack head" who knew no limits; when she got desperate, she would break into and trash anyone's house—including kin. The other sister was an alcoholic, crashing all over town, Jackie said, not coming "home" to family.

Like the generations of her parents and grandparents, Jackie protected herself by living in an enclave with people who were "the same." She lived in Hunky Hollow, across from her mother. Her sisters, by contrast, lived "up there" in Homestead where, Jackie offered, they were subject to temptation, a bad crowd, and dirt. The neighborhood up there, Jackie said, was "shit." As often as possible, she invited her sister's kids to her house, "away from the shit on the hill." Down here, she said, their language "cleaned up" and they didn't "talk black." Alert to the implications of her remarks, she insisted she was not being racist, just factual. "Racism is the riots in Los Angeles."

Words like "dark" and "dirty" to describe the current environment of Homestead came up more openly in interviews in 1991 and 1992. The adjectives complemented straightforward reports of discomfort, fear, and terror on streets that once were totally familiar. "Even during the day, you have that funny feeling, watching your purse, sort of like watching sides, you know, who's on the side or just observing everything or just being on the lookout," a sixty-something wife of an ex-steelworker described her feelings when she walked on Eighth Avenue. "Never can tell," she added. She paused, then lowered her voice, ending in an inaudible whisper: "Oh, I don't know if I should say this or not. . . . There are more [inaudible]." The word "blacks" was so quiet I was not sure I had heard it. She continued: "We didn't have that many in this area and especially up on the hill, we never had any up on the hill there. And now it's polluted there, and it's all [inaudible]. It's not the same. Everything's just going to pot."

"Polluted" was a well-chosen word. It captures the view I heard expressed over and over again that Homestead was "spoiling." "See this neighborhood down there on the avenue?" a white woman asked me while we stood on the corner talking. "It makes me puke. Kids. Can't understand it. White mother, black kids. You know, I mean it might be all right for— you may think it's all right, but what's those kids gonna do?" She repeated what was basically a rhetorical question: "What's gonna happen to those kids? I look at those kids, I get sick. Which way are they going?" As the word *pollution* implies and her reference claims, mixing things up messes things up.

In the 1990s even crime had become messy, crossing the boundaries of what a "bad act" was supposed to be. Not only did an elderly woman have to worry about her prayer book, but a rash of rape cases involving women in their seventies and eighties occurred in 1988 and 1989. Homestead residents who talked to me about those crimes were plainly disgusted, and the crimes drove both the local and the national police into a search that came close to violating the civil rights of residents. Until the ACLU stepped in, every black man in Homestead was subject to seizure and fingerprinting. It was the nightmare climax of Otis's story of "No, no, I never go up there."

On our last tour through town together, Sam discovered a symbol of the pollution spreading through Homestead. Generally upbeat, on this trip he revealed his despair at how "dark" everything had become. This tour took us up to the redone Carnegie Library. We went across the street to small Frick Park with its cupola honoring the steel produced by the Homestead Works. I found the place pleasant, green, and quiet, a peaceful interlude in an industrial town—the sense of calm town planners intended. Sam saw it differently from the way I did. "Now this is Frick Park. And at one time," he paused for a few minutes, then continued: "I told you it was a different world when I was growing up. When I was growing up, that was a fish pond full of goldfish, and nobody disturbed the goldfish. That's the kind of system we were raised in. You could never do that now. It's filled with dirt."

I could end the book on a sad note, as Sam ended his tour of Homestead by pointing to a pond filled with dirt, the goldfish ruined. This was a new kind of dirt, not the soot and smoke that once represented prosperity.

No one now could transform the dark puff from a smokestack into a cloud or find graphite glowing on the sidewalks. Dirt was still symbolic, but of change and decline, of hopelessness and despair. In the face of the present, the old days were remembered as "clean," a time of solidarity and celebration rather than of oppressive work conditions, bitter strikes, and racial and ethnic animosities.

But it would not be fair either to the residents I interviewed or to their histories of the town to end on a note of pessimism. Memories of the good old days, and the self-conscious contrasts between then and now, constitute an affirmation of community and a source of hope for the future. Looking back nostalgically, residents recreated a core of life apart from steel; upon this core, a new community can be imagined. Based on "below the tracks," the proffered image of Homestead as harmonious and "homey" communicates and confirms the values townspeople have held over time. These values were transmitted from generation to generation, not stopping with newcomers like Joy and Flora, who moved in because it was a "good place to raise children."

The frequent use of words like "country" and "homelike" for one of America's most famous industrial towns underlines the quality Homestead had for its residents throughout the century. The close, face-to-face interactions in crowded neighborhoods and the memories of sharing and celebrating *deindustrialized* the town well before USX made its final decision. This is not to deny the devastation of the pullout, but to note that townspeople always envisioned a town other than the one lying in the shadow of the mill. Turning from the great Homestead Works and the intruders who took advantage of its presence and, later, of its absence, residents created an image in which the "garden" equaled the "machine" in significance. Such an image is not new, as *Homestead: The Households of a Mill Town* testifies, but it serves a new purpose at the end of the twentieth century. It is an image for the future, represented in verbal and visual portraits that can carry the once world-famous steel town into a new century.

Memorial to the Homestead strike of 1892.

NOTES

Preface

1. See, for instance, Connerton 1989; Gillis 1994.
2. Byington [1910] 1974, 3.
3. See Trachtenberg 1989.
4. In *Mind's Eye, Mind's Truth*, James Curtis (1989) discusses these and other aspects of the Evans and Agee collaboration.
5. Hareven and Langenbach 1978, 31.
6. Chalfen 1991, 2.
7. The work of Doug Harper (1982) includes sensitive visual portrayals of work; see also Kane, *Works* (1992). There is also a tradition of official "industrial photography" in the United States.
8. Curtis 1989, 30–32.

1. Envisioning Homestead

1. The pictures we discussed with residents included a historical collection from the University of Pittsburgh Archives, Brodsky's portraits, and family albums people brought out during an interview. See preface for further discussion of the use of photography in our project.
2. Dudley 1994, which discusses the closing of a Chrysler plant in Kenosha, Wisconsin, mentions the changes residents noticed in the physical landscape of the town.
3. Paul Krause's 1992 *The Battle for Homestead* is a first-rate account of the strike; it is currently the best source on the events leading to the drama of 1892.
4. Serrin 1992, xxiii.
5. In 1973, the federal government mandated affirmative action hiring policies in the American steel industry, at least formally doing away with racial (and gender) discrimination.
6. Serrin 1992, 278, in general an excellent source on union-corporation relations.
7. See, for instance, Hoerr 1988 and Serrin 1992 for elaboration of this point.
8. The other volumes are Elizabeth Butler, *Women and the Trades* (1909); Crystal Eastman, *Work Accidents and the Law* (1910); John Fitch, *The Steel Workers* (1910); Paul U. Kellogg, ed., *The Pittsburgh District: The Civic Frontage* (1914); Paul U. Kellogg, ed., *Wage Earning Pittsburgh* (1914).
9. Among the exceptions to this view of steel towns are Ruck, *Sandlot Seasons* (1987) and Kleinberg, *The Shadow of the Mills* (1989).

10. "Below" actually contained the First and part of the Second Ward; see Cole 1994.

11. Hinshaw and Modell 1996.

12. See Gaventa 1980.

13. At the time of publication of this book, no (public) decision had been reached about what to put on the empty space where the mill had been.

2. Setting the Stage

1. Concentrating on those who do stay in rust-belt towns, our book shows how complicated both the reasons and the rationalizations for such a decision may be.

2. Pappas 1989 makes a similar point about the residents of Barberton, an Ohio town that lost its tire plant.

3. Shkilnyk 1985, 233.

4. Lakoff and Johnson 1980, 5.

5. Pittsburgh Regional Planning Association 1966, 5.

6. Hoerr 1988, 570.

7. John Friedmann, quoted in Bluestone and Harrison 1982, 20.

8. Some of this reflected deliberate policy on the part of the corporation, as when Andrew Carnegie built his famous libraries and made sure each mill town had a Christmas tree. Later, the corporation sponsored sports teams and other events. See, for instance, Ruck 1987.

9. Bell [1941] 1976, 212.

10. Ibid., 167.

11. Pappas 1989 borrows the notion of "family" from his interviewees; workers "belonged" to Sieberling as if to a kin group.

12. One bar on Eighth Avenue, for instance, had a wall filled with photographs, including several of men standing on top of a huge crane and in front of an oversized ladle.

3. The Curtain Comes Down

1. See Gaventa 1980 for a similar report on the reluctance of laid-off workers to blame either the company or the union.

2. See Bluestone and Harrison 1982 for fuller discussion of these decisions.

3. Hoerr 1988, 594.

4. Pappas writes that the men and women of Barberton similarly hoped the tire plant would resume full employment, as it had after other lay-offs. "Their experience with past recessions made them believe that the present one would pass and the jobs would reappear" (1989, 49).

5. Bluestone and Harrison 1982.

6. Ibid, 79.

7. Pappas reports a similar pattern of early marriage and childbearing in Barberton. "He was married soon after he obtained this good factory job; this is a common pattern among young blue-collar workers" (1989, 49).

8. Wages were, of course, a factor, but must be considered along with the other things mentioned by ex-steelworkers. See Bluestone and Harrison 1982 for the refusal of laid-off workers to take minimum-wage jobs.

9. Pappas 1989, 83.

10. These responses exist elsewhere. See Dudley 1994, Zippay 1991, and Pappas 1989.

11. Bluestone and Harrison 1982, 20, quoting Paul Samuelson.

12. Pappas 1989, 34.

13. See Gillis 1994 for discussions of the importance of physical commemoration.

4. Women's Activities and Men's Work

1. Byington [1910] 1974, is an exception; so is Kleinberg 1989.

2. Like frontiersmen in any setting, the people of the steel valley created various legends and legendary heroes to mark their achievements and conquests; see Dorson 1981.

3. The eight-hour day was instituted in 1923 (Brody 1970, 274).

4. Bell [1941] 1976, 32.

5. See Modell and Hinshaw 1996.

6. Byington talks about the "roll of accidents reported in the Homestead paper" and the facing page includes reprints of front-page headlines: "Hot Metal Fell in Water and Exploded," "Two Men Injured by Chain Breaking" (1974 [1910], 92, 93).

7. Serrin 1992, 62.

8. See Kleinberg 1989 for an account of the importance of boarding.

9. Bell [1941] 1976, 150.

10. "After watching the busy lives and the problems of these women, I came to believe that the woman who can keep her home healthful and attractive on $15 or less a week has in her elements of genius" (Byington [1910] 1974, 79).

11. Byington [1910] 1974, 141.

12. In Portraits in Steel, Rogovin juxtaposes portraits of a woman or man at work with an image of a woman or man at home, letting the contrast speak for itself (Rogovin and Frisch 1993).

13. Komarovsky 1967, 72.

5. Raising a New Generation in an Ex-Steel Town

1. Byington [1910] 1974, 127.

2. The phrase is borrowed from Paul Willis's fine study of working-class socialization in Britain (1977).

3. Byington [1910] 1974, 118.

4. Serrin 1992, 62.

5. Byington [1910] 1974, 126–27.

6. The point that schools educate children in "sociability" rather than "skills" is made in schooling literature and has particular ramifications for children in working-class communities; see, for example, Eckert 1989.

7. Walker 1922, 83. Thirty years later, Walker became director of research in technology and industrial relations at Yale, where he again emphasized the significance of practical, on-the-job training (Walker 1950).

8. Haas 1977, qtd. in Applebaum 1981, 87.

9. Willis 1977, 56.

10. Bell [1941] 1976, 56.

11. Byington [1910] 1974, 126.

12. Ibid., 127.

13. Ibid., 159.

14. Buss and Redburn 1983, 101–02.

15. *The Wall Street Journal,* June 3, 1983, p. 1.

16. In a 1980s study of laid-off steelworkers, Putterman 1985 mentions the same phenomenon; the men and women he interviewed wanted on-the-job training, not government sponsored programs.

17. Some time after this, the Pittsburgh newspapers began to refer to gangs in Homestead, but during the time of my interviews no one used the term: they were "crowds," "bands," and "bunches."

18. Foltman 1968, 69–70.

19. Pappas 1989, 135, 137.

6. Harmony and Discord

1. The *Homestead Daily Messenger* shut down in 1979, when the town could no longer support a paper of its own.

2. Davis 1979, 20.

3. Chalfen 1991.

4. Early in the twentieth century, Kennywood Amusement Park began sponsoring nationality days, when people of the same ethnic background would use the park for their celebrations. This practice has continued into the 1990s.

5. The phrase refers to the title of a book on Pittsburgh. See Bodnar, Simon, and Weber, *Lives of Their Own* (1982).

6. See Miner and Roberts 1989.

7. Bodnar 1982, 63.

8. See also Michrina 1993.

9. The number of Slovaks in the region reached nearly three thousand in 1910, leading to a rapid growth in clubs. (Faires 1989, 12).

10. The distinction between occupational and ethnic taverns comes from Kornblum 1974.

11. Bell [1941] 1976, 209.

12. Byington [1910] 1974, 163–64.

13. Bodnar 1982, 63.

14. Plotkin and Scheuerman 1990.

15. Serrin 1992, 22.

16. Bell [1941] 1976, 185.

17. The term is in Faires 1989, 13.

18. Many of the people I interviewed asked me about my own background, usually wanting to know my ethnicity and my religion.

19. Byington [1910] 1974, 115.

20. Nash 1989 notes that people in the deindustrialized factory town she studied began to market ethnic arts and crafts as a way of reviving the economy. I saw no sign of such a movement in Homestead.

21. Byington [1910] 1974, 149–50.

22. Life-cycle events, like christenings, confirmations, birthday parties, and weddings probably constitute the most common subjects in family albums; see Chalfen 1991. In addition, there are usually studio portraits of weddings to complement, and enhance, the story told in candid snapshots.

23. Bell [1941] 1976, 329.

24. Faires 1989, 13.

25. Bell [1941] 1976, 138.

26. Pritchard 1989, 339.

27. Seiler, Wintersteen, and Baptie 1980, xii.

28. Byington [1910] 1974, 15.

29. Hoerr 1988, 170.

7. Steel and Segregation

1. The notion of official texts and hidden texts comes from Scott 1990.

2. Dickerson's *Out of the Crucible* (1986) is a thorough account of black migration to and settlement in Mon Valley steel towns.

3. Between 1910 and 1930, Laurence Glasco writes, "newly opened jobs at places like Jones and Laughlin Steel enlarged Pittsburgh's black population from twenty-five to fifty-five thousand, while hiring by Carnegie Steel plants in Aliquippa, Homestead, Rankin, Braddock, Duquesne, McKeesport, and Clairton raised the black population in those neighboring towns from five to twenty-three thousand" (1989, 75).

4. Bell [1941] 1976, 330. Interestingly, Bell capitalizes the white ethnic nickname and not the nickname for African-Americans.

5. See Ruck 1987 for an account of sports in towns like Homestead and the significance of Little League to the history of race relations.

6. See Cole 1994 for a description of the demographic composition of the ward compared to the neighborhoods above the tracks.

7. Hinshaw and Modell 1996.

8. In an important essay, Barbara Fields (1982) argues that as an ideological concept, racism develops in situations of scarce resources.

9. Kornblum 1974, 66.

10. Byington [1910] 1974, 14.

11. Dickerson's account (1986) of black steel workers in the Western Pennsylvania area is excellent. He writes as a historian and, as well, a member of a steelworking family.

12. Byington [1910] 1974, 14.

13. Magda 1985, 14.

14. Serrin 1992, 154.

15. Bell [1941] 1976, 243.

16. Bodnar 1982, 128.

17. Quoted in Hinshaw 1995.

18. The Consent Decree was the culmination of several decades of black activism and liberal support for changes in the steel industry. Its provisions included supervision of the steel industry's hiring and promotion practices. For a full account of black efforts to combat racial discrimination in the steel industry, see Dickerson 1986.

19. Quoted in Hinshaw 1995.

20. In fact, cleaning tar was a job frequently given to African Americans.

21. Bidding for jobs was the way a person moved from position to position in the mill.

8. Outside the Mill

1. That blacks had to sit in the balcony of the Stahl Theatre was well known, as was the fact that they were not permitted to swim in the pool at the local Carnegie Public Library (Serrin 1992, 21).

2. Serrin 1992, 21.

3. Duis 1983, *passim*.

4. See Hinshaw and Modell 1996 for a more detailed history of informal segregation in Homestead bars, taverns, and other recreational spaces.

5. Jitney taxis, though illegal, are accepted in Pittsburgh and Allegheny County and provide an important source of income for African Americans.

6. Curt Miner qtd. in Cole 1994.

7. See, for example, Glasco 1989 for a description of the socioeconomic differences among blacks in Pittsburgh.

8. Efforts to clean up the red-light district in Homestead started in earnest in the 1950s and 1960s and were relatively successful; see Miner 1989 and Serrin 1992.

9. Pritchard 1989, 330.

10. See Cole 1994.

11. Byington, [1910] 1974, opposite p. 41.

12. Kornblum 1974, 37.

13. See Hinshaw and Modell 1996; Serrin 1992; Hoerr 1988.

14. He was correct. Munhall, the richest of the three boroughs, has been virtually all white through most of its history.

15. Steel Valley High was built in 1972, an early response to the declining economy, population, and tax base of steel towns along the Mon. It replaced the separate borough high schools and brought students in from a wide regional area.

16. Glasco 1989.

9. Responses in the Valley

1. "In Pittsburgh, the U.S. Steel Corporation called a press conference to announce that it would permanently close down fourteen mills in eight states (principally in Pennsylvania and Ohio) within the year, thus laying off over 13,000 workers. Its reward was an $850 million tax break from the federal government, which it later put toward the down payment on the purchase of Marathon Oil" (Bluestone and Harrison 1982, 4).

2. Bluestone and Harrison 1982, 139, quoting Metzgar 1980.

3. Zippay 1991, 12.

4. Byington [1910] 1974, 98.

5. Zippay 1991, 51.

6. Serrin 1992, 10.

7. Bluestone and Harrison 1982, 156.

8. Buss and Redburn 1983, 128.

9. Rogovin and Frisch 1993, 95.

10. Bluestone and Harrison 1982, 105.

11. Bluestone and Harrison 1982 argue that in few cases do closings result from worker laziness (14).

12. Dudley 1994, 141.

13. I also interviewed the mayor of Homestead as we drove around the mill site. His talk referred more to processes of steelmaking and to the "good" years of Homestead than it did to current conditions.

14. Foltman 1968 describes the same reaction after the closing of a Buffalo steel plant.

15. Bluestone and Harrison make this point in *The Deindustrialization of America* (1982).

16. Hansen, Bentley, and Davidson 1980, 90. A few pages later, the authors point out that the union did nothing either.

17. Bluestone and Harrison 1982, 65.

18. Zippay 1991, 12.

19. Bluestone and Harrison 1982, 11.

20. Jahoda, Lazarsfeld, and Zeisel 1971 [1933], 53.

21. Hoerr 1988, 193.

22. Plotkin and Scheuerman 1990, 201.

23. Serrin 1992, xxiii.

24. Ibid., 347.

25. Bell [1941] 1974, 401.

26. Serrin 1992, 347.

27. Fantasia 1988 discusses worker activism and consciousness in recent American history in *Cultures of Solidarity*.

28. Byington [1910] 1974, 168.

29. Bensman and Lynch 1987, 179.

30. Pappas 1989, 160.

31. Eventually, clothes distribution was taken over by a community organization located in a church around the corner from the Rainbow Kitchen.

32. Pappas 1989, 176.

33. Bars were the exception, still serving the functions they had always served in industrial towns; see, for example, Rosenzweig 1983.

10. Beyond the Closing

1. Serrin 1992, 348.

2. At the time of this writing—1995—the Rainbow Kitchen was still open, running on a shoestring budget.

3. See Gaventa 1980.

4. See Zippay 1991.

5. In her book about the closing of the American Motors plant in Kenosha, Wisconsin, Kathryn Dudley describes the horror with which workers watched boat clubs go up where an automobile plant had stood (1994, 164).

6. Serrin 1992, 368–69.

7. That such a change had been made in the city of Pittsburgh as well did not alter the meaning for him.

8. Even before the mill closings, social workers in the Mon Valley "reported finding both 'underlying racial tensions' and some 'outright hostility.' The investigators suggest that 'if the economic base continues to decline, race relations could worsen" (Cunningham and Martz 1986, 94).

9. See Gaventa 1980, *passim*.

10. *Recovery Plan*, November 22, 1993, p. I-1. The plan was developed for the Borough of Homestead, and did not include Munhall and West Homestead, except as sites of cooperation and consolidation.

11. The recommendation to reduce city council from nine to five members also caused a fairly furious reaction. "We need nine members to handle all the problems there are," was one typical statement.

BIBLIOGRAPHY

Agee, J., and W. Evans. [1941] 1960. *Let Us Now Praise Famous Men*. New York: Ballantine Books.

Anderson, Benedict. 1991. *Imagined Communities*. New York: Verso.

Applebaum, Herbert. 1981. *Royal Blue: The Culture of Construction Workers*. New York: Holt, Rinehart, and Winston.

Barth, Fredrik. 1969. *Ethnic Groups and Boundaries*. Boston: Little Brown.

Bell, Thomas. [1941] 1976. *Out of this Furnace*. Pittsburgh: University of Pittsburgh Press.

Bensman, David, and Roberta Lynch. 1987. *Rusted Dreams: Hard Times in a Steel Community*. New York: McGraw Hill.

Bluestone, B., and B. Harrison. 1982. *The Deindustrialization of America*. New York: Basic Books.

Bodnar, John. 1977. *Steelton: Immigration and Industrialization*. Pittsburgh: University of Pittsburgh Press.

———. 1982. *Workers' World: Kinship, Community, and Protest in an Industrializing Society 1900–1940*. Baltimore: Johns Hopkins University Press.

———. 1989. "Power and Memory in Oral History: Workers and Managers at Studebaker." *Journal of American History* 75(4): 1201–22.

Bodnar, John E., Roger D. Simon, and Michael P. Weber. 1982. *Lives of Their Own: Blacks, Italians, and Poles in Pittsburgh, 1900–1960*. Urbana: University of Illinois Press.

Borchert, John. 1982. *Alley Life in Washington: Family, Community, Religion and Folklife in the City*. Urbana: University of Illinois Press.

Brody, David. [1960] 1970. *Steelworkers in America: The Nonunion Era*. New York: Russell and Russell.

Buss, Terry F., and F. Stevens Redburn. 1983. *Shutdown at Youngstown: Public Policy for Mass Unemployment*. Albany: State University of New York Press.

Butler, Elizabeth. 1909. *Women and the Trades: Pittsburgh, 1907–1908*. New York: Charities Publication Committee, Press of W. F. Fell Co.

Byington, Margaret. [1910] 1974. *Homestead: The Households of a Mill Town*. Pittsburgh: University of Pittsburgh Press.

Chalfen, Richard. 1987. *Snapshot Versions of Life*. Bowling Green, Ohio: The Popular Press.

———. 1991. *Turning Leaves: The Photograph Collections of Two Japanese American Families*. Albuquerque: University of New Mexico Press.

Cole, Lori. 1994. "Voices and Choices: Race, Class, and Identity, Homestead, Pennsylvania, 1941–1945." Ph.D. dissertation, Department of History, Carnegie Mellon University.

Collier, John. [1967] 1986. *Visual Anthropology: Photography as a Research Method*. New York: Holt, Rinehart, and Winston.

Connerton, Paul. 1989. *How Societies Remember*. New York: Cambridge University Press.

Cook, Robert F., ed. 1987. *Worker Dislocation: Case Studies of Causes and Cures*. Kalamazoo, Mich.: W. E. Upjohn Institute for Employment Research.

Cunningham, J., and P. Martz. 1986. "Steel People: Survival and Resilience in Pittsburgh's Mon Valley." University of Pittsburgh School of Social Work report.

Curtis, James. 1989. *Mind's Eye, Mind's Truth*. Philadelphia: Temple University Press.

Davis, Fred. 1979. *Yearning for Yesterday: A Sociology of Nostalgia*. New York: Free Press.

Demarest, David, ed. 1992. *"The River Ran Red": Homestead, 1892*. Pittsburgh: University of Pittsburgh Press.

Dickerson, Dennis. 1986. *Out of the Crucible: Black Steelworkers in Western Pennsylvania, 1875–1980*. Albany: State University of New York.

Dorson, Richard M. 1981. *Land of the Millrats*. Cambridge, Mass.: Harvard University Press.

Dudley, Kathryn Marie. 1994. *The End of the Line*. Chicago: The University of Chicago Press.

Duis, Perry. 1983. *The Saloon: Public Drinking in Chicago and Boston, 1880–1920*. Urbana: University of Illinois Press.

Eastman, Crystal. 1910. *Work Accidents and the Law*. New York: Charities Publication Committee, Press of W. F. Fell Co.

Eckert, Penelope. 1989. *Jocks and Burnouts: Social Categories and Identity in the High School*. New York: Teachers College Press.

Faires, Nora. 1989. "Immigrants and Industry: Peopling the Iron City," in *City at the Point*, ed. S. Hays, 3–32. Pittsburgh: University of Pittsburgh Press.

Fantasia, Rick. 1988. *Cultures of Solidarity*. Berkeley: University of California Press.

Fields, Barbara. 1982. "Ideology and Race in American History," in *Region, Race, and Reconstruction: Essays in Honor of C. Vann Woodward*, ed. J. M. Kousser and J. M. McPherson. New York: Oxford University Press.

Fitch, John. 1910. *The Steel Workers*. New York: Charities Publication Committee, Press of W. F. Fell Co.

Foltman, Felician. 1968. *White- and Blue-Collars in a Mill Shutdown*. Ithaca, N.Y.: Cornell University School of Industrial and Labor Relations.

Gaventa, John. 1980. *Power and Powerlessness: Quiescence and Rebellion in an Appalachian Valley*. Urbana: University of Illinois Press.

Gillis, John R. 1994. *Commemorations: The Politics of National Identity*. Princeton, N.J.: Princeton University Press.

Glasco, Laurence. 1989. "The Black Experience," in *City at the Point*, ed. S. Hays, pp. 69–110. Pittsburgh: University of Pittsburgh Press.

Guimond, James. 1991. *American Photography and the American Dream*. Chapel Hill: University of North Carolina Press.

Hansen, G. B., M. T. Bentley, and R. A. Davidson. 1980. *Hardrock Miners in a Shutdown*. Utah State University: Economic Research Center and Center for Productivity and Quality of Working Life.

Hareven, T., and R. Langenbach. 1978. *Amoskeag: Life and Work in an American Factory City*. New York: Pantheon Press.

Harper, Douglas A. 1982. *Good Company*. Chicago: University of Chicago.

Harris, Alex, ed. 1987. *A World Unsuspected*. Chapel Hill: University of North Carolina Press.

Hinshaw, John. 1995. "Dialectics of Division: Race and Power in American Steel." Ph.D. dissertation, Department of History, Carnegie Mellon University.

Hinshaw, J., and J. Modell. 1996. "Perceiving Racism: Homestead from Depression to Deindustrialization." *Pennyslvania History* 63(1): 17–52.

Hirsch, Herbert. 1971. *Poverty and Politicization: Political Socialization in an American Sub-Culture*. New York: The Free Press.

Hoerr, John. 1988. *And the Wolf Finally Came*. Pittsburgh: University of Pittsburgh Press.

Jahoda, M., P. Lazarsfeld, and H. Zeisel. [1933] 1971. *Marienthal: The Sociography of an Unemployed Community*. Chicago: Aldine-Atherton.

Kane, Martin W. 1992. *Works: Photographs of Enterprise*. Wilmington, Del.: Hagley Museum and Library.

Kellogg, Paul U., ed. 1914. *The Pittsburgh District: The Civic Frontage*. New York: Survey Associates.

———. 1914. *Wage Earning Pittsburgh*. New York: Survey Associates.

Kleinberg, S. J. 1989. *The Shadow of the Mills*. Pittsburgh: University of Pittsburgh Press.

Komarovsky, Mirra. 1967. *Blue-Collar Marriage*. New York: Random House

Kornblum, William. 1974. *Blue Collar Community*. Chicago: University of Chicago Press.

Krause, Paul. 1992. *The Battle for Homestead, 1880–1992*. Pittsburgh: University of Pittsburgh Press.

Lakoff, George, and Mark Johnson. 1980. *Metaphors We Live By*. Chicago: University of Chicago.

Lesy, Michael. 1980. *Time Frames: The Meaning of Family Pictures*. New York: Pantheon Press.

Magda, Matthew. 1985. *Monessen: Industrial Boomtown and Steel Community*. Harrisburg, Pa.: Commonwealth of Pennsylvania, Pennsylvania Historical and Museum Commission.

Marx, Leo. 1964. *The Machine in the Garden*. New York: Oxford University Press.

Maurer, Harry. 1979. *Not Working*. New York: Holt, Rinehart, Winston.

Michrina, Barry. 1993. *Pennsylvania Mining Families*. Lexington: The University Press of Kentucky.

Miner, Curtis. 1989. Homestead: The Story of a Steeltown. Pittsburgh: Historical Society of Western Pennsylvania. Pamphlet.

Miner, C., and P. Roberts. 1989. "Engineering an Industrial Diaspora: Homestead 1941." *Pittsburgh History* 79(1).

Modell, Judith. 1994. "Envisioning Homestead: The Use of Photographs in Interviewing," in *Interactive Oral History Interviewing*, ed. K. Rogers and E. McMahan, 141–61. Hillsdale, N.J.: Lawrence Erlbaum.

Modell, J., and J. Hinshaw. 1996. "Male Work and Mill Work." *International Journal of Oral History*, Special Edition on Gender and Memory 4: 133–49.

Nash, June C. 1989. *From Tank Town to High Tech*. Albany: The State University of New York.

O'Malley, Michael. 1962. *Miners Hill*. New York: Harper and Brothers.

Pappas, Gregory. 1989. *The Magic City: Unemployment in a Working Class Community*. Ithaca, N.Y.: Cornell University Press.

Pittsburgh Regional Planning Association. 1966. *A Neighborhood Analysis for the Borough of Homestead, Pennsylvania*. Pittsburgh, Pa. January.

Plotkin, Sidney. 1990. "Enclave Consciousness and Neighborhood Activism," in *Dilemmas of Activism: Class, Community, and the Politics of Local Mobilization*, ed. J. Kling and P. Posner, 218–39. Philadelphia: Temple University Press.

Plotkin, Sidney, and William E. Scheuerman. 1986. *The Steel Crisis: The Economics and Politics of a Declining Industry*. New York: Praeger Publishers.

———. 1990. "Two Roads Left: Strategies of Resistance to Plant Closings in the Monongahela Valley," in *Dilemmas of Activism: Class, Community, and the Politics of Local Mobilization*, ed. J. Kling and P. Posner. Philadelphia: Temple University Press.

Pritchard, Linda. 1989. "The Soul of the City: A Social History of Religion in Pittsburgh," in *City at the Point*, ed. S. Hays, 327–60. Pittsburgh: University of Pittsburgh Press.

Putterman, Julie S. 1985. *Chicago Steelworkers: The Cost of Unemployment*. Chicago: Steelworkers Research Project.

Recovery Plan for the Borough of Homestead. Prepared for Pennsylvania Department of Community Affairs Resource Development and Management, Inc. 1993. Draft report in author's files.

Rogovin, M., and M. Frisch. 1993. *Portraits in Steel*. Ithaca, N.Y.: Cornell University Press.

Rosenzweig, Roy. 1983. *Eight Hours for What We Will*. New York: Cambridge University Press.

Ruck, Robert. 1987. *Sandlot Seasons: Sport in Black Pittsburgh*. Urbana: University of Illinois Press.

Scheuerman, William. 1986. *The Steel Crisis: The Economics and Politics of a Declining Industry*. New York: Praeger.

Scott, James. 1990. *Domination and the Arts of Resistance*. New Haven: Yale University Press.

Seiler, M. M., D. Wintersteen, C. Baptie. 1980. *Mid the Hills of Pennsylvania: Munhall-Homestead-West Homestead*. Annanadale, Va.: Charles Baptie Studios, Inc.

Serrin, William. 1992. *Homestead: The Glory and Tragedy of an American Steel Town*. New York: Times Books.

Shkilnyk, Anastasia M. 1985. *A Poison Stronger Than Love: The Destruction of an Ojibwa Community*. New Haven: Yale University Press.

Sontag, Susan. 1977. *On Photography*. New York: Farrar, Straus and Giroux.

Strauss, Anselm. 1961. *Images of the American City*. New York: Doubleday Anchor.

Strohmeyer, John. 1986. *Crisis in Bethlehem*. New York: Penguin Books.

Trachtenberg, Alan. 1989. *Reading American Photography: Images as History*. New York: Hill and Wang.

Walker, Charles. 1922. *Steel: The Diary of a Furnace Worker*. Boston: Atlantic Monthly Press.

———. 1950. *Labor Relations*. Ithaca: Cornell University Press.

Willis, Paul. [1977] 1981. *Learning to Labor*. New York: Columbia University Press.

Zippay, Allison. 1991. *From Middle Income to Poor: Downward Mobility Among Displaced Steelworkers*. New York: Praeger.

Bibliography

INDEX

Page numbers in italic denote illustrations.

Accidents, 97

African Americans, 6, 12, 15, 297; crime blamed on, 306, 308–10; jobs of women, 100, 102. *See also* Race relations

Alcoholism, 74, 265–67

Amalgamated Association of Iron and Steel Workers, 5

Amusement park, on former mill lot, 25 26, 76, 304–05

And the Wolf Finally Came (Hoerr), 267

Anderson, Bob, 268–70, 275, 299, 303

"Anglos," 6

Bars: occupational *vs.* residential, 211–12, 231; racial discrimination in, 232–38, 241–42

Bell, Thomas, 32–33, 94, 167, 205; on celebrations, 169–71; and education, 136, 138

"Below the tracks," *26*, 157–58, 161–62, 194–95, 301; community in, 29, 31; meaning of, 11–13, 23. *See also* Neighborhoods

Bensman, Roberta, 271

Blue Collar Community (Kornblum), 211

Bluestone, B., 265–66

Boarders, 98

Bodnar, John, 13, 162, 167

Braddock, Pa., 16, 34, 36, 58, 272

Byington, Margaret, 92, 104, 169, 204; on education, 133–34, 136–38, 142–43, 145; on ethnicity, 166, 180; on families of steelworkers, 8–9; on home life, 90, 142–43, 250, 254

Carnegie, Andrew, 5–6

Carnegie Library, in Homestead, 2, 4, 314

Carnegie Steel Company, 5

Celebrations, 29–30, 165–69

Chalfen, Richard, 160–61

Charity, 308; from churches, 270, 273, 275–76. *See also* Rainbow Kitchen, the

Children, *134*, 311–12; ambitions for, 107–08, 133–36, 138–39, 143–44, 149–52; hopes and fears for, 35–36, 109–10; influence of mill on, 42, 97, 138–40; racial integration of, 197–99; raising, 29, 152, 176–77

Churches, 226–27; charity from, 270, 273, 275–76; and Denominational Ministry Strategy, 299–300; ethnicity of, 174–75, 177; of Homestead, 145–48, 178–79. *See also* Religion

Civil rights legislation, 194; dislike of, 180, 246; effects of on Homestead, 14–15, 206–10, 230–49

Class, social, 11–12, 35–36, 269–70, 297

Community, 13–15, 17, 76, 148–49, 158–60; decline of, 72–73, 295–96, 298–99; deindustrializing, 20, 95–96; nostalgia for, 23–24, 298–99. *See also* Harmony; Neighborhoods

Consent Decree of 1974, 92, 207–09

Consumerism, 27

Crime, 318; blame for, 305–06, 308–10; increase of, 296–97, 312–13

Cultural institutions, "below the tracks," 31

Davis, Fred, 159
Deindustrialization, 3, 95–96, 264, 319;
    effects of, 106, 109, 311; speed of, 257–
    58
Denominational Ministry Strategy
    (DMS), 299–300
Depression, the: nostalgia about, 13, 23;
    women working during, 105–06
Discrimination: against blacks, 6–7, 15,
    196–97, 202–11; against Hunkies, 95,
    167–68, 181; against mixed marriages,
    307–08, 318; ethnic and racial, 172,
    180
Divorce, 73, 266–67
Drinking, 153. *See also* Alcoholism
Drug use, 153; blacks blamed for, 309–10;
    increase in, 296–98, 311–12; proposals
    about, 305, 314; as result of plant
    closings, 73–74, 311
Dudley, Kathryn, 263

Economics, 31, 254, 109
Education, 145; and ambitions for
    children, 107–08; ambivalence toward,
    136–38, 140–42; and changing needs,
    149–50, 303; and learning to labor,
    134–37; as work, 153–54
Eighth Avenue, 25, 79–89, 302; businesses
    on, 33–35; charity institutions on,
    273–74; crowds on, 27, 33; decline of,
    36, 58, 153, 296–97, 312, 314; diversity
    in, 31–33; loss of familiarity of, 15, 156;
    racial integration on, 15, 232, 235–36
Ethnicity: changing rules about, 178–81;
    importance of, 156, 158–61;
    maintenance of, 143–44, 147, 165–69;
    and marriage, 169–71, 173–76;
    stereotypes about, 167–68

Families, *111–31*; decay of, 295–96, 317;
    dependence on in crises, 64, 71–72,
    270–71; discipline of children in, 152–
    55; and home training, 135, 142–43;
    influences on, 74–76, 107–09, 266–67;
    in steel mills, 11, 22–23, 66, 136, 139;
    of steelworkers, 8–9, 90–110; and work,
    153–54
Flannagan, Margaret, 98–100
Flannagan, Michael, 93

Fox, Bruce, 150
Frick, Henry Clay, 5
Frick Park, 318
Frisch, Michael, 257

Gender roles, 101–03; and ambitions for
    children, 133–34; changes in, 101,
    149–50; and changes in household life,
    90–110; effects of plant closings on, 71,
    73, 78, 105–10; religion as women's
    domain, 144–45, 177; in steelworker
    families, 92–100, 135
Government, 256; anger at, 253, 262–63,
    297–98, 314–16

Harmony, 169–71, 247, 295; "below the
    tracks," 158–60, 163; illusions of, 24–
    25, 197–99, 232, 309; loss of, 156, 313;
    nostalgia about, 11, 13, 29; and race
    relations, 194–95, 197–99, 232; in steel
    mills, 202–06, 210–11
Harrison, B., 265–66
Hays, Pa., 163–64
Hays Street, *12*
Health benefits, 63
Heritage House, 274–75
Hine, Lewis, 9, 133, 169, 243; on gender
    roles, 92, 104
Hoerr, John, 181, 267
Hole-in-the-wall, 41–42, *280*
Homes, 9, *26, 111–31, 213–25, 228–29*;
    segregation of, 232, 242–46, 248. *See
    also* Neighborhoods
Homestead, Pa., 4–8, 23–24, 136, 316;
    compared to other steel towns, 16, 34,
    36, 58, 272, 274; continued belief in,
    304, 312–13, 319; identity of, 16, 105,
    303, 319; improvements in, 302, 314–
    16; influence of mill on, 27, 78; map,
    17; newcomers to, 156, 294–95, 305,
    308–10; perceptions of residents, 34–
    35, 58; relation of to West Homestead
    and Munhall, 4, 11–12; reluctance to
    move away from, 70–71, 74; vows to
    remain in, 23–25, 152, 334–35
*Homestead: The Glory and Tragedy of an
    American Steel Town. See* Serrin,
    William

Homestead: The Households of a Mill Town.
   See Byington, Margaret; Hine, Lewis
Homestead Strike, 5–6, 260, 276; women
   during, 91, 250
Homestead Works, *277–93*; closing of, 43;
   demolition of, 16, 24, 62–63, 251–53,
   288–93; effects of closing of, 64, 74–
   75, 155–56, 197, 250; hope for
   reopening of, 62–63; influence of, 11–
   12, 19; perception as too big to close,
   251, 255; process of closing, 251, 256,
   263–64; proposals for reusing buildings,
   303–04; responses to closing, 58, 61–
   62, 250–76. *See also* Steel industry
"Hunkies," 12, 167; discrimination
   against, 95, 167–68, 181

Immigrants: and development of
   Homestead, 6, 12, 195–96; lodges of,
   166–69; neighborhoods of, 161–64; *vs.*
   modern newcomers, 305–06. *See also*
   "Below the tracks"; Neighborhoods
Italians, 163–64

Jackson, Jesse, 269–70
Jackson, Rufus "Sonnyman," 233
Job hunting, 66–67, 69, 154; lack of search
   skills for, 66–67
Job training programs, 69, 150–51, 258
Jobs: difficulty for steelworkers to change,
   68–69, 264–65, 304; layoffs as chance
   to change, 74–75; for women, 100–10,
   142
Johnson, Thomas and Lydia, 199, 232–33,
   238–39, 244–45

Kornblum, William, 202, 211, 243

Layoffs, 74–75, 105, 251, 254, 257–58. *See
   also* Homestead Works; Unemployment
Leisure, 28–30, 94–95, 147, 158, 164–65;
   parks and playgrounds, 133, 298; in
   photos, 25, 276; and racial
   discrimination, 230–49, 232–35;
   relation of to mills, 90–91; in
   unemployment, 63–64
Lower Ward, 13–14, 199–200. *See also*
   "Below the tracks"
Lynch, David, 271

Manhood: effects of unemployment on,
   64, 71, 265; effects of women working
   outside on, 106–08, 110; and steel
   work, 39–40, 66–69, 96, 135
*Marienthal: The Sociography of an
   Unemployed Community*, 266
Meals on Wheels, 275
Military, 150–51
Mon Valley Employment Organization,
   269, 299–300
Morrison, Frank, 302
Moving, 70
Munhall, 78; discrimination in, 196, 232,
   244, 246–47; relation of to Homestead
   and West Homestead, 4, 11–12

Neighborhoods, *213–29*; as enclaves, 13,
   162; ethnic, 29, 144; life in, 11–13,
   161–63; racial discrimination in, 211–
   12, 231–32, 234; racial segregation in,
   232, 242–46. *See also* "Below the
   tracks"
Nostalgia, 159, 319; for earlier harmony,
   168–69, 210–11; and living in the past,
   35 36

Out of This Furnace. *See* Bell, Thomas

Pappas, Gregory, 75, 155, 272–73
Park Corporation, 251–52
Pension plans, 63, 262
Photos, 30, 58, 160; changes in, 276, 295;
   family life in, 92–93; importance of
   wedding, 169, *172*; on men's and
   women's work, 104–06; newspaper,
   157–58, 161; schools in, 132–33;
   women in, 97–98
Pinkerton detectives, 5
Pittsburgh Steel Company, 5
Police, 297–98
Political activism: attempts at, 296, 298–
   99; centers of, 268–69, 299–300; lack
   of involvement in, 76, 150; reasons for
   lack of, 167, 261, 263
Poverty, 30, 32, 76–77, 316
Presbyterian church, 1–2
Pritchard, Linda, 175
Prosperity, 295; connotations of, 42–43;
   effects of, 14–15, 27; for steelworkers,
   57–59, 66–68

Protests: centers of, 1–2, 268–69, 299–300; lack of, 251–52, 298; against plant closings, 251–52; reasons for lack of, 261, 263

Race relations, 193–212, 317–18; in nonwork situations, 230–49; worsening, 306–10
Rainbow Clinic, 273
Rainbow Kitchen, the, 71–73, 77, 267–76, 294–95, 299
Reagan, President Ronald, 77, 109, 262
Recovery Plans, 315–16
Recreation. *See* Leisure
Red-light district, 237–42, 311
Religion: changing rules about, 176, 178–81; importance of, 135, 158–61; and intermarriages, 173–76; as women's domain, 144–45. *See also* Churches
Russell Sage Foundation studies, 9. *See also* Byington, Margaret

Schools: changes in, 132–35, 246–49; of Homestead, 146–49, 248. *See also* Education
Serrin, William, 97, 205, 255, 305; on lack of political activism, 167, 267; on Rainbow Kitchen clientele, 294–95
"Slavs," 12
Smith, Vivian, 102
Social mobility, 138–40
Soup kitchens, 71–73, 76–77, 267–76
Sports, 30. *See also* Leisure
Springsteen, Bruce, 269
Stealing, 31–32
Steel industry, 42; and education, 133, 136–39; entry into, 66–67; influence of, 24, 92, 133; as metaphor, 26–27; mythologizing, 39, 57. *See also* Homestead Works
Steeltown (Walker), 137
Steelworkers: benefits for, 14–15, 57–60; effects of prosperity, 14–15, 66–68; mythologizing, 39–40, 137–38; self-image as, 40–41, 69, 91–92
Stout, Michael, 268
Strikes, 5–8, 204–05; and plant closings, 60–61, 260
Suburbs, 15, 246, 302
Suicide, 265, 267, 296

Tennant, Mrs., 146–47, 177
Thirteen-week vacations, 7, 14–15, 261–62

Unemployment, after plant closings, 36; dangers of, 71; effects of, 28–29, 30, 37, 73–74, 76, 91, 152–53; as hell, 264–67; responses to, 63–64, 254, 300; shock at finality of, 61–62. *See also* Homestead Works
Union. *See* United Steel Workers (USW)
United States Steel Corporation, 2, 5, 7, 14. *See also* USX
United Steel Workers (USW), 5, 205; ambivalence about, 6–8; criticism of, 60, 270–71; perceptions of, 258, 260–62
Urban renewal, 71, 297, 302–05
USX, 2, 37; and blame for plant closings, 60, 258–59, 261–62; effects of plant closings, 30, 37, 63, 178–80; home life separate from, 307, 313; influence on Homestead, 16–17, 161, 201; plant closings by, 8, 43; process of plant closings, 58, 61, 65; race relations by, 195–96, 202–11; relation of steelworkers to, 38–39, 59, 65–67; secrecy about plant closings, 66–67, 251, 253; supporting black vice businesses, 237, 240. *See also* Homestead Works

Wages, collecting, 41–42
Walker, Charles, 137
Weddings, 29–30, 158, 169–73, 199
Welfare, 71–72
West Homestead, 78; discrimination in, 196, 244–45; relation of to Homestead and Munhall, 4, 11–12
Wiesen, Ron, 270–71
Willis, Paul, 138
Women: ambitions of for daughters, 107–08; dangers to around plant gates, 41–42; effects of plant closings on, 73, 78; histories of, 8–10; outside jobs of, 10–11, 100–10, 142; in steelworker families, 92–100, 94–95, 135; training for domestic work, 141–42; working in mills, 39, 91–92

Work ethic: criticism of, 59–60, 208, 260–61; learning to labor, 134–37, 142; of steelworkers, 38–41; of women, 102
World War II: expansion of mill during, 11, 13–14, 25; jobs of women in, 100
Wozeck, Jane, 104
Wozeck, Jim, 104, 176
Wozeck, Mrs., 139, 142; history of, 93–94, 98–100, 103, 174–75

Wozeck, Rosie, 104, 173, 175–76, 313–14
Wozeck, Sam, 39–40, 174–75, 308, 313; as historian, 18, 157–58
Wurtz, Dick, 19–20, 207–08

Yearning for Yesterday (Davis), 159

Zippay, Allison, 265–66

Library of Congress Cataloging-in-Publication Data

Modell, Judith Schachter, 1941–
    A town without steel : envisioning Homestead / Judith Modell : photographs by Charlee Brodsky.
        p.   cm.
    Includes bibliographical references and index.
    ISBN 0-8229-4071-X (cloth : acid-free paper)
    ISBN 0-8229-5676-4 (pbk. : acid-free paper)
    1. Homestead (Pa.)—History. 2. Homestead (Pa.)—Social conditions. 3. Plant shutdowns—
Pennsylvania—Homestead—History—20th century. 4. Steel industry and trade—Pennsylvania—
Homestead—History—20th century. 5. Iron and steel workers—Pennsylvania—Homestead—
History—20th century. I. Title.
    F159.H7 M63 1998
    975.5'816—ddc21   98-9030